Competing for Capital

WILEY SERIES ON SYSTEMS AND CONTROLS FOR FINANCIAL MANAGEMENT

Edited by Robert L. Shultis and Frank M. Mastromano

Competing for Capital
A FINANCIAL RELATIONS APPROACH

BRUCE W. MARCUS

A Wiley-Interscience Publication

JOHN WILEY & SONS   New York   •   London   •   Sydney   •   Toronto

Library of Congress Cataloging in Publication Data

Marcus, Bruce W   1925-
    Competing for Capital.

    (Wiley series on systems and controls for financial management)
    "A Wiley-Interscience publication."
    Bibliography: p.
    Includes index.
    1. Investments—United States. 2. Brokers—United States. 3. Investment banking—United States. 4. Public relations—Corporations. I. Title. II. Title: A financial relations approach.

HG4930.M36   332′.041   75-19280
ISBN 0-471-56863-5

Printed in the United States of America

10 9 8 7 6 5 4 3 2 1

To Mana, David, Michael, Jonathan, Joseph, and Lucy

SERIES PREFACE

No one needs to tell the reader that the world is changing. He sees it all too clearly. The immutable, the constant, the unchanging of a decade or two ago no longer represent the latest thinking—on *any* subject, whether morals, medicine, politics, economics, or religion. Change has always been with us, but the pace has been accelerating, especially in the postwar years.

Business, particularly with the advent of the electronic computer some 20 years ago, has also undergone change. New disciplines have sprung up. New professions are born. New skills are in demand. And the need is ever greater to blend the new skills with those of the older professions to meet the demands of modern business.

The accounting and financial functions certainly are no exception. The constancy of change is as pervasive in these fields as it is in any other. Industry is moving toward an integration of many of the information gathering, processing, and analyzing functions under the impetus of the so-called systems approach. Such corporate territory has been, traditionally, the responsibility of the accountant and the financial man. It still is, to a large extent—but times are changing.

Does this, then, spell the early demise of the accountant as we know him today? Does it augur a lessening of influence for the financial specialists in today's corporate hierarchy? We think not. We maintain, however, that it is incumbent upon today's accountant and today's financial man to learn *today's* thinking and to use *today's* skills. It is for this reason the Wiley Series on Systems and Controls for Financial Management is being developed.

Recognizing the broad spectrum of interests and activities that the series title encompasses, we plan a number of volumes, each representing the latest thinking, written by a recognized authority, on a particular facet of the financial man's responsibilities. The subjects contemplated for discussion within the series range from production accounting systems to planning, to corporate records, to control of cash. Each book is an in-depth study of one subject within this group. Each is intended to be a practical, working tool for the businessman in general and the financial man and accountant in particular.

ROBERT L. SHULTIS

FRANK M. MASTROMANO

PREFACE

The atmosphere, toward the end of the 1960s, was such that three chestnut vendors pushing their stands on New York's Fifth Avenue could band together, readily find an underwriter to take them public, come out at $3 a share on Monday, close at $25 a share on Friday, and sell franchises the following Monday.

In 1970, the American economy entered not only a new decade but a new phase. It may have been just an accident of chronology, although the year found the country's brand new administration bent on dampening the serious inflation that had become the parasite of the booming economy of the 1960s. Nevertheless, the structures, the attitudes and context of the capital markets changed abruptly within the first months of the new year. The economic boom that began in 1961 did not level off so much as it came to an acute reversal of direction.

Which isn't to say that the economy was not still sound. It was merely reacting to a number of administrative measures specifically designed to separate inflation from its host; to allow the economy to continue to expand, but at a slower rate.

Following that brief period, particularly awesome to those who had not lived through a depression and to whom an economic reversal was almost a violation of civil rights, the economy made a rapid recovery. Through the beginning of 1973 it seemed as if the good old days were back. All the promises of economic reform, and particularly reform of the securities industry, were quickly forgotten. Things were once again, it was said, as they should be.

Then it happened again for reasons that no one could quite fathom—although the country was pervaded by such as Watergate, the instability of the dollar, and a rising crime rate—the market took a downturn. What was different this time was that many of these factors were not related to the economy, although much was said about how the market prognosticated the course of the economy. Corporate profits continued to rise and the market continued to drop. There seemed to be none of the normal relationships of cause and effect in which investors could reside with comfort. Suddenly, in the fall of 1973, once more, for no apparent reason, the market turned up again, only to be shot down once again by raging inflation and the stringent measures taken to stem it. By the end of 1974, inflation had led to deep recession—probably the worst since World War II.

Only one thing was certain—that for the corporation dependent upon a consistent source of capital there was no stability. There was no longer the easy way of the 1960s boom.

During the boom years of the 1960s, the prime source of capital was the investor in common stock. The small investor was assiduously wooed by the stock market. Small investors became large investors. Institutions, such as mutual funds, pension funds, and so on, couldn't invest fast enough. The amount of money available to any corporation in need of expansion funds, and willing to give away a piece of equity, was overwhelming.

The number of public corporations in which the investor could buy stock increased from 3999 in 1961 to 9030 in 1970, even allowing for a large number of companies that went public on the strength of great promises, and then went out of business because of great promises unfulfilled.

During this period, the prevailing idea was to get stock prices up as high as possible in relation to earnings. For the investing public, the measure of a company seemed to be the rate at which its stock went up. Some truly great price/earnings ratios were achieved, ratios as awe-inspiring as a leap across the English Channel from a standing position.

Within the context of this economy, high p/e's were of the essence. It made many an instant paper millionaire from a base of virtually no investment. Added to this need for high p/e's was the merger fever of the era in which, as a result of tax laws and accounting procedures that smoothed many a path, there were some 6000 mergers in 1969—the peak year. For the merger or acquisition-minded, for whom stock was currency, the high p/e was the seductive force that made the stock viable as currency.

With all this, the sheer volume of companies competing for the investor's dollar made that competition all the keener. And thus financial relations came into its own as a consequential competitive tool.

Financial relations is the mechanism by which companies marshal and orient those facts about themselves which lead to the judgment of corporate operational ability, and then communicates these facts to the people who are most concerned with investment and investment advice.

The prime target for this activity is predominantly the security analyst —the man whose research is supposed to discover and anticipate those companies whose stock will rise. Competition for the attention of analysts and other investment advisors, both through direct appeal and with the ancillary support of visibility in the business press, was the main substance of most financial relations programs.

And when stock prices rose, it was due, in large measure, to the success of the financial relations practitioner in directing attention to his client in the center arena.

This is not to say that a stock's price could be inflated without some measure of legitimate earnings and growth promise. While there were some spectacular exceptions, the acoustics of Wall Street are too good to have allowed a worthless stock to be touted for more than a brief period. The very best that financial relations could achieve were visibility and focus. Flagrant misrepresentation was the exception, not the rule. But given two stocks of equal value, the more visible one—the stock of the company best known to the public—was the stock that got the higher p/e.

In a market rising at a fever pitch, financial relations served its most useful function in helping a company compete against other public companies for attention. It did not, with exceptions, of itself cause stock prices to rise. The economy did that.

But with the turn of the decade came the slide. In a matter of just a few months, the Dow Jones average slipped from almost 1000 to well below 800. Abruptly, many of the economic growth indicators began to stall in their breathtaking acceleration, and to flutter downward. The supply of money was tightened as the prime interest rate was raised. The shortage of money meant a slowdown of investment for expansion, bringing with it anxiety on the part of the consumer, followed by reduced spending in all quarters, followed by reduced earnings. Also in only a few months, the average p/e ratio in the New York Stock Exchange went from 18 to 13, and ultimately in 1974, to almost 6. The Dow Jones average, which had recently broken 1000, went the other way to break 600.

Without going into pedantic discussions about the definition of recession, we were nevertheless in an entirely new economic milieu. Price/earnings ratios began to reflect more realistically a company's ability to earn. Larger companies in dire need of expansion capital that, due to tight money, was no longer readily available at reasonable rates from banks, had to rely more heavily on equity financing. This meant more shares available for sale in an atmosphere in which there were fewer dollars to purchase these shares.

This cycle, with variations on the same theme, was repeated in 1973, 1974, and 1975.

But a corporation is a peculiar entity, with a life of its own and an insatiable appetite for capital. By a corporation's very nature, and by the nature of our economic system, capital is the fuel for generating corporate profits.

Up until the 1970s, sources of capital, particularly the investing public, were abundant. But in this new economic era, with this source diminished and other sources curtailed, the competition for capital becomes keener than ever before.

At the same time, both the sources of capital and their captains, the investment bankers, have altered appreciably. And while the public source remained essentially the same, the mechanisms for reaching it—both corporate and economic—also changed radically. The investor now buys a different product, sold in a different way—and nobody has bothered to tell him.

This is what this book is about. How have the markets and sources of capital changed? How does a company compete for the diminishing sources of capital? What is the role—and what are the techniques—of financial relations, and how do they serve the corporation in the competition for capital?

Its primary purpose is to apprise the corporate executive of some of the techniques available to him to compete in this highly competitive, shrinking capital market.

It is also a how-to book, in terms of the day-by-day mechanics used by financial relations professionals. For the corporate executive, it is designed to delineate the options available to perform the competitive functions, as well as the arena in which the competition functions. Its aim is to serve the financial professional by helping him to understand and evaluate these options, so that they may be profitably applied to the specific needs of his company.

BRUCE W. MARCUS

New York, New York
June 1975

ACKNOWLEDGMENTS

While writing, as is well known, is a solitary endeavor, no book on a subject of this magnitude is produced without help.

Primary help came from my wife, Mana, who not only encouraged me and read proofs deep into the night, but who gave up countless hours of my presence, as did my children, Joseph and Lucy, while I performed the solitary task.

My partner Ted Pincus not only contributed invaluable criticism, but more significantly, pioneered many of the practices described in this book that are now standard in financial relations.

Close behind in their help were the executives and staff of The Financial Relations Board, including Earle Brown and Arthur O'Reilly.

Much of my analysis of the future of investment banking and mergers stems from ideas germinated by Richard Hexter, of Donaldson, Lufkin and Jenrette.

And then there is my mother, Pauline Marcus; my attorney, Andrew Davis; investment banker Robert Rosen, and all my friends who caught all the typos and other mistakes, and made sure the facts were straight.

Other than that, writing is a solitary task.

B. W. M.

CONTENTS

CONTENTS

Competing for Capital

CHAPTER 1

DEFINITIONS AND RATIONALE

During the bull market of the late 1960s—the Go-Go years—when the stock market was booming and new issues were proliferating at a rate dictated almost solely by the speed of printing presses, financial relations emerged as a consequential factor in the economic community. Financial relations practitioners performed their little rituals and incantations in behalf of their clients, and scratched their bellies with glee as stock prices and price/earnings ratios set new records daily. Corporate executives, sensing the promotional aspect of the market, had some vague notion that there was a direct relationship between financial relations activities and rising stock prices, even at a time when every fiscal quarter produced greater earnings than the last.

There was a measure of truth in that notion. Financial relations did indeed help the stock of one company perform better than the stock of another company with comparable financial and economic configurations. It is, after all, a marketing situation in its most literal sense. With some 9000 publicly traded stocks, obviously those that were more consistently and flagrantly displayed before the investing public were the ones that got the greater attention.

But the Go-Go years are over now. Volume has been down by as much as half, and stock prices have been down by some 50% and more from 1968 highs. An occasional new issue drifts by like a stray bird blown off course from its southward migration. Gone are the shooters; one great name in mutual funds is now running a restaurant. The small investor, who bought odd lots and 100-share round lots in such great numbers as to contribute more than half the volume on the stock market, is gone, gone, gone. The growing corporation, seeking needed expansion capital, must run frantically in other directions.

And in the remnants of the stock market that was and is, and may be again, the question arises—can financial relations serve now? When price/earnings ratios are a fraction of the highs of the past, and double digit prime rates are a closing valve on borrowings, of what value are those rituals and incantations of financial relations? In competing in the capital markets in the context of a low as well as a high Dow Jones average, is financial relations an anachronism—or is it still a useful, effective tool?

In the current market, can financial relations still contribute to effective capital formation?

There is, unfortunately, a tendency to use the phrase "the current market" in a way that implies that 1968 was a normal period. Quite the contrary—and perhaps here lies the beginning of the answer. When the Dow Jones average broke 1000 in August 1972, it seemed to herald a new era. It was, in fact, a handsome bit of pyrotechnic that was the culmination of a drive begun some years ago to bring the small investor into an industry that for generations had been an exclusive club. This drive was sustained by a salutary economic period. But when the economy took a downturn in 1970, what really happened was that the market found a level more consistent with the realities of the economy. This consistency is perhaps a better definition of a normal market than are the numbers of the halycon days of 1968. In a decelerated economy, it is, unfortunately, a market that zaps that relatively new and still unsophisticated American capitalist—the small investor. It drives him from the market in sheer fright.

The equities market of the late 1960s has been replaced by one in which the small investor, who had been lured into the market in the 1950s, has sharply retrenched. More than 70% of stock trading, as of this writing, is being done by institutions—and the institutions, burned by the bear markets of 1970 and 1973–1974, are buying cautiously. Gone are the Go-Go years, in which new issues were gobbled up by investors like small fish in a sea of sharks.

And so we watch the traditional capital markets fade off into the sunset, even as the need for new capital proliferates. James J. Needham, chairman of the board of the New York Stock Exchange, writing in The *Wall Street Journal* on May 16, 1974, points out that aggregate corporate capital needs during the next decade should be well in excess of $3.3 trillion. He said:

> Even if the equities markets are called upon to supply no more than 10% to 15% of the total, we will be asking American investors to pony up an amount roughly equivalent to the entire present Federal debt to keep U.S. business moving forward during the next ten years!

This sentiment has even been voiced by John J. Scanlon, financial vice president of the giant American Telephone and Telegraph, while expressing his anxiety about the source of this capital. With the vast AT&T concerned about capital, what chance is there for the smaller company?

If the major portion of the remainder of this needed capital is to come from retained earnings, it must be noted that the profits from which come retained earnings are also the source of dividends. This distribution of earnings becomes an investor relations problem, since shareholders must then be made to understand the balance between profits to be distributed and the need for profits to be reinvested.

The capital markets, it would seem, are not merely diminishing, they are changing rapidly. (Never mind the securities industry itself, which is undergoing its greatest upheaval in decades, and seems destined to emerge in a considerably different form than we have known traditionally. Where it's going and in what shape it will emerge, is anybody's guess.)

And if the capital markets are changing so indeed must the approach to reaching those markets change. The competition becomes keener. The need is greater, the sources of capital are fewer, and the locus of capital, once so firmly rooted and clearly visible, keeps shifting like (and sometimes to) the sands of Araby.

Competing for this diminishing, shifting capital obviously requires infinitely more realistic and sophisticated skills, more intensively applied. With new targets there must be new techniques of communication; new strategies in reaching the sources of capital; new ways for a company to demonstrate its ability to appreciate the invested dollar.

There is, in other words, an even more intense need for financial relations now than there was in the years of the great bull markets. Moreover, the need is for financial relations programs that are more technical, more flexible, more sophisticated than any in the past. As the prey diminishes in number, so must the hunter increase his speed, skill, and cunning.

But does it work?

We know that financial relations, even in the most raging bull markets, contributes by virtue of its ability to expose and to focus attention. How then does it work in a market where the average New York Stock Exchange trading is half of its former peak? How does it work in a securities industry in which vast numbers of individual investors have left the market and more than 300 New York Stock Exchange firms have disappeared since the end of 1968? Can financial relations serve the smaller company, as well as the larger one, in a financial community that has grown accustomed to a concept of two tiers of stock, blue chips in one and everybody else in the second? What can it do for the company with a float (number of shares available for public trading) of under a million shares?

In the early days of financial relations—the 1960s—the financial relations effort was relatively simple. Analysts' meetings. Releases. An occasional story in the major business and financial journals. Annual reports that were all color and pretty pictures and few tangible facts. All mindless and mechanical.

But now companies must function in a market in which the average price/earnings ratio of the Dow Jones stocks has gone from a peak of 17.3 in 1971 to as low as 6 in early 1975—roughly a 60% cut. This equities market is still the prime target of financial relations.

While it is true that the equities market supplies only 10 or 15% of the total capital needed by corporations, its contribution to total capital formation is infinitely greater than just its dollar volume.

First of all, the contribution by equity represents a significant segment of the total capital formation in terms of its application. It acts often as a base for all other financing. Equity capital most frequently represents the capital used for significant growth or expansion. At the time it is acquired (and aside from some of the ancillary reasons for going public, such as the personal needs of individual owners, capitalizing on personal assets in a rising stock market, etc.), it is usually used to move a company from one level of operation to another. While normal operational growth can frequently be financed from retained earnings, equity capital is used for the spurt; for the expansion of either operations or markets; for the acquisition program that sharply increases the size of a company. Moreover, equity capital is permanent, and not subject to credit crunch.

Secondly, a company moving from the private into the public market finds itself with a visibility that enhances its access to other sources of capital—banks, private investors, larger debt issues, and so on.

Thirdly, a public company is a regulated company, which implies that, since its operations are publicly observed, there must therefore be greater credibility in its financial reporting.

To the lender—banks, institutions, and private investors—this implication of credibility also enhances the sense of stability about a company, and makes it a more attractive investment vehicle.

It is assumed that the local bank extends its line of credit solely on the evaluation of financial statements. Unfortunately, and to the surprise of many a corporate executive, this is not universally and forever true. It becomes less true as the prime rate goes up and as the amount of money available from any institution goes down. Even granting the primacy of the balance sheet, the lending committee of any bank must make a final decision predicated upon an assessment of intangible factors—off-balance sheet factors that indicate a company's ultimate ability not simply to repay a loan, but to maintain an ongoing strength. To more and more banks, the lessons of the Penn Central Railroad's bankruptcy became abundantly clear.

For many corporations—and not just the giants—foreign sources of capital enter into the picture, including Eurodollars and foreign money. Since most sources of foreign capital use American investment banking firms to help them to determine those companies in which an investment is to be made, these American representatives become a prime target for information about the company.

It is difficult to speak of foreign money without recognizing that for many corporations a defensive position must be taken, in that one of the results of dollar devaluation has been the frequency of tender offers for American companies by European or Japanese corporations. An alarmingly large number of corporate executives have suddenly awakened to find tender offers for their company's stock from foreign companies. It is precisely at this point that a successfully informed, wooed, and won roster of shareholders is most necessary. It is also precisely at this point that informing, wooing, and winning shareholders is too late.

And so the mere size of the contribution of equity to the total capital structure belies its actual effectiveness. A corporation's position in the equity market is of far greater importance to the financial community's total view of the company than may be surmised from the proportion of equity to other financing. It is for this, as much as any other reason, that the prime concern of a financial relations program never strays far from its focus on the equities market.

As for "the current market," it is best viewed in terms of Lot's wife who is admonished, as Lot and his family departed from Sodom and Gomorrah, not to look back. She did and was turned into salt.

The market is *always* the current market. It does not matter that it was once better or worse, or even that it will ultimately be better or worse. The needs of the public corporation—immediate, near-term, and far-term —must constantly be faced, regardless of the Dow Jones average at any given moment.

A basic reality is that the stock market, for all its mystique, for all its implied wisdom by virtue of its self-imposed notion of fiduciary concern, is a vast, complex, and cumbersome structure. At best it reflects not considered individual opinion predicated upon wise conservative consideration, but rather masked emotional reaction. It is an auction market and functions like one. Stock market values bear no one-to-one relationship to facts, so much as they reflect an overreaction or an underreaction to the news at any given moment, or to a dream of possibilities of the futures.

A case in point is seen in the events of December 1973, the time of the Arab oil embargo. The market, anticipating correctly that there would be a downward adjustment in the economy resulting from a shortage of energy, did not stop to assess the degree of that effect. It merely overreacted. There was a tremendous sell-off and stocks fell sharply. Among those stocks to feel it first were the stocks of truck leasing companies. Obviously, the reasoning went, if there was a shortage of fuel and a sharp increase in fuel prices, the earnings of the truck leasing companies would be acutely affected. In its overreaction, the market did not take into account the fact that most of the truck leasing companies had been anticipating the shortage for months, and had been stockpiling or making other arrangements. More importantly, it was not recognized until months later that most truck leasers have built-in escalation clauses to correspond with increases in fuel costs. Granted that there was a period during the first quarter of 1974 when it was difficult to pass along some of these increases because of price controls, but the price controls were short-lived, and most truck leasing companies' margins, and therefore profits, tended to be sustained. For those major companies that did not sustain profits, there were reasons other than the energy crisis. But it was the energy crisis that caused the stock prices to go down irrationally. This is a market reaction.

In viewing the stock market in this context, one other observation must be made. There is a tendency to view the market not in the perspective of the individual companies that comprise it, but as a whole. Stock market movement is reported in terms of an average. A Dow Jones average. A Standard and Poor's Index. A New York Stock Exchange average price per share. It must be recognized, surely, that while these averages in a down market represent more stocks whose prices go down than up, there are stocks whose prices go up or remain stable. This is a significant point in considering the possibility of upside performance in a down market for a successful company.

For the individual corporation, viewing the possibility of improving the performance of its own stock in even the worst of the markets, certain basic facts must be recognized:

1. Regardless of the price of a stock at any given moment, or the low to which the Dow Jones average—or any other average—may sink at any moment, there is still a market. It opens every morning and it closes every night. Granted, volume has diminished sharply, but liquidity—or at least the structure for liquidity—still exists.

2. The number of firms in the securities industry has been sharply reduced. But the industry hasn't ceased to exist. From 1971 to July 1974 the number of firms doing business in the securities industry went from 4461 to 3390, but there were still 3390 firms. From 1971 to 1974 the number of security analysts, those people responsible for analyzing a public corporation's potential for success in the stock market, went from 15,000 to 10,000—but there still were 10,000 analysts reporting to work every day and seeking new companies, and new facts about old companies, to evaluate as potential investments. There were 8000 fewer stock brokers

in 1974 than there were in 1971, but there were still 33,000 brokers out beating the bushes for new buyers every day.

3. The structure of the securities industry in all aspects is now in its greatest state of flux since the stock market began in the 1700s under the Buttonwood tree on what is now Broad Street, but it still has not departed from its basic occupation of buying and selling securities. Institutions now seem to control the greatest proportion of stocks traded, but the largest individual institutional investor manages approximately $26 billion of assets, of which about $20 billion is invested in common stocks—and this represents only 2% of the value of all common stocks. Furthermore, it must be recognized that institutional decisions about a stock are predicated, to a major degree, upon the prognosis for that stock's ability to appreciate in market price. In an auction market, liquidity—the ease with which a stock can be sold or purchased—is a major factor that ultimately determines the increase in stock price. The institutions themselves must face the reality of destroying the liquidity of their own holdings. If their purchases go too far into the total number of shares available for trading, it is like killing the goose that lays the golden egg.

4. As the securities industry shrinks, internal structures for evaluating, buying, and selling securities change. With the advent of negotiated rates for commissions on buying and selling stocks, new concepts for evaluating research capabilities as part of the total trading package have come into being. New questions arise, such as, should research be paid for separately? Many firms—not necessarily the smaller ones—now raise questions as to whether the security analyst who merely analyzes and does not make a direct contribution to the income of the firm should be viewed as a luxury. Large firms such as Merrill Lynch, which for years have had large research staffs that were relatively insulated from other segments of the securities industry, are now changing their operations by adding top-notch industry specialists, and analysts who can double as institutional salesmen. And as brokerage houses attempt to reduce cost by eliminating research departments, a greater burden for research falls upon brokers and traders. The picture changes. The old ways and the old approaches no longer apply.

5. The focus of purchasing power continually shifts. If there is diminished volume, then liquidity must be maintained by broadening the trading base. If there are no more 10,000-share purchases by one firm, then 10 firms must be found instead that will make 1000-share purchases. The effort must be fluid, and shifted to where the purchasing power is at any one point. For example, when the individual investor and odd-lot trading are strong in the market, then the focus is on the retail houses. When they are weak in the market, then the focus might shift to the pension funds,

which have a constant pressure to keep invested for the long term, but not necessarily the pressure to perform on a short-term basis, as might a mutual fund.

What it comes down to is that the equities market may be changing and shifting, but it continues to exist. And so long as it exists there is a necessity—as well as an opportunity—to represent the corporation to the market not only to maintain that high level of visibility necessary for success in all aspects of the capital market, but as a responsibility to shareholders as well.

In view of the current structure of the capital markets—its changed configurations, its new sources of capital and the relative dormancy of all sources, the sharply diminished equities market, and the shifting prime rate—what precisely is the rationale, and what are the techniques, for a financial relations program?

Both the bull market of the late 1960s and a bear market have one thing in common. They are both markets, regardless of texture, regardless of the volume. Shares of stock are still being bought and sold, and money from other sources is still being invested and lent. Under any circumstances, this capital must be competed for against hundreds—thousands—of other corporations.

If a corporation of any size has need for capital beyond its own cash flow, it must be prepared to compete for that capital.

In order to compete for that capital, any corporation must be prepared to demonstrate—clearly, forcefully, honestly, and skillfully—those factors about itself which indicate that an investment in it is warranted.

And if the sources of capital are diminishing, and if stock trading activity is at its lowest ebb, then that effort must be refocused and redoubled in order to eke the most out of the least. As long as the capital market exists, whatever its configuration, there are still ways and techniques of reaching it effectively.

Furthermore, the marketing effort in the capital markets is very much like a hoop—it keeps rolling only as long as you keep hitting it with a stick. The minute you stop, it stops and falls over.

Nor can it be assumed that a company's record will speak for itself. True, there are rare occasions when a company's superior performance is discovered, recognized, and rewarded in the market place. But for each such company there are dozens of companies whose presidents moan in frustration that the price of their stock in no way reflects the company's performance. Under the best of circumstances nobody is watching. Under the worst of circumstances there is a lethargy and a suspicion that precludes the independent investigation that might turn up a corporate gem and follow it, quarter by quarter, through superior performance.

Moreover, the printed record is only half the story. It merely demonstrates where the company has been—not where it's going. Nor does it ever adequately expose the management team—the people who made the record possible and upon whom the investor must depend to sustain the record.

One of the most compelling reasons for an intensive financial relations program during a down market—as well as during an up market—lies in the basic nature of security analysis itself. The greatest part of analysis is based upon intangible and unmeasureable factors, such as management and the company's ability to project and meet its objectives. The more precisely and clearly the elements that define these intangibles are projected, the more readily the company's ability to appreciate the invested dollar will be understood. The more readily this ability is understood, the more likely the acceptance—and investment—by the financial community.

Essentially, the successful financial relations program seeks to demonstrate three basic things. It's true that security analysis and the attempts to judge a company's ability to succeed in the future depend upon an extraordinarily complex configuration of characteristics, but still they all evolve to three basic points:

1. Earnings.
2. Management.
3. Plans.

Earnings are, after all, what a corporation is all about. They represent the return on the investment. They signify the company's ability to succeed as a corporation. But at best, earnings constitute only a small portion of the measure of a company's viability, and they demonstrate not so much where a company is going, but where it has been. If earnings were the sole measure of a company's performance, there would be no auction market. It would all be done by computer. One could very well have bought the stock of a buggy whip manufacturer in its last great year before the invention of the automobile. What's more to the point is not just the earnings record of a company, nor even the consistency of its earnings growth. It's the degree to which the pattern of earnings demonstrates the ability of the company to continue to earn that must be projected.

Second is management. A corporation may by definition have a perpetual life, but its ability to operate successfully is a function of its management during the life of that management. This is as true of a $2 million company as it is of IBM, for all its vast size and greatness. If, during the next few years, the president of IBM makes a decision about the computer industry that differs from his predecessors, it will alter the entire structure of IBM for many generations to come. And what is it that must be projected about management? Not just the skill, intelligence, vigor, and clear-sightedness of its officers, but its ability to see the company, the industry, and the economy clearly. It's the ability of the management team to deal with the day-by-day problems of the company, and its ability to develop and implement realistic long-range plans. It's the ability to fathom all aspects of management—operations, administration, production, marketing, distribution, finance. It's the ability to deal with contingencies in changing situations. Is the management that brought the company from $10 million to $50 million in volume capable of dealing with the same company when its volume reaches $100 million, and therefore with an entirely new set of problems?

Third is plans. Not just what the company is going to do tomorrow or five years from now, but rather its programs. Where is it going? What are its objectives—long, medium, and short range? How does it mean to finance its plans? Are its plans realistic in terms of the industry, the market, the economy, and the company's financial condition?

When all of the elements about a corporation that can possibly be compiled in these three categories are projected and understood by the financial community, and when they are projected believably and consistently, then that company can expect to compete successfully in the capital markets. In fact, there is a premium that accrues to predictability.

And how is success in a financial relations program measured?

It is measured in a feedback of knowledge and understanding about a company by those segments of the financial community that are most important to a corporation.

It is reflected in the relative ease with which a corporation can deal with the capital markets, ranging from banks to the equities market.

It is reflected in a realistic price/earnings ratio, in relation to the overall average price/earnings ratio of the stock market at any given time and, more significantly, a corporation's own industry.

It is reflected in increased liquidity—the comparative ease with which sellers find buyers and buyers find sellers, even in a sparse market.

It is reflected in increased and enthusiastic sponsorship and more market makers.

Assuming successful performance by a corporation, or at least a clear and honest reason to believe that the corporation's efforts are leading ultimately to success and profitability, there is no way that a company can compete successfully in all aspects of the capital market except through an intelligently designed and skillfully executed financial relations program. As any businessman knows, the theory of the better mouse trap no longer functions in a complex competitive economy.

CHAPTER 2

SECURITY ANALYSTS AND OTHER CONDUITS

On the face of it, the role of the security analyst is to determine those companies in which an invested dollar will appreciate at a reasonable rate or better. That's on the face of it.

The reality is very much different. The security analyst is, to varying degrees, part of a sales effort. He is either directly involved in selling stock to his customers, or indirectly in supplying research to a broker who must sell stock. If the analyst is part of an institution, in which he is recommending stock to be purchased by the institution, his position is still the same. The stocks he recommends must go up. They must go up generally, specifically, or, under the worst of circumstances, go down less than other stocks. The point is that no matter what he does, or how he does it, or for whom he does it, the security analyst's job is to divine which stocks will increase in price at the greatest possible rate in relation to the stock market in general.

And since the stock market is an auction market, and stocks don't increase in a one-to-one relationship to earnings, what the analyst is really doing is not determining those companies in which an invested dollar will appreciate at a reasonable rate. He's really trying to fathom which companies the market will bet on to increase stock price.

The difference between trying to gauge companies whose stock will rise as a reflection of the companies' abilities and trying to gauge companies whose stock will rise as a function of an auction market and the mass reaction is a significant one, even though the end result may often be the same.

On the one hand, certain fundamental factors of corporate analysis are basically applied in security analysis. These are supposedly primary elements that, despite many variables within the economy that are beyond the control of the corporate management, are basic business indicators and gauges. On the other hand, the analyst is trying to fathom public opinion. But ultimately, it's public opinion based upon a broader and less sophisticated assessment of those very same elements that goes into the judgment of a company's prospective ability to continue to thrive.

This may all seem like an academic discussion except for one thing. With exceptions so rare as to not warrant concern, the analyst is the person who does the basic research to warrant the specific recommendation that results in stock being bought or not bought. His role must be understood if he is to be dealt with effectively.

It can be argued that the stock market has relatively little to do with the direct capitalization of industry. After all, when one person buys shares of IBM stock from another person, the money that changes hands doesn't go into the IBM treasury. The stock is by then probably many times removed from its original sale to the public, which did supply capital for IBM. But if there were no liquidity, if there were no market in which people bought or sold shares of stock even many generations removed from the company's capital structure, then the likelihood is very great that the original market for stock—that market the proceeds of which *do* go into a company's capital—would not exist. The sale of stock for capitalization would be a very difficult job indeed without that liquidity. Without the auction market American industry could never have been capitalized to have grown as mightily as it has since the founding of the country.

If the investor had no liquidity, if he could not readily change his mind about an investment and either withdraw his money or increase his participation at will, he would be extremely hesitant about investing. If he could not see the appreciation of his investment by the trading up of its value in an auction market, he would undoubtedly be reluctant about buying stock. For the risk of investing, he wants—and is entitled to—substantial returns. Naturally, when there is limited liquidity and the auction market is not bidding his stock up, he withdraws from the market with great haste. For most investors, dividends are rarely enough. He measures the return on his investment more in terms of increase in stock price than in dividends. If his total yield—stock price appreciation plus dividends—is not as high as it might be in some other investment vehicle, he switches. Fast.

There are a great many stocks from which to choose, and the elements that determine the likelihood of a company's succeeding—and therefore of its stock increasing in value—require some rather detailed analysis. This is why the security analyst, for all his strengths, weaknesses, shortcomings, and susceptibilities to the same fads and misconceptions as is the ordinary investor, has become the primary target and conduit for communication to key sources of capital.

WHO IS THE SECURITY ANALYST?

Who, then, is this paragon of corporate wisdom? What is the structure of this segment of the securities industry that puts people who are sometimes just a year out of business school in a position to judge a company's ability to succeed? What is the training and what are the abilities of this group of people, most of whom have not 10 minutes of experience behind a corporate desk, and yet are so crucial a key to the capitalization of a company?

It's difficult to view analysts as a group, any more than it is valid to attempt to define the people in any occupation as a group. There are 10,000 analysts currently practicing in the United States. In 1971 there were 11,500 analysts, but the exigencies of the stock market have sharply diminished the number. It is almost reasonable—*almost* reasonable—to assume that those who remain are all superb at their task. This is hardly so.

Most analysts have a business school background and many have come up through the ranks of the securities industry. There was a time, during the bull market of the 1960s, when the need for analysts was so desperate that some of the large brokerage houses were taking bright college graduates with degrees in other areas and training them in-house. That practice, happily, seems to have diminished.

Ideally, the analyst has trained for his job in terms of those elements which offer the best assessment of a company's ability to succeed and thrive; to appreciate the invested dollar. Naturally, a company's ability to do this includes a large number of variables and intangibles. For example, the best run company will lose ground when economic conditions change abruptly and to such a degree that the company cannot correct its operations in a short time to meet those changing conditions. Witness the effect of the 1973 Arab oil embargo on automotive companies. Faced with the possibility that gas would be in very short supply for several years to come, and certainly higher in price, consumer purchasing of automobiles dropped sharply. Manufacturers of larger automobiles—General Motors, Chrysler and Ford—suffered the most. American Motors, which had a more popular line of smaller cars, thrived. But there was a catch there, too. Not having anticipated the crisis, American Motors had to scurry to meet production schedules set by the new onrush of business. While American Motors' sales increased, there was a greater call on their capital to expand to meet increased sales.

Unanticipated high interest rates in the early part of 1974 were another element beyond the control of even the best managements. Any company with large interest payments, and certainly those that were highly leveraged, found their earnings sharply reduced to an unanticipated degree. Many hitherto sound companies, in fact, found themselves seriously in trouble.

Changing economic conditions also alter, over the years, the value of the basic elements of analysis. For example, the judgment of a company in terms of its leverage is one thing in a boom economy, where profitability is high, margins are high, and thus cash flow is more than enough to meet payments on debt. It's yet another thing in a somewhat depressed economy where margins are lower, cash flow is less, interest rates are higher, and meeting payments on a loan saps a greater proportion of the profits.

THE ELEMENTS OF ANALYSIS

Still and all, the analyst is taught to view a company in terms of some rather specific elements, some of which are measurable and some of which are questions of judgment. Among those factors that enter into the analysis of the company are:

1. Financial structure of the company.
2. The economic context in which the company operates.
3. The nature of the industry in which the company operates.
4. The management of the company.
5. The company's own projection of its plan for growth.

Perhaps the best delineation of the technical aspects of security analysis is found in the superb work *Security Analysis* by Benjamin Graham and David L. Dodd. Benjamin Graham is considered to be the dean of analysts, not only for his success as an analyst, but by virtue of the fact that his book was one of the first, and certainly the most masterful, to set forth the basic elements of security analysis. Even if his precepts are honored in the breach, they are still a standard.

Basically, Graham believes that no company should be considered as an investment vehicle unless:

1. The company is prominent and conservatively financed. Current assets should be at least two times current liabilities, and debt should be not more than 110% of net current assets.

2. The company has been a consistent dividend payer. The more conservative investor would want to see dividends going back 20 years.

3. There has been no deficit in the last five years.

4. The price-earnings multiple is low. In a soft market, and with high interest rates, he suggests a maximum price of eight times current earnings per share.

5. The stock is selling at one half of its previous high.

6. The stock is selling at a price that is no more than two thirds of net tangible assets.

Obviously, these are very stringent factors. Under many conditions, this would eliminate all but the smallest segment of publicly traded companies. And while very little argument can be taken with any of the points he makes, it can certainly be argued that the spectrum of investment possibilities is much greater than companies that fall within his parameters.

At the same time the realities of the stock market, and the range of reasons for investments, dictate some rather more lenient considerations in analysis of a company.

VARYING ANALYTICAL POINTS OF VIEW

Certainly the bank trust department, functioning in a fiduciary capacity, must be infinitely more conservative than the speculator who is going for high return and who is willing to take a greater risk for it. The individual investor views a company rather differently than does the fund manager who must recognize that he is dealing with other peoples' money and will be held accountable for the results. The tape watcher who looks to make his profit with every movement of the tape sees investment possibilities very differently than does the long-term investor who is willing to buy a stock at a very low multiple, but with long-term growth possibilities.

Analysts, too, face the problem differently. The analyst for a bank trust company considers companies rather more conservatively than does the analyst for the hedge fund. The analyst for the mutual fund functions in terms of his fund's charter. The hedge fund analyst is looking for companies which he thinks the market will become enamored with, and whose stock the market would drive up rapidly. The analyst for the growth fund is looking for more substantial growth with long-term staying power. The analyst for the pension fund is looking for companies that will not only grow steadily and appreciate over the longer period of time, but have a measure of safety. The bank analyst has another problem in that bank portfolios are so large that the ability to liquidate in volume is strictly limited.

Some years ago, an economist at a very large bank identified a problem in the airline industry at a time when the industry was doing very well and airline stocks were flying high. He passed the information on to the trust department, which then calculated that it had a year to get out of the stocks before the market turned. If they had sold off their entire holdings at once, they would have been the cause of a sudden and steep drop in airline stocks. By slowly and quietly cutting back their portfolio, they had managed, by the time the prophecy came true, to sell off only 50% of their airline stock holdings.

The analyst for the large retail house must deal with the broader spectrum of companies because the retail customers have different portfolio needs.

ANALYZING ECONOMIC CONDITIONS

Analyzing economic conditions is an infinitely more arduous task. There are two aspects of it—the general economy and the industry.

The least readily discernable of the two is, of course, the economy in general. For all its apparent sophistication, economics is a most inexact science. Just when everybody thinks he's got it licked, some new and unforeseen element enters into it. A war. Currency devaluations. Political uncertainty, such as the Watergate situation. An oil embargo. A decision by the Federal Reserve Bank to tighten up the money supply. A beef shortage. A drought. A bankruptcy by a major company such as Penn Central. And on and on and on.

Everyone knows where the economy has been and sometimes people even know where the economy is. But nobody knows where it's going. Obviously this throws even the best analysis into a cocked hat. It moves it out of the realm of the economic certainty of a balance sheet, and the historical value of the earnings records, into a vast world of major uncertainty. It's not without its charm, however, in that it offers analysis the excitement of prognostication that one rarely gets with slide rule or the electronic calculator.

Prognostication for an industry is somewhat easier, at least within a limited range of time. If consumer spending is down as a result of inflation, for example, it is reasonable to assume that retail purchases in certain industries, such as appliances and apparel, will have trouble achieving earnings records. If there are basic material shortages, with no relief in sight, it is reasonable to assume that those industries using those materials will have problems. When transistors were invented, transistor manufacturers enjoyed a boom in those products which used the transistors, such as miniature portable radios and portable tape recorders. But then as the industry became saturated with transistor manufacturers, it became impossible for any company to compete successfully and with very high margins, and the transistor stocks fell on their faces. Color television suffered the same cyclical fate as the first reasonably priced color television sets hit the market. But the market was quickly saturated and started to diminish. Color television stocks stopped their rapid rise abruptly.

On the other hand, when the petroleum crisis hit the country at the end of 1973, the only stocks to show a rapid rise were those of companies in any way connected with the industry, from production and distribution to exploration. Prior to that, petroleum stocks were not particularly glamorous and the course of their growth was predictable. Afterward, the multiple of any company in any way connected with the petroleum industry enjoyed a heyday. Premiums were paid by institutions and brokerage houses for analysts who specialized in petroleum stocks and who had any understanding of the industry.

Industry analysis is not without its problems. It tends to exclude, for example, the company that is outperforming its industry. In 1973 and 1974, the apparel industry was considered to be depressed. Most companies were functioning on very low margins and could anticipate a cumulative annual growth of only 6 or 7%. Apparel industry analysts were universally bearish about the industry and as a group would recommend no apparel stock. Some apparel companies, at that time, were, however, performing brilliantly. College-Town Inc., a relatively small Boston based ladies sportswear manufacturer, had grown at a cumulative annual rate of 27% for five straight years, and was still growing. Its margins were averaging between 20 and 30%. While the techniques of dealing with this kind of situation are discussed elsewhere in this book, it should be noted here that industry analysts, even recognizing College-Town's superior performance, would not recommend the stock. Industry analysts tend to think, and unfortunately to act, as a group. The result is sometimes a self-fulfilling prophecy in that industry group.

Sometimes industry analysts find themselves susceptible to the same kind of short-term response to which the individual investor is victim. One of the groups to be hit when it was first announced that the plastic, polyvinyl chloride, was a factor in producing cancer in both the PVC industrial worker and the consumer was the plastics industry. Plastics analysts felt that most plastics manufacturers would be subject to regulation that would either curtail production or involve large capital investment in safety equipment. It took a considerable amount of time, during which plastic stocks were adversely affected, for the analysts to sort out those companies that were unaffected, or had already built safety factors into their production.

The problem of environmental pollution lends itself to a similar potential for overreaction. Many industries—paper, steel, chemical, utilities—are now subject to production strictures that will affect their processes, and attendant costs, to varying degrees. But there are relatively few facts available on how these strictures are to be defined or how to judge the costs for individual companies, much less specific industries. Very little research has been done in this area, and without facts, overreaction is found to be the rule.

ANALYSIS OF MANAGEMENT

The analysis of management is an even more difficult problem. Not only is it intangible, but it is highly subjective.

Management is about as exact a science as is weather forecasting. The elements of management are definable. What is not definable is the way the configuration of those elements will function in terms of results.

A good management must have a grasp of a great many things—finance, marketing, administration, production, distribution, and the economy in general. And even within the context of these elements abilities are limited and alter with changing conditions.

A man who invents a cure for the common cold may be a thoroughly bad manager in terms of marketing, production, or finance. The entrepreneur who invents a useful and valuable item in his garage may be capable of managing the company he develops with his invention until sales reach a level of $10 million a year. As his company continues to grow the shape of the company alters, his production needs change, and so, then, do administrative needs. A company in transition is at its most vulnerable point. The entrepreneur who is capable of building it to $30 million may not have the capabilities to build it from $30 to $100 million. Or from $100 to $200 million, or to $500 million. The management of a one-product company that decides to expand its product line or to diversify suddenly faces new and generally unfamiliar problems and may not be able to cope. A one-plant company that becomes a multiplant company or goes into an international market faces an entirely new set of management problems.

Other potential problems predicated on both personality and the capabilities of management further cloud the issue. When economic conditions are good and sales are coming easily, and the company is adequately financed and there are no production problems, a management team can be perfectly capable of showing profits. But how can you judge how that same management will function when money becomes tight, when competitors start hitting the market, when a strike hits the plant, when there is a material shortage, when there is a takeover attempt by another company, when there are price controls, or when—as in the case of the transistor problem—the market becomes saturated with its product? When a company has the only water hole in the desert for 200 miles around, a manager doesn't need a degree from the Harvard Business School to know how to sell water. But most companies function in a competitive economy. The history of American business is laden with managers of major companies who made the wrong decision. Sewell Avery of Montgomery Ward came to the conclusion that there would be a depression immediately following World War II. He refused to build additional stores. Sears Roebuck, on the other hand, anticipating economic growth, put up stores as rapidly as was economically feasible. The decline of Montgomery Ward was almost as fast as the rise of Sears Roebuck. What factors could a security analyst work out on his slide rule that would have gauged Montgomery Ward's major management mistake as compared to Sears Roebuck's salutary decision?

ANALYZING PLANS

Yet another intangible in which corporate evaluation must be made is the company's own plans. Any analyst with 12 minutes experience has learned to make a distinction between plans and dreams, even though dreams occasionally come true. There are, after all, businessmen named Ling, Bluhdorn, and Steinberg.

Fortunately, the experiences of the past decade have sharply diminished the number of corporate presidents who attempt to fool sophisticated analysts by passing their dreams off as valid projections or plans. It should be recognized that the acoustics of Wall Street are magnificent, particularly as it pertains to bad news or direct misrepresentations.

What is specifically of the essence here are the legitimate and carefully formulated plans and projections of a company that express more than just its wishes for the future, but are rather the blueprint and road map of company policy for continued profitability, expansion, and growth. The future is, after all, what the analyst is concerned with. He knows what the present and the past are. He may find the management of a company to be charming, sincere, bright, intelligent, highly motivated, ambitious, and trustworthy. But as an analyst he must make an assessment of how these virtues are going to be applied to appreciate the invested dollar.

In some cases the plans available for the analysts to consider are relatively simple and unsophisticated. "We are planning to grow through a program of acquisitions and our experience in the past has demonstrated that we can do this. This is the kind of acquisition we are planning to make, this is how we are going to buy the companies, this is the size company we are looking at." And so on and so on . . . Most of the factors, management is saying, are there for the analysis.

Or so it would seem. There are still many judgments to be made as to the validity of the program. One company in the office cleaning services business in the late 1960s had a very simple concept and seemed to have the capabilities to fulfill that concept. It was in an industry made up of predominately smaller privately held companies. The company simply went around the country combining the smaller companies into the larger one. Cash flow was good up to a point. It was an industry management knew and understood very well and seemed capable of managing. The stock was selling at a reasonable multiple, the issue was sufficiently large to allow a considerable amount of it to be used as a currency for making the acquisitions, and the banks and the institutions were in a mood to be generous. It worked very well for a while, and every analyst following the company could visualize the successful configuration of both tangibles and intangibles. But then the acquisition momentum outpaced both the ability to manage the rapidly growing company and to finance the continued growth. The company fell on its face. It ultimately had to sell off some of its properties in order to revitalize its balance sheet and make payments on its debt.

Corporate planning is itself a very complex business. At best, even supported by sophisticated thinking, it is precarious. Necessary, but still precarious. To distinguish the dream from the plan requires as much luck as skill. The larger companies—the General Motors, General Electrics, and the AT&T's—have a far greater capability to control their economic environment, and do plan more effectively than does the smaller company. General Motors, after all, controls a lion's share of the market, has the wherewithall to finance any reasonable plan, has the scope and diversity to offset and survive most economic swings, and has the marketing capability to expand and develop new markets virtually as needed. As major companies they control their own sources of supply of raw material, and as significant factors in their industries they receive little surprise from labor. Moreover, they have vast sources of input of economic information, not only domestically but worldwide. They have full staffs of economists to both gather and interpret material, and they have relationships in every corner of the world.

In other words, when General Electric, or any company of comparable size, develops a one-year or a five-year or a ten-year plan for its growth, it does it with infinitely more certainty than one applies to planning next Sunday's picnic.

And yet when the Arabs established their oil embargo, General Motors was hit as suddenly and as sharply as was the ordinary motorist. The first quarter of 1974 for General Motors was a shock. An industry that needs a lead time of two or three years for design of its products alone found that suddenly large cars were anathema to the general public, and was ill prepared to meet the sudden demand for small cars.

If a vast and sophisticated corporate machine like General Motors could fail in its corporate planning, what can an analyst expect of a company a fraction its size? A small company can blueprint, to a certain degree, its market opportunities and its plans to seize those opportunities, its capital expansion and the means for financing it, the normal growth patterns of its prospective markets and its ability to capitalize on those growth patterns, and so on. Some of these plans may be perfectly valid, but not in an unforeseeable economic climate. Other plans may be reasonable, but perhaps not for the management as it is presently constituted. The projections may be unrealistic in terms of potential shortages of raw materials or foreseeable problems in distribution patterns and so on. The smaller company may at best have a fine grasp of its own operation and its industry, but its input in terms of the larger economic context and facilities for capitalization down the line are sharply limited, and the company is, of course, more likely to be buffeted in a rough economic sea than is the large corporation. This is the very element that gives a greater appearance of stability to the giant company—the so-called blue chip stock. The same elements that portend stability and reliability for long-term performance for the larger company are the elements that make it easier for the larger company to plan for the longer range.

It is precisely these elements that the analyst must assess as part of his job in determining the ability of the company to generate a profit on the invested dollar in the near-, medium-, and long-range future.

THE CHARTIST

The kind of analysis—and the analysts—described thus far are merely one segment of the industry. These are analysts that concern themselves with analyzing fundamentals. There is yet another group—the technicians, or chartists.

The technician is concerned not with the company, but with the stock itself. He believes that stocks behave in a particular pattern that may be charted to project their future behavior. He concerns himself with such elements as the history of the stock's movement, a statistical analysis of the market's behavior, volume, and so forth. He believes that by charting a stock's historical pattern, he can project the pattern for the future.

Naturally there is a great deal of controversy among analysts and other observers of analysis about this approach. The chartist is irrelevant to this discussion, however, since he views the stock, not the company.

While the security analyst is the prime practitioner of corporate analysis, he is not, however, the sole conduit of information to the capital markets. There are many others.

THE BROKER

The broker is the direct contact between the customer—investor—and the company. The stock broker, or registered representative, is primarily a salesman. He has passed a simple basic examination that determines his ability to understand the fundamentals of the securities industry. His basic education beyond that need not be extensive, although some brokers are highly sophisticated. But the broker is essentially a salesman. He works either on commissions or, in some cases, on a salary predicated upon his sales quota. Essentially he must rely upon his firm's research department for basic information about a company and for the intensive analysis necessary to make a sound judgment about a security.

It is very difficult for a broker to function within the securities industry, even on its outer perimeter, without getting a strong feeling that he knows infinitely more than he does. On the one hand, he is a repository of all kinds of random information derived from other brokers, from research reports, from rumors brought to him by his customers, from his own inquiries of corporate officers, and from his general reading of the business journals. On the other hand, he is rarely equipped to make judgments based upon the fundamental factors used by the trained and experienced analyst. Many brokers, constantly watching the tape, tend to be gut reaction chartists.

Few investors make investment decisions based upon their own analysis, and then merely instruct the broker to execute the order. They are more likely to come to the broker with the name of a stock they believe, for one reason or another, to be a good one. The broker may then inquire of his research department or simply give his own reaction to it, based upon knowledge and feelings he has gleaned from the rumors, the tapes, and so on.

The broker's job is the most precarious in the securities industry. Regardless of the general condition of the stock market, his job depends upon his customers' buying and selling stock, from which he earns commissions. If the market is down generally and if the small investor is not investing, the average broker obviously does very little business. If the stocks he recommends, based on whatever factors, do not go up, or the stocks he recommends to be sold do go up after the sale, he loses his customers. Since it is relatively easy to become a broker, and extraordinarily difficult for a broker to make a good living in anything but a bull market, the turnover in brokers is overwhelming. In 1971 there were 53,000 brokers functioning. In 1974, with the market down, there were 33,000 brokers.

Nevertheless, with brokers as the focal point for the customer, it is almost as important that brokers understand a corporation as do analysts, regardless of the degree of sophistication involved in that understanding. An enthusiastic broker wtih a large following of customers can place a substantial amount of stock. Thus it becomes almost as important to consider brokers a target audience for corporate information as analysts.

THE INSTITUTIONAL SALESMAN

Institutional salesmen, while like brokers essentially salesmen, are dealing with an infinitely more sophisticated and knowledgeable customer. More and more the institutional salesman is being drawn from the ranks of the analysts, and many brokerage firms are converting their analysts to institutional salesmen. With the change from fixed to negotiated commission rates on stock sales, the picture has begun to change considerably and the question of unbundling begins to arise. Unbundling, in this context, means separating the research function from the sales function and charging the client or customer separately for each. In the past, when an individual or an institution purchased stock, the commission on the purchase was considered to cover the cost of research. But as competitive rates enter the picture, the move is now toward a separate fee for research. This is particularly important in institutions that do their own research and want to pay only for the execution of stock purchase. The line is still fuzzy since institutions, always eager for new ideas, still may depend upon the institutional salesman for information, even though the institution may ultimately do its own final research.

THE MONEY MANAGER

The money manager is a person who makes the final decision in a stock purchase. He may be the head of a mutual fund, or a bank trust department, or a pension fund, or hedge fund, or a small pool of private investment capital, or a discretionary account for a brokerage firm. Most money managers tend to use the basic research supplied by their own or other research departments, to which they apply their own judgment. It, too, is a precarious job, since it is directly performance oriented, with very little margin for error. Thus the money manager tries to be as informed as possible in order to have a basis for judgement of the research factors.

THE ECONOMIST

A little known factor in corporate analysis is the economist for the major bank, the larger brokerage houses, and the major corporation. While the economist is primarily concerned with larger economic trends, he relies to a large extent on industry information, and the performance of companies within that industry, for major elements in making his projections. His output then becomes an important framework for security analysis.

CORPORATE PORTFOLIO MANAGERS

Not to be overlooked are the corporate portfolio managers. While most corporations depend on outside sources for advice, they still participate in making final stock purchasing decisions.

THE TRADER

Since the configuration of the market has changed considerably, a segment of the financial community that has become increasingly important in stock trading, and therefore in the analysis of stock, is the trader. In the past, most traders—the exceptions were a few leading traders at the larger houses—were concerned solely with trading on the instructions of others. Today, with sharply lower volume, the trader in over-the-counter stocks plays an infinitely more important and independent role. Frequently, the over-the-counter trader, his job facilitated by the NASDAQ system, will take small to medium positions in a stock in which he has faith in order to make a market. Frequently he is armed with no more than the information he is basically required to know by securities regulation, which is little more than the company's most recent financial performance. More and more he must rely upon his own judgment. Most of the smaller trading firms do not maintain a research staff to keep him informed in very great detail. Thus the onus for keeping the trader informed must fall upon the corporation.

All of this is on the equity side. But the greatest source of capital in industry is debt—the bank loan, the debenture, commercial paper—the full range.

ANALYSIS FOR CREDIT

The analysis of a company for equity investment differs sharply from the analysis of a company for credit. The equities investor is concerned with the ability of the company to give him a profit on his invested dollar. The creditor is concerned with the ability of the company to repay the loan, no matter how long or short the period.

While the approaches to analysis in each case are significantly different, there are many overlapping factors. Essential to both is a judgment of the viability of the company.

The fact that many debt issues are rated for quality by Moody's Investors Service, Standard and Poor's, or others does not mean automatic acceptance or rejection by individual bond or commercial paper buyers, banks, or other institutions. The competition for capital via debt is no less keen. And certainly no banks automatically lend to any company, no matter how apparently sound, that applies for it. Investors in debt issues have choices to make, even between two bonds rated AAA.

Thus the effort to reach debt investors must be no less intensive than for equity investors. Virtually every element about a company that is of interest to an equities analyst is of interest to a debt issue analyst, whether it is an individual, a bank lending officer, an analyst at a bond house, or an institution. The company story must be just as carefully formulated, and as energetically presented, as for an equity issue. This holds true, incidentally, for a municipal bond as well as for an industrial or utility bond.

The rating services themselves are not infalliable. They function predominantly from set formulas which give little consideration to subjective factors of judgment and which can be just as valid a measure of a company's potential to repay debt as are subjective factors. What this means, realistically, is that ratings can sometimes be upgraded by an intelligent presentation of facts to rating service analysts.

OTHER ANALYTICAL TARGETS

Those segments of the financial community that have been described here constitute the main body of specialists to whom the elements of a company's potential must be communicated. Naturally, nothing in this area is monolithic. While the bulk of investment decisions rest with analysts, money managers, and others, there are still fragments of the securities industry whose opinions and impressions are important. The role of external means of communications, such as the financial press, will be dealt with later. The concern here is with specific focal points of judgment within the securities industry. There is, for example, value in having the head of the corporate finance department of a brokerage firm or investment banking firm aware of a company's profile, since he is frequently a man who is sufficiently respected within his own company to have his judgment considered. The man in charge of mergers and acquisitions for an investment banking firm is frequently looked upon as a source of new investment ideas, since the nature of his work brings him into exploratory situations with a great many companies. Within this context the merger and acquisition man has another interesting potential value. A merger is a form of investment of corporate assets. The mergers and acquisitions specialists can frequently put corporate information to better use in behalf of a corporation than can many other people in the investment community.

THE FOREIGN MARKET

There is a somewhat larger foreign market for American securities than many people realize. American securities are purchased by banks, investment funds, and other institutions, as well as by individuals. Foreign purchasing is usually in smaller blocks and is frequently for the longer term. As may be expected U.S. stocks are purchased by generally more sophisticated investors. Considering the state of the securities market at any given time, the foreign market can be a good one for many companies not now selling outside of the United States.

Most foreign investors in American securities purchase stock through American brokerage houses, particularly those that have offices abroad, or through U.S. securities affiliates of foreign banks and brokers. By the end of 1973, approximately 140 U.S. banks had branches or affiliates in 150 foreign countries, and 168 foreign banks from 38 countries were represented in the United States. These affiliates, while not allowed to join the New York Stock Exchange, are frequently members of regional exchanges or trade actively in the third market. In some cases, they purchase through American brokers. Some larger U.S. companies find it valuable to list their securities on foreign exchanges.

Aside from the techniques described in this chapter, which will effectively reach the American outlets for foreign securities, support can be achieved by working directly overseas. Companies such as European Financial Forum (2 Carlos Place, London W1, England), a financial relations firm that works with American companies and is run by former American investor relations specialist Leonard Baker, have the capability to establish sound and valuable relations between American corporations and the European financial community.

While the diversity of target groups for corporate information is wide, there are certain basic factors which must be communicated universally. The strategy of dealing with the different groups will be discussed in Chapter 10, but basically the information needed for analysis is definable.

REQUIREMENTS OF ANALYSIS

Essentially, the requirements of analysis of a corporation fall into three categories—financial data, management, and plans.

Financial data is, of course, the simplest to define. Although there are still areas of operating information that many companies seem reluctant to disclose, for a public company there is relatively little to which an interested observer cannot become privy. The corporation that tells less in its annual report than it does in its Form 10K, the mandatory report filed annually with the Securities and Exchange Commission and available to the public, deludes itself. More significantly, it deprives itself of any opportunity that may exist to view the company favorably. It also leaves itself open to a serious credibility problem. Most analysts feel that if a company is reluctant to disclose and broadcast information of any nature, and particularly information to be found in a 10K, the reasons for doing so must be negative. And since most analysts tend to recoil at the least bit of negative information, any attempt to hide anything causes an almost immediate overreaction.

Furthermore, the SEC, in recent years, has been absolutely assiduous in its efforts to increase disclosure. Ultimately there will be relatively little that a company can legally fail to disclose in its annual report, much less its Form 10K.

The overriding factor still remains—the more that is known about a company the more readily it will be understood, believed, and favorably viewed.

In analyzing a company at least the following financial information is essential:

1. *The earnings record.* Since earnings, and the ability to project earnings, are the ultimate aim of analysis, earnings history is a basic tool. It should be clearly remembered, however, that the numbers for earnings never stand alone. Earnings are relative to many other factors. Certainly, earnings are meaningless except in relation to revenues and as a percentage of revenues. What is significant in analysis, then, is not just the earnings figure, even when there is a steady increase over the years. It is more important to note the degree of consistency and growth in earnings and margins. And even this doesn't stand alone, since a growing corporation is affected by many different factors during the course of a year. A sharp growth in earnings may be the result of astute management and a marvelously improved production, distribution, or marketing structure. It may also reflect a merger or acquisition, or a change in accounting practices. In recent years, accelerated by the efforts of two analysts, Thornton L.

O'Glove and Robert A. Olstein, a new and meaningful term has come into use—quality of earnings. This is an analysis of earnings predicated upon factors which are not immediately discernible, such as accounting changes which can alter the measure of earnings in ways that do not accurately reflect the company's actual performance. Prime examples are changes in depreciation method, or capitalizing versus expensing certain expenditures. For example, the measure of loss or gain from the sale of a segment of a corporation's operation is a function of the reserve set up for the disposal of those operations—and there is virtually no way to determine from most financial statements the basis used for establishing the size of that reserve. Historical earnings in the pure sense are of themselves of little value in gauging the ability of a company to continue to earn at a consistent rate. Properly analyzed, however, the factors behind a consistent earnings history are a measure of contributing elements to ongoing earnings growth.

2. *Revenues.* Revenues are a measure of the size of a company—a way of categorizing the economic sphere in which it functions. Obviously, it may be readily inferred that many factors about a $500 million company are different from those of a $25 million company. The large company is generally older and better established and would seem to have a greater potential for growth and survival. It probably has a better grasp of its markets. It probably has a larger number of shares outstanding and a greater liquidity in the stock market. It probably has a greater ability to withstand broader economic difficulties. Yet it must not be taken for granted that a very large company has any greater ability to be successful than does a smaller one. The number of giants that have fallen on hard times in recent years is too large to take size alone as a measure of investment safety. Witness Penn Central, Litton Industries, Pan American World Airways, LTV, Lockheed, Chrysler, and others.

3. *Margins.* Normally, margin—the percentage of net income to revenues—is relatively simple to measure. It is a major factor in determining both the efficiency of a company and its ability to cope with costs and expenses—a constantly changing factor. It becomes even more significant in a period of raging inflation, when margins reflect vast swings in the cost of raw material and labor. In 1973 and the first quarter of 1974, the margins of many companies were severely hit by a federal price control structure that in many cases did not allow them to pass on to their own customers the high cost of certain basic materials. The quality of earnings became a serious concern in 1974 in relation to margins, when many companies sold from inventories that had been built up at lower costs, and were reported at inflated prices. In many cases, this resulted in a distorted picture of the company's realistic margin, since it was difficult to discern the consistent level of future costs for the same items. Many

companies changed their method of depreciation to affect accelerated inflation.

4. *Return on equity.* In terms of investment, this is a most significant measure of a company's success. It is, after all, what investment is all about. If the return on an investment in one company isn't as high as it is in another—and assuming that the difference isn't offset by dividend yield or that the company isn't so highly leveraged that it is threatened by high interest rates—then what is the point in investing in the company with the low return?

5. *Balance sheet.* An accurate balance sheet is still the best picture of a company's financial position—*as of the date of the balance sheet.* If the balance sheet of Penn Central, which reported an extraordinarily heavy debt, had been carefully read, then its favorable earnings reports issued immediately prior to its bankruptcy might have been viewed with a bit more skepticism. The balance sheet does—or should—tell the analyst a great many things. It also poses a great many questions. And it behooves the corporation to anticipate these questions in order to prevent misunderstanding or misinterpretations, as well as to clarify the position of the company. There may very well be justification for a very high inventory or a substantial increase in inventory from one year to the next. The balance sheet alone will merely indicate the size of the inventory. It will not explain it. A reduction of cash from the prior year against a reduction of debt implies that the cash was used to reduce the debt. Without explanation it is merely an implication. Certainly any disparity from one year to the next in accounts receivable or accounts payable warrants an explanation, even if it's an unfavorable one.

While the notes to financial statements usually clarify the debt structure, questions about debt—both long and short term—go much beyond the balance sheet. The balance sheet, it must be remembered, is as of a particular date. Debt can be increased or decreased the day after the closing of the balance sheet, as can any element of the assets or liabilities. This is a prime example of why a balance sheet never speaks for itself in describing a company; the analyst wants to know more. And with accounting standards rapidly changing, the company must be prepared to defend its accounting methods.

6. *Ratios.* The analyst, with his slide rule or electronic calculator, can compute a headspinning number of ratios, many of which, like astrological symbols, have meanings of varying depth for different people. The ratio of current assets to current liabilities, if it is less than two to one, sends a red flag flying. If the debt/equity ratio is too high, the analyst immediately wonders about the drain on future earnings by debt payments. The range of ratios is extensive. The ratio of return on total capital. The ratio of

depreciation and depletion to sales. The ratio of earnings paid out in dividends to earnings. And this is exclusive of ratios of various factors such as earnings, dividends, assets, and sales to the market price of the stock. Graham, in his book, *Security Analysis*, leans very heavily on ratios as a measure of company performance.

The point is that ratios without explanation frequently imply a picture that, in view of changing conditions and other factors, may not be accurate in terms of the corporation's actual operations. Ratios, like any statistics, are a still picture of a corporation frozen at the moment the picture was taken, while the corporation continues to move on. It is extremely important that any ratio that differs from the industry norm, either up or down, is a signal for the need for elucidation and explanation.

7. *Cost of capital.* Some aspects of the cost of capital, such as the prime rate, are fairly evident. The company that must function heavily with short-term borrowing, such as a leasing company or an importer who depends upon revolving credit lines, will find itself in serious trouble when the prime rate gets up around 11 or 12%. The company that is fairly heavily leveraged—has a very high debt in proportion to its equity—is also in serious trouble. The expansion-minded company is always viewed in terms of its financial ability to expand either internally or externally. Even in an atmosphere that allows for additional capital through equities, the analyst must consider the cost of a company's equity capital in terms of its price/earnings ratio. This whole area then becomes a matter of major concern for analysts, and therefore of major concern for the corporation that wants to explain itself.

8. *The industry.* For a company to represent its financial situation independent of the industry in which it functions, or even the larger economy, is to delude itself. Even the company that is out-performing its industry for one reason or another must still realize that it is being judged in terms of its industry. No company president functions without intensive knowledge of his industry. But too often companies are presented to analysts without a clear explanation of comparable performances, common and uncommon problems and solutions, costs of raw materials and distribution, potential markets, and so forth.

9. *Specialized industries.* The evaluation of companies in certain industries, such as banks, insurance companies, finance companies, leasing companies, public utilities, and so on, requires analysis of some additional elements, and a different emphasis on common elements. Sources and uses of funds and revenues differ. Accounting methods differ. Nevertheless the same rules of communication apply. Ratios and changes require explanation, and nothing should be taken for granted.

There is yet another problem in that the analysis of specialized industries usually falls on a small segment of analysts who specialize in that industry. This poses two serious concerns. First, the judgment of a company by industry specialists, no matter how well it is performing, is often given the same general market value as is the industry itself. If the industry is depressed, a superior company within that industry faces serious stock market problems.

Second, the number of analysts who fully understand the ramifications of a particular industry is rarely sufficient, and often not representative of a sufficiently large investment public, to affect broader trading in most cases. It therefore becomes necessary to deal with analysts functioning in other contexts and in other organizations who are not sufficiently well versed in the ramifications of a particular industry to make sound judgments. The communications effort then becomes doubly hard. Not only must the company be explained, but the complex specialized differences in dealing with the company and analyzing it must be made clear.

This problem also arises frequently in dealing with companies with large international operations. Few analysts feel they have the broader international economic background to properly assess a company with significant international activity. Their tendency is to ignore such companies and move on to those they do understand. There are, after all, more companies in the broader economic sphere than any one analyst can deal with. If an analyst doesn't understand something readily he will move on to something he does understand.

10. *External economic factors.* During the Arab oil embargo in December 1973, when gasoline became scarce and available stocks increased rapidly in price, an automotive analyst did not have to wait for General Motors' or Ford's figures to understand what was going to happen to automobile sales. When, a few years ago, the use of DDT as an insecticide was banned, an analyst did not have to wait for the next quarter's results to know that those companies that were major producers of DDT and other insecticides were going to suffer.

But unless the company itself supplies the guidelines for evaluating the effect of these external economic factors, the judgment by analysts will almost invariably be an overreaction. The responsibility for putting any economic news in perspective, even before its effect is felt by the company, resides with the company.

These are the significant financial factors that must be communicated in the judgment of a company. It should be clear, however, that in dealing with analysts and others who judge companies, numbers should never be allowed to speak for themselves. They never do. They require elucidation and explanation. It cannot be repeated too often—a corporation's statistics freeze the picture as of the date of those statistics, and corporations are moving entities.

JUDGMENT OF MANAGEMENT

The intangibles of a company that must be judged are its management and its plans. There are in American industry today many large companies that began as small companies. There are also many small companies—and many that no longer exist—that were started at the same time as companies that are currently large. One difference between two companies that started small and of which only one thrived is capitalization. The other and major difference is management.

The broad definition of management is the subject of a full library. What is of the essence here is the ability to project, believably, a corporate management's ability to manage its company, to cause it to thrive and to grow, and to survive, especially in difficult times.

The question of credibility becomes a very significant one here. A company president can hardly stand in front of an audience of security analysts and boast of his abilities. It is good form, on the other hand, for him to describe, in speaking and writing, his management team as being excellent, forward-looking, and skilled. But why should he be believed? It's true that some corporate leaders are clean-cut, strong-jawed, and clear-eyed—obviously exciting and believable men—at least at the moment they are talking. Other extraordinarily competent corporate leaders are shy, reticent, introspective, and poor public speakers. Some of the most striking photos of chief executive officers appearing in annual reports show men of vision and forcefulness, obviously the kind of people in whom widows and orphans should invest their faith and savings.

In fact, credibility is a function of three things—corporate performance, consistent truth, and a willingness to deal forthrightly with the public and those who analyze securities in behalf of the public.

It is absolutely imperative, for success in the capital markets, for an executive to build a record of truthfulness. Any misrepresentation will not only be readily found out, but will reverberate throughout the financial community like a lion's roar. Furthermore, the number of eyes on a public company are many. A public company is under constant scrutiny. It took only one disgruntled employee and one astute analyst to topple the fraud-ridden Equity Funding empire. Any corporate executive who thinks he can deal with the investing public by misrepresenting facts or by refusing to disclose pertinent material necessary for the judgment of his company will not long succeed in the capital markets.

The best gauge of management is still track record. How successfully has management performed? What has it achieved in the growth of the company? How has it survived and dealt with problems? What opportunities has it seized upon and how were those opportunities capitalized? How has management restructured itself to meet changes in its corporation and its environment?

These and other elements of management capability are intangibles that are projected in real ways. The history of the company, however brief, can be told in terms of management decisions. "When we realized that the next decade would see a population growth in the number of women between the ages of twenty-eight and thirty-five, we decided to design a special line of sportswear and merchandise it to that group."

"When we recognized that we were just a few years away from market saturation for our product, we began to explore feasible areas of diversification into products the design and production of which were within our experience and existing capabilities to exploit."

"As our company reached the fifty million dollar mark, we recognized the need for broadening the management base, expanding middle management, and changing the nature of our management reporting systems."

"As we recognized that the average age of our management team was approaching fifty, we began a recruiting and training program to develop the men who would ultimately be our successors."

Yet another way in which management can project itself is in the clarity of presentation of facts about its company. The erudite company president, surrounded by his executive vice-president and vice-president of finance, who clearly recites facts and figures about his company's operation, clearly delineates its present financial structure and its plans for future growth, and obviously has a grasp of his industry and the economy at large, is much more believable than the company president who merely recites, either by rote or from the printed page, material that has already appeared in his annual report.

The company president who demonstrates the ways in which he has constantly broadened the management base to meet the growing needs of his company, and is constantly divesting himself of responsibilities by delegating them to other able people, inspires infinitely more faith than the president of a company who is obviously a one-man band and keeps everything to himself, regardless of the number of underlings he has hired to do his bidding. The future of a one-man company is no greater than the length of the president's arm, and every analyst knows it.

PLANS

Despite what has been said about the precarious nature of long-range planning, a company's plans are an essential part of its evaluation and should be clearly expressed. As has been noted, however, there is a significant difference between plans and dreams. The president of a company with $1 million in sales may have dreams of heading a billion dollar multinational corporation, but may not have the foggiest idea of how to increase his sales to $2 million. On the other hand, a company president who recognizes the potential in certain aspects of home furnishings, is planning to expand his existing marketing and production capabilities to meet that potential, who hopes to supplement that capability with an acquisition or two, and who recognizes the limitations of his ability to finance those plans, should clearly delineate his corporate ideas. He should recognize publicly the dimensions of the potential market, the need to divest himself of certain unprofitable operations, however painful and without emotional consideration, the ways he intends to finance the growth and how much he expects it will cost him, the kind of management changes he is going to have to make, the kind of economic climate in which he expects to function, and the down side risks.

There is among analysts a built-in skepticism that was ingrained during the glorious years of the 1960s. Too many presidents saw the world as a boundless cornucopia and were free in their declarations of a utopian future for their companies. They had, after all, achieved marvelous records so far. The names of a very large number of these men still come to the mind of too many analysts for them to believe any projection of glory that is not specifically documented in terms of how those plans are to be accomplished, predicated upon a record of achievement and comparable activities.

THE MECHANICS OF DEALING WITH ANALYSTS

Given the substance of what is to be communicated there remains only the mechanics of communicating it.

The strategy of selecting the specific techniques to be used, people to be dealt with, and timing, is discussed in Chapter 10. The mechanical structure of dealing with the financial community consists essentially of the following:

1. Security analyst meetings.
2. Meeting with or talking to individual analysts.

3. Issuing a background report.

4. Preparing and distributing printed material, including annual and quarterly reports, for distribution to the financial community.

5. Regular and periodic mailing of information about the company to the financial community, including copies of press releases.

6. The financial press.

7. Corporate advertising.

8. Handling unsolicited inquiries.

ANALYST MEETINGS

Setting up an analyst meeting is like good tightrope walking. It looks easier than it is. It would seem that the simplest way to hold an analyst meeting is to select the names of 15 or 20 likely analysts from the directory of the Federation of Security Analysts (available from the Federation of Security Analysts, 219 East 42nd Street, New York, N.Y. 10017, $25.00), arrange for an appropriate dining room and catered luncheon, and invite them. This is like saying that the way across the river is simple. You walk to the edge of the river, take off your cloak, strike the water, and when the water parts you walk across. Simple.

The selection of analysts is described later on in this book in the chapter on strategy. There are some basic considerations that should be dealt with here, however.

The number of analysts should be kept manageable. Sometimes, if the meeting is to be held in a city rarely visited by the management group, as many as 20 or 25 analysts are appropriate. Otherwise, 15 is a large number, certainly in terms of the ability of everyone present to ask intelligent questions and to allow time for questions to be answered.

A luncheon meeting, which is the most common way of doing it, has some specific elements. It should be held in a private place, preferably a luncheon club or restaurant with private rooms. The club or restaurant should have some measure of experience in dealing with meetings of this type or else service will extend well into the period allotted for the presentation.

Timing is most important. While most analysts are delighted to attend a luncheon, particularly if it's a company in which they are especially interested or even if they know it will be attended by other analysts with whom they will have the opportunity to talk shop, they are still away from their desks during the time that the market is functioning. The rule is very simple. Luncheon meetings should be called for noon. Cocktails should be served until virtually all of the invited guests have arrived, and certainly no later than 12:30. Lunch should be over not one minute later than 1:15, the presentation should begin over dessert, and the meeting, including questions, should end promptly at 2:00. Anyone who has the time beyond that point will stay around afterward to chat with management, but that should be a personal option.

An attempt shoud be made to determine whether any meetings are scheduled for other companies in the same industry, which would draw analysts who might find themselves in a conflicting situation. This is done by phoning one or two analysts you plan to invite and asking them if they know of any other company in the industry they follow that's planning to have a meeting on that date. Once the list of analysts is determined and the date selected, simple invitations to attend the meeting should be mailed out. This is done two to three weeks before the meeting. A few days after the invitations are mailed out, there should be a phone follow-up to develop a preliminary list of those who plan to attend. Those who have accepted the invitation should then be sent a kit of printed materials on the company. This should include the latest annual report, subsequent interim reports, the Form 10K, releases issued since the annual report, reprints of material about the company that have appeared in the financial press or the trade press (or even articles from the consumer press if they demonstrate the company's claim to product superiority or widespread promotion), reprints of an important and significant trade or consumer advertising campaign, business biographies of top management, and, if pertinent, product material. While it is rare that every one of the analysts who accepts an invitation a week or two before the meeting will actually attend, the phone follow-up gives the first basic idea of what attendance is likely to be. There is usually a 10 to 20% drop-off.

The morning of the meeting, every analyst who has accepted the invitation should be phoned to remind him of the meeting that day and to verify his attendance. Here, too, there are usually dropouts or substitutions.

Following the phone calls on the morning of the meeting, convention style badges should be made for everyone who is to attend, including management. While it would seem that these badges have a gala aura about them, there is rarely any objection, and they serve several extremely valuable purposes. They allow the company officers to be readily identified and to be able to address analysts by name. They allow the analysts to identify one another and to build the valuable acquaintanceships among themselves which are of great importance to them in an industry in which interchange of information is extremely important. By noting which badges are used and not used, the mechanics of taking attendance is reduced to a very simple matter. All that is necessary is that a representative of the company be on hand to write out badges for the substitutes and uninvited guests that show up.

Including the press at analysts' meetings is generally not preferred, although opinion varies. Unless the meeting is going to be used to impart important new information, the two should be kept separate. Societies and splinter groups should be specifically queried.

These are the mechanics of the meeting. Preparation for it poses an entirely different problem.

PREMEETING PREPARATION

Whether a prepared speech or an outline is used is the personal choice of the executive who is to make the presentation. Of the two, the outline is preferred, if for no other reason than it demonstrates more readily the executive's grasp of his company. It is too easy to assume that a speech was written by someone else.

The organization of the presentation is extremely important. A typical outline can be found in the Appendix. It begins with a very brief history of the company, sufficient only to give a context for the present and the future. If appropriate, it can delineate those problems that the company has had or that the industry has faced. It then describes the company as it is presently constituted—what it is, what it makes, how it distributes, the size of its markets, why it is in those markets. It then discusses the company's financial structure in terms described earlier in this chapter. This can be followed by the management structure and then the plans for the company. The meeting is then opened for questions.

It is absolutely essential that no company executive attend an analysts' meeting without having anticipated every possible question that might be asked by the analysts and having prepared an answer. It makes no difference how silly, ancillary, or painful the question is. It should be anticipated and the answer carefully thought out beforehand. The most impressive presentation can be destroyed in a moment by one question that is badly answered.

THE PRESENTATION

The tone of the presentation should be honest, forthright, and positive. Negative factors should be expressed clearly and in no way avoided, however, they need not be dwelt upon inordinately and out of proportion to their importance to the overall picture. Hostile questions should be handled patiently and forthrightly and, even if the answer is negative in terms of the total presentation, should be ended on a positive note.

It should be recognized that despite all care taken in developing the invitation list, a certain number of analysts will invariably show up who really don't care about the company, even if they discover it during the course of the presentation. They will seem uninterested or ask cursory questions. It should also be recognized that not everyone present will see the company in the same way, nor with the same degree of sophistication. In any meeting of 10 or more analysts, there will almost invariably be three or four silly questions—questions asked because an analyst feels he must say something to make his presence known or because he frankly doesn't understand. These questions must be handled with the same patience as the more serious and delving ones.

A great many company stories are well told by visual presentations—a short film or slide presentation. This can be useful and effective if it is carefully done. In the Appendix is a typical script for one such slide presentation. It is pertinent, tight, and to the point. It is useful in visualizing product and service, as well as in the graphic presentation of complex financial material.

The visual presentation, however, should never preclude a personal presentation of the chief executive officer. It should merely visualize that which is best visualized—the star performer should always be the chief executive himself. How else can he demonstrate those factors about his own management's capabilities than by his own physical presence?

Despite the fact that each person invited has been sent a kit of materials about the company, a duplicate kit should be placed on each seat before the luncheon. Many analysts will have forgotten their kits or there will have been substitute analysts to whom no kit was ever sent. A fatal mistake, incidentally, is to include a copy of the chief executive's presentation in the kit. There is nothing more distressing to a speaker than to look up and find 10 or 15 people following his words on the printed page, or reading ahead of him. It is good practice, on the other hand, to record the presentation and transcribe it for distribution to interested analysts who did not attend the meeting for one reason or another.

ANALYST SOCIETY MEETINGS

In major cities, local analysts' societies hold regular meetings to which companies are invited to make presentations. The question almost invariably arises as to the value of the company's requesting an appearance before an entire city's society.

The problem with meetings of most analysts' societies is that they are attended by vast numbers of analysts who do not follow any but a selected number of companies. This means that, except for the very largest corporations, the overwhelming percentage of the audience is attending only out of curiosity. For the smaller OTC or AMEX company, the only value in a meeting before New York, Chicago, or Los Angeles societies is the prestige of the reprint of the presentation. In most cases, those analysts who can best serve the company are readily identifiable, can be singled out, and can be dealt with in other ways.

Splinter groups—segments of the analysts' society that specialize in covering a specific industry such as real estate, apparel, insurance, and so on—are increasing in number. For the medium or smaller company, appearance before the splinter group makes infinitely more sense. For the larger company, its value is obvious.

THE POST-MARKET-CLOSE MEETING

Not all analyst meetings need be luncheon meetings. For companies with an especially interesting story to tell, a post-market-close meeting can be useful. Analysts are selected and invited in the same way as for a luncheon meeting, but the meeting is held at 4:30 P.M., after the market closes, as either a cocktail party or, if convenient, at the offices of the company itself.

A variation of this is the single-firm sales meeting. Frequently, the sales manager of a brokerage house can be persuaded to invite a corporate management to the brokerage house's office after the close of the market to make his presentation to his staff of registered representatives. The rules of the presentation are the same as for the analyst meetings, except that it should be anticipated that the questions are likely to be somewhat less sophisticated than those from the analysts, and will dwell more heavily on the movement of the stock, which is, after all, the broker's prime concern.

EARNINGS PROJECTIONS

One basic point that should be seriously considered is the problem of earnings projections. There are many schools of thought on this.

An earnings projection by management that can be given any substance or validity is an analyst's dream. It gives him something to focus on. In fact, the SEC has from time to time considered making earnings projections mandatory. The assumption is that any well-managed company can make at least a short-term projection of how it is going to perform, give or take a few percentage points.

On the other hand, earnings projections have several inherent dangers. They are an implied promise of performance that may well preclude factors beyond the company's control. They place the company's credibility precariously on the line and are frequently misjudged. A projection of $1.30 that comes out as $1.23 can cause the market to overreact irrationally. A projection of $1.30 that comes out to $1.40 can cause the market to overreact on the up side.

An earnings projection also places an additional psychological burden on the management team by causing it to focus its energies on operations toward meeting that projection, which is not management's job.

What almost invariably happens, on the other hand, is that the analysts themselves will make a projection in the form of a question. If management chooses not to make a projection of its own, it can simply ratify the analysts' projection as "being in the ball park" or otherwise too high or too low. If management has decided to make no projection, it should in no way be bullied into it. There are sufficiently sound reasons to explain the refusal to do so if the remainder of the presentation has been forthright.

The SEC is seriously considering mandatory inclusion of projections—including "ball park" assent—in the Form 10K, the annual report, and registration statements. They would also insist that a Form 8K be filed should a projection be made.

There is one important point regarding all analyst meetings, and, in fact, any form of financial communication. Although it will be dealt with in greater detail in Chapter 4, the rules of disclosure of the SEC very clearly apply here. Any statement made in an analyst meeting, whether it be before one or many analysts, that is significant in judging the company and that has never been made before must be publicly released as quickly as possible. If management intends to make such statements at a meeting, whether it be an earnings projection or a merger announcement or a major diversification plan, a release should be prepared well beforehand for public distribution at the time of the meeting. This is extremely important.

MEETING WITH INDIVIDUAL ANALYSTS

In addition to meeting with analysts in groups, it is frequently valuable to meet with them individually. Since this can be tremendously time consuming, this kind of meeting should be limited to analysts representing a significant segment of the investing public. This includes analysts for very large retail houses, funds, or investment advisory services. The meeting can be held at lunch, or in the office of the chief executive, or in the office of the analyst. Here the presentation, while as complete as for the larger analyst meeting and as well prepared, can be somewhat less formal. The questions tend to be more searching and the executive should be more guarded, since his answers are likely to be more detailed than they would be in response to questions from the floor of a larger meeting. Here, too, the company must be prepared to release publicly any information of consequence that had not theretofore been public knowledge. A record of the meeting—even on tape—should be kept so that it can be shown that no inside information was given.

Frequently a company (and especially those that for one reason or another prefer to remain obscure) will capture the eye of an individual analyst without any effort on the company's part. The analyst then calls the president and asks a lot of searching questions. In the case of larger companies the inquiries may be welcome, and sometimes more so at one point than another. Sometimes an individual investor will feel lonely and concerned and will take it upon himself to call the company president. Nothing inappropriate about it, but sometimes a surprise.

These inquiries should be anticipated by the management of every public company, and prepared for in much the same way as is the presentation for a full-scale analyst meeting. An individual analyst who surprises a company president and gets the wrong answers can do considerable damage to a company's stock, no matter how well the company is doing. There is no need for it.

All inquiries should be treated courteously and in detail. The company should follow up the inquiry by mailing the same material that it distributes to analysts at meetings. If the analyst represents an important enough faction of the investment community, it's certainly appropriate to invite him to come in for a personal visit and a plant tour.

It is extremely important, in anticipating inquiries and preparing the presentation, that the company story be uniformly understood and told by any member of the management team who is likely to get such an inquiry. In some cases it's appropriate for the chief executive officer to insist that all such calls be passed on to him or to the vice-president of finance. In some cases this may seem like a put-off, which in itself is an attack on credibility. It then behooves the chief executive officer to be sure that everyone who might receive such an inquiry is fully informed of the company's point of view, method of presentation, and proper answers to questions.

When the company is some distance away from a major city, when there is a story of particular interest to tell, and when a tour of the company's operations can contribute to the analysts' knowledge, one or several analysts may be invited to visit with management at the company's plant. This is frequently done at the company's expense, although a large number of analysts prefer to pay their own way. Analysts also make field trips on their own, touring a particular area and the companies within that area.

FOLLOW-UP

Apart from these formalized analyst meetings, a properly run financial relations program, whether performed internally or with the aid of a financial relations agency, must include a concerted effort to build and service a following of analysts.

Merely to address a meeting of analysts is not to solve a financial relations problem. The corporation is, after all, competing against hundreds and thousands of other companies, not only for capital, but for the analysts' attention as well. This competition is a continuous effort. Simply because an analyst has met with management and heard its story once, and even if he is impressed, there is no reason to believe that his interest will be sustained or that he will not be distracted by six other companies that command his attention. This is done by putting every analyst who attends a meeting—or expresses any sort of interest—on a continuous mailing list.

He must then be contacted periodically, updated on material, reminded of recent information that has been released, and have his questions answered. It is an ongoing process that, to be effective, must be consistent.

RESEARCH REPORTS

A constant aim, in dealing with analysts, is to generate research reports by brokerage houses or research services. These are reports, issued periodically, for use by both brokers and investors. They may be either brief discussions of the company or intensive, detailed research studies. They almost invariably conclude with a purchase recommendation—either to buy or to sell—or a recommendation to hold the stock for the longer term. A favorable recommendation by a major firm can be a virtual guarantee of increased buying.

A successful financial relations effort includes constantly developing new interest for a company in the financial community. A knowledgeable consultant will be aware, by virtue of his consistent efforts in the field, of what analysts are following what companies, the many changes among analysts and their affiliations, and the current basis for viewing companies. He will spend a considerable number of hours every month talking to analysts to determine those who are likely targets to hear the company's story. He will follow up earlier contacts to keep them updated and to help maintain their interest. He will develop a constantly expanding following for a company and eliminate those analysts no longer interested or no longer available to be interested. This also leads to developing sponsorship for a stock, as well as new market-makers.

FEEDBACK

What is just as important is the consultant's ability to supply feedback of market reaction to the company. By frequently speaking to analysts who follow the company, as well as those who are no longer interested in following it, he supplies an extraordinarily valuable view of how Wall Street sees the company. He will identify the problems to be anticipated in telling the company's story, and will be invaluable in determining strategy for meeting objections and for developing sustained interest. Although the general function of the financial relations consultant is dealt with in another chapter, it should be noted here that the more effective consultants are those who are specialists not only in the techniques of dealing with the Street, but whose intensive involvement with the largest number of analysts gives them the basis for a constant two-way flow of information and intelligence.

The effective consultant will also supply the company, on a regular basis, with reports of each Street contact made in the company's behalf. This includes a report of follow-up discussions with each of the analysts who attended any meeting. The report covers the date of the contact, the person who was contacted and his affiliation and position, what was said by both the consultant and the contact—including negatives—and the consultant's impression of the discussion. This kind of report gives the company an effective and continuous feedback of financial community reaction.

THE BACKGROUND REPORT

Another effective device for reaching the financial community is the company-prepared background report. This is a succinct summary of the financial information needed by analysts to understand and evaluate a company. While in many respects the background report is similar in form to the research report prepared by analysts, it is by no means the same thing, nor should it purport to be. It should be clearly identified on the front cover as having been prepared by or for the company. It should not render an opinion that might be construed as part of an offer to sell stock. This would be illegal.

The purpose of this report is to summarize and focus, in professional form, that data which the analyst himself must search out before he can make a judgment on a company. It differs from the annual report in that its format is much more succinct and much more in the order preferred by analysts themselves. It costs considerably less, and can be more widely distributed. It includes no statements by the president nor any illustrative material. Aside from the basic financial data, the report contains a brief summary of the company's position, a description of its business, an account of its recent performance in the market, a description of recent significant events, a description of some of the problems the company has faced and overcome—or is facing and how it is overcoming them—and a brief description of management.

The background report is used as part of the kit of materials given to analysts who attend meetings or is mailed to analysts. Because of its terse presentation of facts, many analysts find it more useful than the annual report, not only as a research document and supplement to the annual report, but, in the case of those who have not been hitherto exposed to the company, as a primary tool in determining the degree to which they might ultimately become interested.

PRINTED MATERIAL

Printed material, including the annual and interim reports, reprints of significant press articles, reprints of speeches, and information folders on significant new products, is a useful tool in keeping analysts informed of a company's progress. This material is not only distributed directly to analysts at meetings or in person, but should be mailed to them at regular intervals.

Also to be mailed regularly to analysts are copies of any financial press releases as soon as possible after they are issued by the company. It should not be assumed that any analyst has seen or retained material about the company that has appeared on the Dow Jones, Reuters, or any other news service. In many cases the analyst will not have seen it at all on the wire. In other cases he will have seen it only fleetingly, when his mind was on something else. In some of the larger houses there may be several people interested in the company and only one copy of the Dow Jones or Reuters tape. By mailing the analyst a copy of the actual release, he can focus on it and retain it for his own files.

MAILING LISTS

Considering the amount of material in the course of a year that a corporation sends to each person on a mailing list—the annual report, quarterly reports, releases, and so on—the cost can easily mount up to $15 or more per name. For companies that accumulate names on mailing lists without ever reviewing the list, the cost can mount and become exorbitant. It is essential that mailing lists be reviewed at least quarterly, and certainly before every mailing. Lists are built in several different ways. The basic press list is easily derived from several directories (see Appendix). Financial community lists can be put together from the directory of the Financial Analysts Federation, from analysts and brokers who have phoned or written in to inquire about the company, and from lists of people who have attended meetings. Other names are added as a result of random inquiries and requests for information about the company from shareholders and prospective investors. In some cases the company has advertised the availability of its annual report and has added those names to the list.

Every major financial relations firm and every major financial mailing house maintains general lists of the financial press and the financial community, usually with the financial community categorized by specialty of industry interest (apparel industry, oil industry, generalists, investment counselors, etc.). The Financial Relations Board, for example, maintains on computers the most complete and up-to-date list possible, which allows extensive mailings within 24 hours.

There are a number of serious problems with mailing lists which, in view of the frequency of changes and the high cost of mailing, require considerable attention. Mailing lists are the nuisance of the financial relations industry. They are a basic tool which must be kept honed, and yet they require attention far out of proportion to the total role they play in a financial relations program. Some of the significant problems of mailing lists are:

1. The turnover in the financial community is horrendous. A comparison between the Financial Analyst Federation Directories from any one year to the next would show a startlingly high turnover of names and addresses. Analysts leave the business and change jobs with great frequency and rarely a day passes without at least half a dozen changes.

2. While turnover in the financial press is not as frequent, it still exists to a very large degree. Press people change jobs, leave or enter industry, or change assignment at a very high rate.

3. In the past several years the number of brokerage houses that have merged or gone out of business completely is, as has been noted, startlingly high.

4. Analysts' interests change. An analyst who has been following electronics may switch to petroleum. An analyst may no longer be interested in following a particular company for any number of reasons, ranging from the size of the company, to its listing, to his own impression that the company's performance no longer warrants his interest, and so on.

5. Many individuals inquire about a company on a random basis or out of curiosity, and once their curiosity is satisfied they are no longer interested.

6. Shareholders who are sufficiently interested in following a company closely will ask to be put on the mailing list for press releases not ordinarily sent to shareholders, and then sometime sell their holdings and cease to be interested in the company.

The point is that it is very easy to add a name to a list and very difficult to find a basis for removing it.

The standard practice in the industry, in periodically weeding out lists, is to take three steps:

1. Amend the list upon any indication of change, such as a returned release or a news announcement about an individual's reassignment.

2. Visually review the list to eliminate those individuals known to be no longer interested or those firms known to have merged or gone out of business.

3. Periodically include in a mailing a stamped self-addressed return postcard (see Appendix). The return of these postcards is never more than 10%. Failure to return the card with any indication one way or the other, then, cannot be construed as a reason to remove a name from a list. Of those postcards returned, a certain percentage will indicate that they are no longer interested in receiving material on the company. These names should be removed from the list, although they should be reviewed to determine whether any of the individuals are sufficiently important to the company to warrant a follow-up phone call to determine the reasons for the lack of interest. Another portion of the cards will indicate changes of address. And the largest portion of cards will simply reaffirm interest.

A question always arises as to whether firms should be included on the list if there is no specific name. This is a highly subjective decision. It takes only a postcard to the company from a firm or an individual to ask to be included on a mailing list for material. But considering the high cost of mailing it pays to be selective. For example, should research departments or libraries of brokerage firms be included on lists? In most cases the answer is yes, since these files are central reference points for individual research people. On the other hand, should business school libraries be included on the list? Here the question of cost comes into play. If there is any notion that the interest on the part of the school is for its own investment portfolio, then obviously the answer is yes. If the school librarian appears to be just building files for the sake of files, the answer is no.

THE FINANCIAL PRESS

The financial press, which is dealt with in detail in the next chapter, is a significant means of communication with all segments of the financial community. It serves three purposes. The first is to impart up-to-date information. The second is to afford an independent editorial view of the company. The third and, in a way, most significant value of the financial press is that it is a powerful weapon in the competition for attention. Obviously a company that is written about in public print with some measure of frequency is better known, and an object of greater attention, than one which is not. Where appropriate, financial publicity should be sought in the most expert and assiduous way possible. Reprints of such publicity should be mailed to the financial community regularly.

CORPORATE ADVERTISING

Corporate advertising is a controversial subject. Many companies spend a considerable amount of money on full-page ads in the financial journals, using the space either for institutional advertising—"Our company does great things"—or to impart specific information, such as a summary of the latest annual report.

As is the case in all advertising, it is difficult to measure the contribution made by corporate advertising, particularly in relationship to its price. Certainly there is one basic factor that is frequently overlooked in all advertising. Success in advertising is a function of repetition. Rarely does any single ad make sufficient impact to stand alone without the support of additional advertising or other promotional efforts. It is one thing for a major corporation such as Mobil, Fuqua, or General Electric to take a full-page ad in the *Wall Street Journal* extolling its corporate virtues or to announce its latest financial results. These companies are already well known and are supported by a consistent program that keeps their visibility high. It is yet another thing for a small company with no consumer brand name franchise to buy an ad one time. It will be overlooked and forgotten.

Furthermore, the use of advertising by a small company to sing the praises of its latest financial results is an expensive buckshot load. With very few exceptions, the number of people in the financial community who are concerned about a company to the point of doing anything effective about it is limited. Very few advertising media focus that intensively on an audience, and so even in the smaller financial publications the likelihood is that the ad will be seen by many more people than can possibly be interested. When the ad is priced on a dollar per reader basis, it turns out to be very expensive indeed.

It can be argued that this kind of advertising reaches individual investors. However, there is a very serious question as to the sources of information for judgment by individual investors. Will a man with $5000 to invest in the stock market read an ad reporting the financial results of a company and then, without considerable consultation with his broker, invest his money in that stock?

Unfortunately, there are many more opinions and myths about the validity of corporate advertising than there are facts to sustain arguments in favor of it.

For all the professional elements that go into the judgment of a company, analysts are human beings with the same strengths and weaknesses as human beings in any other industry. They expect to be dealt with intelligently, courteously, and forthrightly, and they have every right to expect it. This is certainly true if a company must in any way compete in the capital markets. It must also be recognized that as individuals they differ one from the other. Their motives, points of view, intelligence, skill, and experience range from idiocy to brilliance; from astuteness to ineptitude; from humility to presumption. For the public company, every one of these people is a conduit to a capital market and must be treated as such. In the final analysis, only when a company is fully understood, and when its presentations are credible, will it compete successfully in the capital markets.

CHAPTER 3

THE FINANCIAL AND BUSINESS PRESS

The financial and business press is the major conduit of news about companies. No view of the press can begin without an attempt to understand, first, what news is, and second, how news really affects the capital markets.

All news is relative. It is more than just the report of an event or an activity that has never been publicly reported before. Every day the editor of even the largest newspaper must review all reported events of that day and make a subjective judgment as to which of those events will concern or interest his readers sufficiently to warrant the allocation of rare and precious space. On any given day the news of the bankruptcy of a company of, say, the proportions of a Penn Central will garner more editorial interest than will the news of a very large privately held company selling shares of its stock to the public. This in turn will preempt in importance the decision of a company to build a $5 million plant. And this in turn will preempt the news of record earnings for a $25 million company (unless the company is the major industry of a small town in which its success or failure affects a great many local jobs). Lower down on the list is the appointment of a new vice-president. Yet sometimes, if not very much has happened in town that day, the news of the vice-president may be the most exciting thing the newspaper has to report as business news.

Even feature material—general background or general interest stories about a company or its individuals—has its editorial stringencies. For all but the least consequential of the business publications, even the feature story must have its news hook—a fresh basis for writing it.

Moreover, every segment of the press, financial and nonfinancial, has its own target audiences and therefore its own point of view. *Forbes* magazine superbly and assiduously pursues those stories about companies or industries which portend significant change for the future. An industry about to face a major shortage or recovering from one, a company with a serious management problem that is not generally known, an individual manager whose plans would seem more grandiose than his ability to fulfill them—these are *Forbes* stories.

Barron's prefers to update current knowledge and thinking about entire industries, new schools of thought about finance and the stock market based upon recent information or theories, or, in its occasional looks at individual companies, how the company relates to an industry and where the industry is going.

Both *The New York Times* and *The Wall Street Journal* report general business news. But *The New York Times*, with its very limited space for business news, must necessarily deal only with major economic news or very important stories about companies. While *The New York Times* is considered to be the newspaper of record, it is not necessarily the newspaper of business record, since its limited coverage cannot possibly do more than skim the surface of any day's economic activities.

The Wall Street Journal, on the other hand, covers reports of individual companies much more extensively. It, too, has limited space, and neither *The New York Times* nor *The Wall Street Journal* will run any but the most earthshaking stories on any domestic company whose stock is not quoted regularly in their stock tables. The *Journal*, like the *Times*, effectively covers broad economic news which it thinks will serve as a background for understanding the total economic picture at any given moment. The *Journal* occasionally reports material of a tangential nature to business which touches the economic news in ways that are somewhat mystical if interesting. It also covers general news very briefly, and predominantly as its editors feel it serves as a background for understanding the economy.

The news that makes the nonbusiness sections of the press is news of either a magnitude that affects the economy at large, such as a major steel price increase, or scandal and crime, such as illegal price fixing agreements in an industry, or a large-scale business swindle involving prominent businessmen and other public figures. One such case was the Home-Stake Production Co., in which many people who, by virtue of their positions, should have been expected to know better than to invest in a company that turned out to be fraudulent.

Part of the problem in reporting business news lies in the fact that most business reporters—both good and bad—have very little business training. With exceptions, they come to business journalism from the general news side of the press, rather than from business. While there are many good and astute business news reporters, there are still a great many whose understanding of business and finance is shallow and superficial. There are, for example, very few really good investigative reporters of the ilk of *The Washington Post's* Bob Woodward and Carl Bernstein, who uncovered the Watergate scandal. Those who do exist function for just a few major newspapers and business and financial publications. But generally, the state of reporting business news in the press—and certainly on radio and television—is not equal to the needs of the public.

Considering all factors, then, a review of the total spectrum of all business publications would make it very difficult indeed to produce a definition of news that would be applicable across the board.

HOW NEWS AFFECTS THE MARKET

A second and perhaps more significant aspect of news is the way in which it affects the capital markets. The distinction between pure business and economic news and general news sometimes tends to fuzz a little. The news, in 1974, that Consolidated Edison was cutting its dividend had an electric reaction not only on Con Edison stock, but on the stock market itself. Since it portended rate increases, it also concerned the general public. Every time the prime rate hits a new high the market reacts. And when President John F. Kennedy was assassinated, on the surface a non-economic event, the market plunged dramatically with its sharpest drop in decades.

One thing is certain. The market—the stock market as well as all other money markets—does respond to news. In their excellent book on the subject, *News and the Market*, Frederick C. Klein and John A. Prestbo, two *Wall Street Journal* reporters, explored that relationship in great detail. They say, "It certainly makes sense to believe that the stock market responds to the news. Movements of the market as a whole and of the stocks that make it up spring from the decisions of thousands of investors. These people, be they steely-eyed fund managers on Wall Street or little old ladies in Dubuque—read the newspapers, watch television and so on, presumably are affected by what they see and hear. If the United States seems to be getting along well with other nations around the globe and the economy seems to be functioning smoothly, it stands to reason that they will feel well disposed towards sharing in the bounty. If the opposite conditions obtain, a savings and loan account or hole in the ground might seem more secure."

In his very popular book, *A Random Walk on Wall Street*, Princeton Professor Burton Malkiel covers virtually all theories of stock market analysis and relates virtually all significant stock movement to news. Both books deal with time lag—the time between the reporting of news and its reaction in the stock market—an extremely important factor. The company issues a quarterly report that shows earnings lower than those of the same period for the prior year. The stock shows no motion or perhaps even advances a little. This frequently means that the market has anticipated the reduced earnings and sold off in proportion to them, or that the reduction is smaller than had been anticipated and that other events warrant stock purchase. The important thing is that all segments of the capital markets, from the individual investor to the manager of a major fund·or trust department to the lending officer of a bank, are responsive to news. And since the general nature of virtually everybody in every segment of the capital market tends to be skeptical, the response is usually to overreact.

CATEGORIES OF NEWS

Seeing news and its relationship to the capital markets in this context is absolutely essential in formulating an approach to the news media. It breaks down as follows:

1. *General news.* This may appear on the surface to have no relationship to buying and selling 100 shares of the stock of a small over-the-counter company, or of a bank's lending a small company $200,000 to buy a new machine, and yet it clearly sets a context for judging the ultimate economic reaction to that news. It is not difficult to see the signing of a peace treaty in the Middle East in terms of its meaning in international oil affairs. Obviously, any discussions about the impeachment of a president imply an ultimate economic context in which the country will function.

2. *General economic news.* This more readily poses the background for judging the performance of the general economic community. Raging inflation. An increase in interest rates. The devaluation of the dollar. Or even more specifically, news of changes in the financial markets themselves, such as the changeover from fixed to negotiated commission rates for brokerage firms, or changes in banking regulations that permit banks greater latitude in selling securities. Or certainly, the activities in the control of supply of money by the Federal Reserve Bank.

But these are news events over which few businessmen have control. Affected as every businessman might be by the kind of events that make this kind of news, few businessmen as individuals are in a position to influence vast sweeping activities, the results of which affect the overall course of commerce. There are exceptions, of course. A businessman in a lawsuit, for example, may obtain a decision that has consequences reaching farther than his own company. And it's also true that it's usually just a few individuals that are behind events of such magnitude as an Equity

Funding debacle. But there are rare occasions when an individual corporation or executive can effect such events by design.

NEWSMAKING ACTIVITIES

There are a large number of newsmaking activities that do, on the other hand, come within the purview of the individual corporation:

1. *The front-page news story.* When Mobil Oil Corporation makes a bid to purchase a majority of the shares of the giant Marcor Corporation, the consequences of the activity are of such magnitude as to warrant its being extensively reported in all media on other than just the business pages. This is news by any definition. The first time a major automobile manufacturer publicly announced the recall of certain of its models to correct defects, certainly the first public admission of automotive corporate fallibility, it was consequential news. If a major company decides to close down a very large plant, this can be considered to have consequences that could affect a larger portion of the economic community than just the company. And this kind of news need not be generated by large companies alone. A smaller company announcing that it plans to compete with a larger and more established company in a particular field is sometimes of consequence. And certainly when the relatively small Telex Company sued the giant IBM for antitrust activities, it was front-page news.

2. *Major corporate news.* This second category is important business news regarding a company or an industry. The company can be of any size. The magnitude of the event is measured in terms of the effect upon the general financial community. An unusual merger, an exceptionally high record earnings report, the appointment of a well-known public figure, from government or otherwise, as head of a company. Few people outside of the industrial community had heard of Arthur D. Little, the management consulting firm, until the noted war hero, General James D. Gavin, was appointed its president. When an obscure Japanese automobile manufacturer by the name of Mazda announced that it was going to market the first cars with the Wankel engine, that was news. (It was also news, incidentally, when General Motors announced that it was delaying the use of the Wankel engine in its cars for several more years.)

3. *Routine financial news.* The rules of disclosure which dictate the kinds of information that must be disseminated, and the timing, under the regulations of the SEC and the Exchanges will be dealt with in another chapter. Essentially the basic news that is of consequence is financial data —reports on latest financial results—and news of any activity the results of which could possibly be construed as affecting the economic future of

the company. While this category of news is vital to investors, and is almost invariably reported on the Dow Jones and Reuters news tickers (for at least those companies whose stocks are quoted in the tables of the *Wall Street Journal*), its importance to the media and its coverage is dictated first by the size of the company and ultimately by media space considerations. Nevertheless, under the rules of disclosure the news must be released whether it is printed or not.

4. *Lesser company news.* This is a category of news that tends to be more important to the company, the trade, a local community, or an industry than it is to the business editors of most major media. Fewer and fewer executive appointments are announced in the financial pages. *The New York Times* has virtually eliminated such announcements for most companies, and even so will rarely report the appointment of any officer lower than president unless the company is a giant or the individual is notable in some other capacity. This is not to say that these announcements—along with similar reports of new products, new plant, discontinued operations, and so on—should not be reported. They have interest in areas other than the major news media. But the decision of a $25 million company to open a $1 million plant in the Midwest is not going to throw the financial editor of *The New York Times* into paroxysms of excitement.

5. *Feature material.* This is the descriptive article about the company, its management, and its activities that appears in the range of business and financial journals that go from *Fortune* magazine—read by captains of industry—to the *Over-The-Counter Market Chronicle*, whose coverage of small over-the-counter companies tends to make it a favorite of investors in smaller companies. It ranges from a broad-based, well-researched, and elaborately detailed company profile to a few simple paragraphs describing the company's recent performance, and perhaps quoting authoritative sources, inside or outside the company, on the directions in which the company is moving. It ranges from the brief, perceptive, and frequently skeptical searching of the short article in *Forbes* to the succinct page or page and a half review of a company's newsworthy activity in *Business Week*, to a company profile in *Financial World*, to a terse half column in *Time* or *Newsweek* reporting on a startling company event.

It is very easy to see that imparting news about any company can have several immediate salutary effects (unless the news is adverse, in which case the reaction is adverse). The news itself adds further information for the investment decision. The appearance of the news keeps the company name prominent in the minds of those who make investment or lending decisions—certainly important in an arena, in which the competition is keen not only for capital, but for attention. This is perhaps the most significant point, since in the competition for capital those companies that are best known and understood are those likeliest to succeed.

HOW NEWS IS RECEIVED

What is harder to fathom is the way in which any news—and all news— will be received by the financial community.

First, it should be recognized that since news itself is relative, most news is viewed in a total context. Nothing is absolute. News of an FTC decree to divest a division is bad news if the division is profitable, and not such bad news if the division isn't. (It can be argued that no order to divest is absolutely good news; if it takes an FTC decree to get a company to unload an unprofitable division, then certainly a closer look at the company's total operations is warranted.)

Second, it must be recognized that the diverse nature of the capital markets is such that there is never a reaction to news—there is only an over-reaction. The market almost invariably recoils at bad news in anticipation of the worst possible consequences. It is just as likely to overreact, in a burst of optimism, in the other direction at the announcement of good news. The problem is that the overreaction is rapid, and the adjustment to reality, if it comes, is slow.

Beyond that, the reaction depends as much upon the type of news as the news itself. Some news, for example, is anticipated and discounted. While it can be tremendously frustrating to a company president to announce record earnings for a quarter or a year only to see virtually no reaction in his stock—or perhaps a reaction on the down side—the fact is that his earnings have probably been anticipated by those who follow the company. Then the announcement itself is not news at all, but merely an affirmation of what had been anticipated. This, incidentally, is part of the problem with projecting earnings. If analysts anticipate earnings of $1.50, they predicate their recommendations on that. When earnings of $1.50 are announced, the effect of the earnings on the price of the stock has already been taken into consideration, and, in effect, the good news is no news at all. If the analysts have anticipated and projected earnings of $1.50 and the actual figure comes out to be $1.45, this can be a disappointment, with an adverse effect on the stock price, even though the $1.45 may be a rec-ord. Nobody ever said the market was rational.

Even this is an oversimplification. Since the news of record earnings can be qualified by other factors, such as an understanding that the earnings are derived from inventory profits and not improved operations, analysts know that the high earnings are not an accurate reflection of the com-pany's actual performance.

News, then, is never quite pure and simple. It is always qualified by other factors. This, too, is a basic reason why news cannot and should not be manipulated. There tends to be further analysis and adjustment within a day or two, with a loss of credibility which adversely touches all company announcements for a considerable time to come. Credibility cannot be overemphasized as a major factor in all relations with the financial community.

The straightforward announcement of even the most favorable news, then, does not offer a clean-cut cause and effect in terms of the capital markets.

It must also be recognized that, with the exception of very large companies or smaller companies that for one reason or another are constantly in the news, no single news announcement is going to make much of a dent on the financial community except for those who are already interested in the company. While it is always possible that a single salutary announcement about a company that is not widely known will attract someone's eye and engender an interest, it is merely the beginning of a process of investigation for this person. It is not likely that an investor of consequence will read a salutary piece of news about a company that he knows little of and make an investment decision on the basis of that announcement—even if it reports a cure for the common cold. It may cause him to investigate further. But between the announcement of the news and the investment decision, there is a considerable amount of investigation.

This is not the case with the better known company, to which each news announcement is an addition of one more fact to what is already understood.

THE AUDIENCES FOR NEWS

There are actually two audiences for news. The first, predominantly for smaller companies, consists of those who already know the company either as investors or potential investors, or as analysts following it for one reason or another. The second is the larger segment of the financial community. For this group, ordinary news falls on disinterested ears unless it's startling, or itself gives reason to warrant further investigation.

The feature material that appears in the vast range of business publications from *Fortune* magazine to the business section of the Sunday *New York Times* offers a different point of view of a company. There is no question that frequent coverage makes a vast difference. With some 9000 plus companies traded, obviously those that are better known get the greatest attention from the investment community. When two companies are performing equally well, the difference between the higher stock price or price/earnings ratio of one company as compared to another is a function of its being better known by a broader segment of the investment community. For the better known company, the simplest positive news announcement will have beneficial results.

The broader reputation engendered by feature material can stem either from press recognition of the sheer brilliance or uniqueness of a company's performance, or it can just as validly be the result of an organized and carefully executed financial publicity program. Its result is to draw attention to a company repeatedly. Repetition is absolutely essential. While a single press appearance of an announcement about a company may gladden the heart of the company's president, if it is isolated and the company has never been heard of before and is not heard of again, its effect on any segment of the financial community that is not directly involved with the company is nil.

There is another major distinction between the news announcement, such as the earnings report or the report of a merger, and the development of a feature article in *Fortune, Forbes,* or *Business Week.* The news announcement is required by the rules of disclosure of the SEC. As long as the company is large enough to be included in the stock tables of *The Wall Street Journal*, the likelihood is that the announcement will at least be carried over the Dow Jones and Reuters ticker tape wire services. If the company is not large enough to be listed, then the news will be made known by direct mail from the company to investors, analysts, and prospective investors.

In the case of feature material, the fact of editorial judgment comes into play—and this remains the purview of the editor, not the subject of the news. The company may only beseech the editor. There is no effective external power beyond that, and the judgment of the editor who must serve the needs of his readers is paramount.

AIMS OF FINANCIAL PUBLICITY

Nevertheless, the value of visibility through feature material is high and warrants the specific effort that must go into achieving it. Its ultimate aims are:

1. To achieve and sustain visibility for the company and its activities.
2. To project the company's capabilities in ways that demonstrate its ultimate ability to appreciate the invested dollar.

3. To demonstrate specific capabilities about the company—its abilities to earn, the capabilities of its management, its future plans, its grasp of its industry and markets, its ability to control costs and ultimately increase its margins, and so forth.

4. To demonstrate the consistency of the company's performance, as well as the credibility of its management in the veracity of all its representations of the company in the past.

It is very rare that a company, by virtue of its positive performance, will generate sufficient interest to warrant ongoing and continuous appearances in the financial press. A company in trouble, if the trouble is flagrant and the effect of the trouble is significant enough to a large segment of the financial community, has no problem in getting itself broadly covered by the financial press. Witness the Franklin National Bank. Since few companies purposely generate this kind of interest, professional efforts must be used to discern those elements about the company and its operation which are consistently newsworthy and valuable to these publications. This material must be presented to the publications in rather specific ways. Financial publicity on a consistent basis is at least a hard sell, best performed by experts, with full knowledge of not only the techniques of dealing with the press, but the individual requirements of each publication. There should also be a basis of experience that warrants credibility with the press for the financial relations practioner, as well as for the company he represents.

WORKING WITH THE PRESS

Dealing with the financial press breaks down into the following specific segments:

1. News released under the rules of disclosure of the SEC and the Exchanges.

2. Major news events beyond routine financial announcements.

3. Feature material.

4. Inquiries from and stories originated by the press.

DISSEMINATING BASIC NEWS

The rules of disseminating basic material required to be disclosed are essentially simple and mechanical, yet if professional format is ignored, the effect will be sharply diminished.

In dealing with the financial press—or any press for that matter—certain simple rules apply universally:

1. The judgment of news value by the press is made by its editors. Even in those publications which cross the line that delineates news from advertising, the publisher knows that if his editorial content does not consistently interest readers, the number of readers will diminish, as will credibility of his publication. This is invariably followed by a cutback in advertising revenue, which is inevitably followed by bankruptcy. A primary factor in any publictaion, then, is its editorial judgment.

2. Each publication is predicated on a different editorial format—for example, *Fortune* magazine does not print routine earnings reports; *Financial World* rarely does personality pieces, and so on. The editorial point of view of every publication must be discerned and understood before any approach is made to it.

3. Competition for news space is extraordinarily keen. Editors receive five and ten times as much news as they can possibly print. Therefore, the form of presentation of news to a publication is extremely important. It must attract attention for its essential news value in the shortest possible time. It must be in a format traditionally acceptable to publications. Wherever possible, it must be written in a journalistic style acceptable to most editors.

The rules of disclosure dictate that certain material shall be released as rapidly as is mechanically feasible. Information most frequently considered in this category is financial material and operating results. Other such news may include merger announcements, consequential changes in a company's business, divestiture, an important change in management, the discovery of a new mine or oil well, and so forth. The rules of disclosure are considered satisfied when this information is released, as soon as possible after it is known to management, to either the Dow Jones news service and *The Wall Street Journal*, or Reuters news service. In some cases, immediate release to a major newspaper, such as *The New York Times*, may be considered acceptable. What is essential is that the news is released through the broadest possible media spectrum reaching the largest number of investors or potential investors.

This is best achieved by the following procedure:

1. Simultaneous release, by telephone, teletype, or hand, to both Dow Jones and Reuters news service. This is necessary because the two wire services are highly competitive and each is as important as the other. Neither likes to lose the advantage of time to the other and each is quick to say so. Simultaneous release is the simplest and fairest way.

2. Distribution via PR Newswire. PR Newswire Associates, Inc. is a private organization owned by Western Union with direct wires into every major financial publication in the United States, as well as the general wire services, general publications, and major brokerage houses. There are also regional private wire services. It is the fastest and most efficient way to disseminate news. Following simultaneous distribution to Dow Jones and Reuters, the news is then given to PR Newswire. The release may be sent by teletype, by Xerox telecopier, read over the phone, or hand delivered. It takes about half an hour following distribution to the two major wire services, Dow Jones and Reuters, for PR Newswire to move it out over their lines. This is precisely the lead time that the two financial news services request.

3. Depending upon the nature of the news, it is frequently a good idea to hand deliver a copy of the release to the business editor of the local newspaper. While he will ultimately receive the news from Dow Jones or Reuters, or PR Newswire, it is a courtesy editors appreciate. Furthermore, only in rare instances do Dow Jones or Reuters run the full release. It is essential that major news be distributed early enough in the day to warrant its being received by editors in the early afternoon to meet the deadline for the following morning's papers, or early morning for deadlines for the afternoon paper. The same is true of wire service distribution.

4. In some cases, if you are known to the local editor, it is not a bad idea to call him by phone and alert him to the fact that the news is coming to him either by wire or by hand. Considering the amount of news he must deal with on any given day, this call focuses attention on your news and can sometimes make the difference between its being printed or not. Issuing unfavorable earnings reports very late in the day or managing not to be prepared to release them until Friday (for Saturday's paper) is bad practice. In the first place, it's illegal to hold any news of that nature for one minute longer than is absolutely necessary for the broadest possible dissemination. Secondly, it fools no one. Bad news reverberates as quickly and as loudly as a firecracker in St. Patrick's Cathedral at high mass.

For companies in trouble there is no place to hide. An earnings statement or some other news of urgency can sometimes be given in an exclusive interview to Dow Jones or one of its reporters, such as for use in *The Wall Street Journal* column "Heard on the Street." The decision to do this is based upon desired effect. The "Heard on the Street" column, for example, is very widely read and frequently the news it reports results in an almost immediate stock reaction. While this does not strictly follow the procedure for broadest possible dissemination, it is considered sufficient disclosure under the SEC rules of disclosure.

Following the distribution of the news in this way, the release should then be mailed to analysts, brokers, the trade press, sharesholders (if appropriate), and any other interested parties. It is extremely important to mail the release even to those segments of the financial press and the financial community that might have received it over the Dow Jones or Reuters wires. First of all, it is unlikely that Dow Jones or Reuters will have carried the release in its entirety, even though PR Newswire will have done so. Secondly, there is no way to guarantee that the individual at either the publication or the Wall Street house you are interested in reaching will have seen it on the wire. Thirdly, it gives a file copy to those individuals in both the financial community and in the press that are following the company. And fourthly, it is one more legitimate opportunity to make the company name visible.

PRESS RELEASE FORM

The form of press releases is deceptively simple. Properly done, it looks easy. Nevertheless, it requires a substantial measure of expertise and experience.

The form should be that which is accepted and traditional in most newspaper city news rooms. It should be remembered that most city news rooms receive hundreds—sometimes thousands—of releases every day. The editors charged with pouring over these releases grumble over the volume of releases they receive, and invariably most of the releases end up in the wastebasket. They appreciate, however, those releases that are professionally prepared and which make their arduous job simpler. There are some basic rules:

1. *The printed news release letterhead.* The subject of the printed release head versus the plain blank sheet is a matter of more debate than one would find at an economists' convention. Obviously, there is an element of silliness in the printed head that has the big words "NEWS FROM XYZ COMPANY," and then reports that John Jones has been appointed assistant foreman of the third shift. "NEWS FROM GENERAL MOTORS" or "THE WALTER E. HELLER INTERNATIONAL CORPORATION," on the other hand, is likely to warrant the editor's attention. The letterhead of a major financial relations firm that uses the words "NEWS BULLETIN" is more likely to receive attention, since if it is a creditable firm, the editor knows that the release will at least have been professionally prepared. In the best formats (see Appendix), the name, address, and telephone number of the company contact appear in a conspicuous place right at the top, with the name, address, and phone number

of the account person in the financial relations firm who is the firm's point of contact. The name of the company contact is essential because the wire services and major financial publications insist upon verifying most financial information with an officer of the company, regardless of the credibility of the financial relations firm. In other cases, an editor or an analyst might want some clarification or additional information that he feels doesn't warrant bothering an officer of the company. Having both names gives the recipient of the release an option.

It also is useful to put the stock exchange or NASDAQ symbol conspicuously in the heading. This allows an analyst to quickly check the current stock price.

2. *The headline.* Newspapers write their own headlines. Furthermore, the headline is never written—except perhaps in the smallest newspapers —by the man who writes the story. The purpose of the headline in a news release is to summarize the meat of the story, so that the editor can make a quick determination as to whether the story warrants his further attention. It should consist of no more than two lines, stating briefly and succinctly what the release is about—for example, "DEVCON REPORTS RECORD THIRD QUARTER SALES; EARNINGS." It should be centered, all in caps, at the head of the release.

3. *Dateline.* Following the format used by virtually all daily newspapers, the first words of the release should be the dateline. This means the city of origin of the story and the date of the issuance of release: "Pompano Beach, July 10. . . ."

4. *The text of the release.* All releases should be double-spaced, with paragraphs indented. This makes it easier for the editor to read, to mark up, and to indicate notes in the margin. While newspapers have long since gotten away from the traditional five w's—who, what, when, where, and why—as elements for the lead of the story, it is nevertheless extremely important that the lead paragraph—the first paragraph—get as quickly to the point of the release as possible. A good technique is to cover up everything but the first line or two of a release and try to see it with the editor's eye. Does it impart something that is genuinely news in those first two lines? Does it get to the heart of the matter? The name of the company is not news—the facts are. The best possible first sentence is, "Record third quarter sales and earnings were reported today by Devcon International Corporation (OTC)." This is more effective than "Donald Smith, president of Devcon Corporation (OTC), reported record sales and earnings, and so on." The first mention of the company's name should be followed in parentheses by the company's listing—(AMEX), (OTC), (NYSE). This immediately tells the editor whether the company is listed or not, and on what exchange.

The text itself should be written in the journalistic style of *The Wall Street Journal* or *The New York Times*. It should be succinct and to the point. It should be written in simple English, grammatically correct, in the active—not passive—voice, and should not read like a legal contract. Its job is to impart news, not merely to fulfill a legal commitment.

Each topic of the story should be given its own paragraph for simple editing. Each paragraph should cover the points of the story in descending order of importance—the lead paragraph with the primary news, the second paragraph with the next item of importance, and so on. Stories were once edited by cutting from the bottom. This is no longer the case. The purpose of writing in descending order of importance, however, is for interest.

While the release should be written interestingly, a news release should not be confused with a feature.

It should be straightforward and should not in any way editorialize. Opinions, projections, and other subjective points of view should not be reported as facts. They should either be put in quotes or otherwise attributed to an officer of the company by name.

The last paragraph of the release should be a simple one- or two-line statement describing the company's business.

The release is then ended with the traditional ending marks, . . . # # #. The old telegrapher's ending mark—30—is quaint but has long since gone out of style.

Releases should be written by people who are experienced in release writing, or who otherwise have journalistic skill. Unfortunately, since most financial releases are issued under the rules of disclosure, they are too often written by lawyers. Lawyers—even the most literate—should not be allowed to write releases. With rare exceptions, they tend to confuse releases with contracts, out of fear of being misinterpreted, misconstrued, or any of the other things lawyers worry about.

This is not to say that every release should not be cleared by a lawyer. It certainly should. Financial releases can have legal consequences, and it is this potential for trouble that should be reviewed by a lawyer. But the lawyer's purview is not literary style. It is fact, and the possibility of misinterpretation of facts as stated.

Releases sent to the financial press should be addressed to a specific editor by name only in those cases where it is known that the editor to whom the release is addressed is in fact the appropriate person to receive the release, is still employed at that publication in that capacity, and is in residence and at his desk the day the release will be received. If it is important that an earnings release get into the hands of a specific editor at, say, *The New York Times*, the release should not be mailed; it should be sent by messenger and followed up with a phone call to make sure that it is not stalled at the financial department's reception desk. Otherwise, the release should be addressed to the Financial Editor or to the City Desk.

Except under extreme circumstances, it is bad form to call a newspaper to find out why your release was not printed. The chances are that it was not run because the editor didn't think that it was important enough to print in his limited space, in relation to other information he received that day. No newspaper is legally required to print any news, no matter how important it is to the company, and pestering an editor will only incur animosity and risk that subsequent releases will find their way directly to the wastebasket. It is, however, appropriate to phone ahead, talk to the particular editor, and advise him that the release is on the way. In view of the large number of releases received every day, if the news is important enough the editor will appreciate it and watch for it. It will not, however, guarantee that he will print it. There are times when it seems obvious that a release should have been printed and wasn't. It would be surprising, for example, if the earnings report of a major company in the apparel industry were not published by *Women's Wear Daily*. Under these circumstances, it is perfectly appropriate to phone the editor—not to ask why the release wasn't printed—but merely to confirm that the release was received. This is a subtle difference and frequently the publication will appreciate it if the editor has reason to believe that news he should have received never reached him.

Radio and television should not be overlooked. Many stations carry some business news, although considerably less than most newspapers. The measure is the importance of the news to the largest number of viewers or listeners. The newspaper reader disinterested in business can turn the page; the listener cannot. This is why radio and television editors choose only major business items for their newscasts. In most cases, it is pointless to send routine releases to radio or television stations. If there is reason to believe that something is particularly newsworthy, the station's news editor should be dealt with in exactly the same way as the newspaper editor. It should be noted that most broadcast media newsrooms receive Dow Jones, Reuters, and PR Newswire reports.

MAJOR NEWS COVERAGE

Major news can sometimes be treated somewhat differently than routine releases. If the news is of sufficient consequence to warrant greater attention than just routine release, there are other techniques that can be used.

1. *The press conference.* The old style press conference for routine financial or corporate news has gone out of style. Newspaper people are too busy to spend several hours away from their desks to attend a press conference. They get particularly disturbed—and appropriately so—if they are invited to a press conference and are led to believe that they will be given news of greater importance than it actually is. The fact that they are wined and dined is not of the essence. There is no law that says that a newspaperman who drinks your Scotch and otherwise accepts your hospitality has to print your story. Newspaper people are further annoyed by being invited to a press conference to be given news that can just as easily be covered by a press release or even a telephone interview.

A press conference should be called only when:

A. The news is monumental.
B. There is some clear reason, such as a demonstration of a new product or the need for an elaborate explanation, why the news cannot be covered in a press release.
C. Full understanding of the news requires questioning and elaborate answers.

If a news conference is warranted. there are some basic procedures to be followed:

A. *The invitation.* The invitation should be sent out several days to a week in advance of the event. It should state the purpose of the conference, the time, and the place. If there are specific visual aspects to the story, this should be indicated and a separate invitation should be sent to the photo desk of the publication if there is one. If the news is important and urgent enough, invitations can be sent out by telegram, but certainly not a week before the event. The urgency of the news as implied by the telegram is defeated by the time lag. It is a good idea to telephone the invitees on the morning of the conference to remind them and to verify their attendance.
B. *The place.* The place should be appropriate to the event. If it is convenient, the best place is always the office of the chief executive. Next best is a private room at a restaurant or club. It should be obvious that a public table in a restaurant is an inappropriate place to hold a press conference. The room should be large enough to hold everybody comfortably, but not so large that crowd seems dwarfed and the room seems empty. It should be set up and prepared well beforehand to assure that all speakers are visible, can be clearly heard, and that all graphic material is easily presented.
C. *The time.* The time for a press conference is determined by news-

paper deadlines. The best time for a press conference is late morning, lunch, or very early afternoon. A 10:00 A.M. press conference will make both the afternon and the mowning newspapers. If it is a major story the afternoon newspapers, which in most cities are not as widely read as the morning newspapers, will preempt the story, which will not please the morning papers. On the other hand, it is better if a major story makes the financial wires while the market is still open. This means that time should be allowed for everybody not only to hear the news but to write it. Newspapermen still go back to their offices and pound typewriters. Only in the movies do they rush to the phones to call the city room.

D. *Preparation.* A complete press kit should be prepared for every newspaperman attending. This should consist of a basic release, a background sheet on the company, any financial background material such as an annual or quarterly report, biographical material and photos of executives, and product data sheets. While the press kit should be as complete as possible, care should be taken not to overload it with so much material that a reporter can't find the facts for all the paper.

E. *The format.* If cocktails or coffee are to be served, the length of time allocated should be just sufficient for everybody to arrive. It should last no longer than 20 or 30 minutes. The press conference can begin while people are still drinking. Reporters' time, remember, is valuable. If a lunch seems in order, it should be treated exactly the same way as an analysts' luncheon—20 minutes to a half hour for cocktails, a rapidly served lunch, and the conference to begin over dessert.

The presentation itself should be short, simple, and to the point. While there is a great temptation to dramatize, few newspapermen are impressed by this. The drama should come from the material. The material should be simple, to the point, and graphically illustrated. It should take no longer than 30 to 40 minutes to present. Time should be allowed for questioning. Immediately following the press conference, the officers of the company should be prepared to spend a few minutes to answer questions of any reporters that may linger behind the others. The chief executive officer should also be available in his office for the remainder of the day to answer any questions that may occur to a reporter back at his desk writing the story.

2. *The individual interview.* There are times when the most effective way to break a major story is to give it to a single reporter in an exclusive interview. This may be effective, but it has an inherent danger. If there

is any information imparted that comes under the rules of disclosure, that reporter's lead time must be strictly limited, since the rules may require that the story be distributed to the general public within a reasonable period of time—and certainly the same day—as it is released to an individual. This is a matter to be discussed with the company's attorney. An exception is a *Wall Street Journal* or Reuters interview which, as has been stated before, is accepted by the SEC as having broad enough coverage to be considered adequate under the rules of disclosure.

Here, too, the rules for the interview are the same as the rules for the press conference—no nonsense, to the point, and frank discussion.

In both the individual interview and the press conference there are two basic rules to consider:

1. Be prepared for full disclosure. Never voluntarily subject yourself to an interview if there is any question a reporter might ask that you can't answer. If a reporter feels you have anything to hide, it will nullify every positive effect that the story might otherwise have. Certainly, as in an analyst meeting, all possible questions should be anticipated and the answers prepared beforehand. There should be no surprises.

2. Absolutely nothing should be stated off the record unless its pertinence to the story is for background only. An off-the-record statement places an unwarranted burden on a reporter. His job is to print information—not to be a repository of facts. It is a burden that reporters rarely appreciate. Furthermore, it almost invariably leads to the impression that something is being hidden. If you don't want a reporter to know something, don't tell him—on or off the record.

FEATURE MATERIAL

The approach to developing feature material in business and financial publications, as well as the general press, is considerably different than it is for the straight news announcement. The attempt, in feature development, is to project a somewhat detailed and rounded picture of the company or some aspect of it, and to do so in a favorable way. The value of feature articles about a company lies not only in the general exposure of the company to the publication's readers, but in explaining the company with some measure of depth; to engender the impression that the company is functioning well.

In approaching this kind of press coverage there are several basic rules and guidelines that are imperative. These rules apply whether the story is generated internally by the company or by the financial relations or public relations consultant.

1. The target publication must be clearly understood. Several issues of the publication should be studied to determine the kind of material it seeks, its point of view, its style, its editorial viewpoint, and its apparent taboos. Any attempt to try to convince a publication to print a story that is not in keeping with its general editorial policy is not only a waste of time, but could lead to a singularly adverse reaction by the editors to the company or the financial relations consultant.

2. Even a feature article must have a newsworthy point of view. Sometimes this is a hook—an event or activity that serves as a focal point for the story; an indication that the timing for the story is appropriate. Or it can be an angle that is at least unusual and perhaps unique, such as company's new approach to financing or the development of a new production or distribution technique that should result in significantly altering the direction of the company. Or the reorganization of a management team to take into account the changing economic conditions under which the company must function.

3. The story should delineate, in one aspect or another, a significant change in the company's operation. It is only under the rarest circumstances that a publication will publish a story about a company in which absolutely nothing significant has happened, or in which the company is shown to be no different than any other company in its field. An exception might be when lack of change is significant and salutary in itself, such as when every other company in the industry has made significant changes with unfavorable results and the subject company, by changing nothing, has outperformed the industry.

The development of feature material for publication usually requires a measure of skill, if not artfulness. Some time ago it was deemed valuable to develop a feature article about a medium-sized insurance company. Basic investigation indicated that the company's operations seemed no different than comparable companies in its industry. Furthermore, an additional obstacle existed in that newspapers infrequently find stories of insurance companies of sufficient consequence to print. (This was the situation that existed at the time and is not to be construed as universal.)

A careful exploration was made of every aspect of the company's business in the attempt to fathom some point that was unusual and newsworthy. There came to light the fact that the company's return on its investment portfolio was higher than most other insurance companies', including some of the giants. Further investigation showed that this was a function of the investment department's imagination and daring. It was company policy to seek out unusual situations, perhaps with somewhat more risk, and to be considerably more venturesome than is traditionally expected of the insurance industry. The company, for example, was one of the first to invest in the then embryonic cable television industry.

This extraordinary success in portfolio management became the focal point of a proposal to *The New York Times*, which resulted in a large feature story on page one of the Sunday *New York Times* business section.

When a man murders his wife it takes no public relations skill to get his name in the paper. The skill is in fathoming the unusual in an otherwise usual story, and projecting it as the basis for a feature article.

Approaching the publication requires some relatively simple procedures.

1. Once a target publication has been selected and its editorial policies analyzed, the story is developed specifically for that publication. The same general story may function for several different publications, but each approach must still be tailored.

2. The proper editor is determined either by reading the masthead, or by calling the publication and inquiring. In some publications, such as *Business Week*, there are specific areas of specialty. In a smaller publication, the ranking editor on the masthead is the first point of contact. In larger magazines, such as *Fortune*, several people are given the specific responsibility of reviewing all story ideas.

3. A letter is written to the editor describing the story. In some cases the letter may be preceded by a phone call or even a meeting with the editor. Almost invariably, and with very few exceptions, the story will ultimately have to be presented to the publication in written form. Sometimes the letter can be prepared before the first contact. Sometimes, if a discussion with the editor beforehand is feasible, the letter should be written only after the meeting, and should be patterned on the guidelines set forth by the editor.

The letter should be concise and to the point. The editor is busy and businesslike, and even the fact that he has been bought a sumptuous lunch at an expensive restaurant is not going to preclude the necessity he faces to maintain the level of his publication. The essence of the story should be stated in the first paragraph, with emphasis on the reasons why this story is newsworthy and warrants his consideration. The remainder of the brief letter should include facts to support the basic premise. It should indicate the availability of the people involved, and of graphic and visual material, if appropriate, that is available or can be made available to supplement the story.

The letter should *not* begin with the sentence, "John Jones, president of XYZ Corporation, is going to be in New York City at two o'clock next Wednesday afternoon and is available for an interview." If this is the case, then Mr. Jones' visit to New York should be stated further along in the letter—after the story idea has been clearly delineated.

4. A few days after the letter has been sent it is appropriate to follow up with a phone call to determine the editor's interest, to answer questions he might have, and to make arrangements for whatever interviews or further discussions are necessary.

5. The course of all interviews should take precisely the same form as interviews for major news events, and should follow the same rules. The executives involved should be prepared to be frank and open. Nothing should be off the record except material that is necessary for background, but not necessarily newsworthy in itself. Questions should be anticipated and careful preparation made for each answer.

NEWSPAPER FEATURE ARTICLES

There is relatively little difference in the approach to a feature article in a newspaper. In the case of smaller newspapers, or papers in other than the 10 largest cities in the United States, the letter may ultimately turn out to be unnecessary. Arrangements can be made by phone. If an executive is planning to be in Birmingham, Alabama, next Thursday and there is reason to believe that there is a newsworthy aspect to either his presence in that city or to his company, it is perfectly appropriate to phone the financial editor of the *Birmingham News* a few days ahead, to indicate the fact that the executive will be in Birmingham next Thursday and to go on to delineate the basic points of the story in exactly the same way as is done in the letter. Arrangements for the interview are then made by phone.

In some cases an executive may be appearing in a city for purposes other than strictly company business. For example, the company president may be appearing in town to make a speech before a local organization. The procedure is to phone ahead to the editor and inform him of that fact. If the editor is not short-staffed and can afford time for coverage of the event, arrangements should be made. If possible, prepared material should be made available to the editor at the time of the interview. If the story is still considered newsworthy, but the editor is unable to assign a reporter to cover it, it is worth the effort to prepare a news release covering the event and to hand deliver it to the editor on that morning.

LISTING IN STOCK TABLES

Extremely valuable to any company is its listing in the stock tables of newspapers. For the listed company, this is no problem in any paper that carries the complete listing. For over-the-counter companies the listing is supplied by the National Association of Securities Dealers. The NASD

Most Active National List includes the 1400 most active NASDAQ issues, determined upon the basis of average weekly volume, as long as there is also a minimum representative bid quotation of $2.00 in the NASDAQ system. This is the list carried in most major newspapers, as well as *The Wall Street Journal*. There is also a supplemetnary national list which appears weekly. It includes the 900 next most active NASDAQ issues. In addition, the supplemental list requires that the bid quotation at the time of compilation of the list, multiplied by the average weekly volume, equal or exceed the sum of $10,000. These lists are distributed to approximately 30 large metropolitan newspapers.

An issue must also have 1500 shareholders wtih a minimum distribution of 300 shareholders in two of four regional divisions or as an alternative, a minimum of 2000 shareholders throughout the nation.

NASD does supply the wire services with the quotations and volume on substantially all of the approximately 3500 issues in the system. Nobody prints this entire list except *Media General Financial Weekly*, a national financial publication. It is useful, however, to local newspapers, which frequently print the bid and asked quotations of over-the-counter companies located in their area.

Occasionally a company may feel it is eligible for inclusion in the Most Active List by virtue of changed circumstances, such as an increase in price or an increase in the number of shareholders. Since the NASD monitoring system is not as fast as a company might desire, the company can make direct application to the NASD and ask to be included on the list by virtue of the changed circumstances.

There are two aspects of news coverage that are extremely important to businessmen, even as they pose potential danger. The first is the story developed by the publication for reasons that might appear to be unfavorable to the company. The second is the routine press inquiry.

THE UNFAVORABLE STORY

Forbes magazine is noted for ferreting out unfavorable stories about companies—or so it would appear. *Forbes* prides itself in anticipating danger points in industry or the economy, or potential disasters in companies. Their reporters are thoroughly professional and well trained. *Forbes*, in dealing with a story on a company in trouble or potentially in trouble, has often been accused of doing a hatchet job. This is rarely the case.

A *Forbes* editor will hear of a potentially negative story about a company. In the course of investigation one of the first things the editor will do is call the company's chief executive officer. The chief executive officer, aware of *Forbes'* straightforward and irreverent attitude, becomes defensive. He tries to hide facts or to sugarcoat them. He sometimes makes himself or his executives unavailable. To the *Forbes* editor this is a red flag. It indicates that there is more to the story than meets the eye and that something is being hidden. The article will then be developed on the basis of *Forbes'* own research, without benefit of the company's side of the story. The result is a negative report written in *Forbes'* breezy style. The company views it as a hatchet job. It isn't.

Unless the company truly has something to hide, the first reaction to an inquiry from an editor of *Forbes*—or any other publication—should be complete openness. Experience with any major responsible publication, including *Forbes*, indicates that a publication is responsive to an open presentation of the facts—both positive and negative—by the company. No responsible publication ever refuses to hear the company's side of the story. This is not to say that the negative facts will not be printed. Very few publications will be deterred from printing pertinent facts, negative or positive. But at least the negative side of the story can be cushioned by the company's point of view.

It should be recognized that for the public company there is no place to hide. It is the most destructive form of self-deception to believe that there is any way in which a negative story, once it has been discovered by a publication, will not come out in its worst aspects. It should also be recognized that no company ever takes a consistent straight line to success. Not all decisions are correct, nor is every chief executive perfect. What is more important is that if the total story is told and told honestly, the resultant article may not read like a puff piece, but at least the company will come out ahead.

It would be naive not to recognize the fact that not all reporters, editors, or even publications are honest. There are reporters on the take. There are hatchet jobs. There are publications that are unethical. There are publications that tie their editorial columns to their advertising sides. This is unfortunate and frequently illegal, particularly for a financial publication that purports to present honest investment advice. It is just as bad to tie advertising to favorable news without in some way making clear to the reader that the editorial material is not objective or that it has been paid for in some way.

There is nothing that can be done about unscrupulous publications except to vigorously resist all blandishments to tie advertising or any other revenue—including gifts and junkets (free press trips)—to editorial material. For the company in trouble, it is a short-term solution to a deeper problem. Since, as has been noted before, the acoustics of Wall Street are magnificent and bad news reverberates loudly, there is no such thing— regardless of popular lore—as cosmetic public relations, particularly in business news. Other than protesting vigorously, which is usually a waste of time, the only recourse a company has to an unscrupulous publication that prints an unfavorable story is to deal more intensively with the honest publications in the attempt to disseminate the truth. Yes, it takes twice as much truth to counteract falsehood. But it's worth the effort.

Incidentally, the notion that newsmen can be bought is nonsense. It's true that a newsman who has friendly relations with either the company or the company's financial relations firm can in some small way extend a minute measure of editorial favor to the company. But in the final analysis, the publication is almost invariably bigger than any of its editors or any story. In order to survive, the publication must be editorially consistent. True, there are exceptions. And occasionally, favor can be curried with a newspaperman or an editor resulting in a favorable story that might otherwise not have appeared. But no public relations program can ever be built, nor sustained, on such a structure. In other words, don't depend upon it.

THE UNEXPECTED INQUIRY

The unexpected inquiry should also be dealt with in a straightforward manner. No attempt should be made to hide or dissemble—it will only make matters worse. The company president who is called by a newspaperman or an editor and asked to comment on an unfavorable rumor should react calmly and rationally. If the facts are clearly at hand, he should state them simply and straightforwardly, with no attempt to influence the editorial stance. If he does not know the answer he should say so, take the reporter's name and phone number, get the information as soon as possible, and return the call with the facts. If warranted, he should invite the reporter to discuss the question in detail, and here too the same rules apply as for any other interview. It is absolutely imperative that every company have a basic news policy. Specific executives should be designated as spokesmen for the company. The corps of spokesmen can be broad, consisting of specialists in each field, but they should not be arbitrarily selected.

There should be a clear and simple directive from the chief executive officer to all executives and employees of the company that spokesmen have been designated and that all inquiries should be referred to the appropriate spokesman. Under no circumstances should an unauthorized person be allowed to supply vital information to the press, and this should be made clear not in terms of authority alone, but rather for the simple reason that only the spokesmen have all pertinent facts and policy at hand. It should be made clear that it is as unfair to an unauthorized person to allow him to supply information as it is to the company, since it puts the unauthorized person in an untenable position. Unauthorized personnel should be advised to deal with all inquiries politely, to indicate that they are not sufficiently armed with the facts to answer the question, and then to indicate the name and phone number of the designated spokesman.

Designated spokesmen should be kept abreast at all times of company news policy and procedures. They should be briefed as well as possible on all potential inquiries and the appropriate answers. They should know company policy and the limits of the information they are authorized to divulge. They should be made to understand clearly the basic procedures for answering inquiries in terms of dealing with reporters politely, rationally, unemotionally, and openly. When a question exceeds the limits of a spokesman's authority, he should politely say so and refer the reporter to the proper executive to handle that inquiry. All inquiries and the answers given should be made known—preferably in writing—as soon as possible to the chief executive officer.

Except in terms of training and motivation to do their jobs as well as possible, newspapermen are no different from anybody else. The range of the capabilities, understanding, and limitations is about on a par with the total population. There are competent newsmen and there are incompetent newsmen. There are a great many reporters in the financial press who seem remarkably ignorant of business and finance. There are a greater number who are remarkably well versed in the field. Editors and newspapermen are no more exempt from hostilities, bad days, fights with their wives, and toothaches than anybody else. Nevertheless, if they are dealt with professionally they will function professionally.

The editor and newspaperman have no ax to grind. The realities of the world are that they react as humanly to a confrontation as does anyone else. Few newspapermen, however, will react unfavorably to an honest, simple, and straightforward presentation and to an unflinching response to even the most cutting questions.

The proper function of a financial relations consultant in dealing with the press is not to act as a spokesman for the company—unless he has been properly trained and specifically designated in this capacity by the chief executive officer—but to act as an intermediary, smoothing the way for direct relationships between the company and the press. Nor should the financial relations consultant ever be used as a buffer—as a shield behind which the company can hide. The press resents this and rightfully so. Yet the major source of company news is still the financial relations consultant. If there were no financial relations industry, every editorial body in the United States would have to treble its staff to ferret out the massive amount of news that is now brought to the attention of the press. Most newspapermen recognize this. Some newspapermen, however, given reason to feel that the financial relations consultant is inserting himself between the company and the press, will rightfully and vocally resent it.

The press, when properly dealt with, is an important conduit to the financial community. It is worth the effort of every corporate executive to learn to use the press properly.

CHAPTER 4

THE SEC AND THE EXCHANGES

All securities of publically held companies are regulated by the United States Securities and Exchange Commission, a federal regulatory body established by Congress under the Securities Act of 1933. Its chairman and board members are appointed by the president of the United States. It has a very large and keen staff, with offices in major cities throughout the United States, as well as in Washington, D.C. Its major assignment is to regulate and monitor securities practices for virtually all public companies, stock exchanges, and securities dealers in the country. It does its job well and assiduously. While the commission tends to take on the character of its chairman in its emphasis on any particular aspect of securities regulation, it never strays from its basic purpose.

Each state also has its body of securities laws and regulations, most of which are enforced by the state attorney general. These laws are known as "Blue Sky Laws," since they were originally designed, many of them prior to the establishment of the SEC, to prevent unscrupulous securities dealers from promising and selling investors everything but the blue sky.

All companies selling securities to the public must conform to the laws and regulations of both the SEC and every state in which those securities are sold.

All exchanges have strict codes governing practices of companies whose stock is listed on—sold through—those exchanges. Naturally, these regulations often develop with SEC and state regulation. They do, however, frequently define or expand them for listed companies. Securities of companies not listed on exchanges are further regulated by the National Association of Securities Dealers.

The vast body of regulations covers every aspect of security practices, including company practices relating to information about the company that affects the value of that company's stock in the public market. The concern here is principally with the legal aspects of the dissemination of that information—the rules of disclosure.

While the subject of securities regulation is complex, particularly as it pertains to corporate relations with the financial community and the general public, there are two basic points that are foremost. All of the rules of disclosure, whether formulated by the SEC, the Exchanges, or the National Association of Securities Dealers, are designed to cover two major points:

1. All material information necessary for an evaluation of a company and its suitability as an investment vehicle must be made public and available to all interested parties.

2. No material information about a company or its operations that could affect the evaluation of a company or its suitability as an investment vehicle, or that might influence the sale or purchase of its stock, may be known by only a limited number of people. All such information must not only be made available to every segment of the financial community and the investing public, but it must be done by those means most likely to broadcast it to the widest possible degree. Furthermore, timeliness is of the essence—any such pertinent information known to a few people must be made generally known as quickly as is mechanically possible. This means, quite specifically, within hours.

In any segment of securities regulation or public corporate activity, these two basic points apply universally and without exception.

Primarily, the burden of securities regulation remains within the purview of the attorney. Unfortunately, securities regulation is not only complex, it is not always completely clear. There are areas in which judgment must be exercised, as for example, the moment at which prospective mergers become likely and must be disclosed. Since these judgments are invariably made within the framework of law and code, and are amended by a wide variety of regulatory and judicial decisions, they are best made only by an attorney.

Nevertheless, the primary burden for compliance with disclosure regulation remains with the corporation, its attorneys, and in the area of communication, its financial relations counsel.

DISCLOSURE PHILOSOPHY

Because the body of regulation is so elaborate and so much of it is a question of judgment, much of the direction necessary to make those judgments is not codified. In some cases the SEC in effect says, "Do it first, and then we'll tell you whether you should have done it or not."

While the ultimate decision resides with attorneys, the corporation and its financial relations counsel should nevertheless adopt a basic philosophy that should pervade its disclosure program. This philosophy should include two basic points:

1. The company should be prepared to disclose any and all information that could conceivably affect a judgment of the company as an investment vehicle. If there is any question—disclose. Certainly, this includes any activity that warrants filing a Form 8K with the SEC. The Form 8K is used to report significant changes in corporate activity, policy or practice.

2. No pertinent or disclosable material should be held from release for more than a few hours from the time the information is known by any officer of the corporation. The machinery for disclosure should be well established beforehand, whether it's done by the company itself or through the auspices of the financial relations counsel. It should then be a routine matter to prepare and disseminate any information.

For many corporations, this kind of policy may seem harsh and arduous. But aside from the basic responsibility to investors and potential investors on the one hand, and the value of competing in the capital markets by disseminating every element of information that assists in the judgment of a company on the other, it should be clearly understood that administration of the rules of disclosure can be rigid and assiduous. The SEC and the Exchanges, it should be perfectly clear, mean exactly what they say. Furthermore, as understaffed as the SEC or any other regulatory body may be at any given moment, the agency is rarely lax in the enforcement of securities regulation.

And let us dispense immediately with any question of secrecy on the basis of competitive advantage. While the SEC has frequently said that it has no intention of putting any company at a competitive disadvantage, it considers the dissemination of material information more important under the rules of disclosure. This can sometimes raise thorny points for a corporation asked to break down its performance by product line or by division, or for the corporation that feels that premature disclosure of merger negotiations might adversely effect those negotiations. The SEC is quite clear. Disclose.

Furthermore, the influx of individual and presumably unsophisticated investors into the market in recent years has caused the SEC to become increasingly concerned with protecting those investors. Purely and simply, the SEC wants no investor or prospective investor ever put in the position of buying, holding, or selling stock on the basis of incomplete or inaccurate information. The drive is toward greater and greater disclosure, however painful this may appear to be to corportaions, or however time consuming this may be to corporate officers.

THE SEC AND FINANCIAL RELATIONS CONSULTANTS

Nor does the SEC exempt from its regulations agents of the corporation. For many years it has been the practice of companies to use financial relations consultants and public relations firms as mere conduits of information. Traditionally, corporate presidents relied on financial relations consultants to simply take the information supplied to them by the company, cast it into its appropriate release form, and disseminate it. Financial relations consultants, since they are seldom accountants or lawyers, are without the means or facility to judge the validity of information supplied to them. They have relied on their clients to supply them with complete and accurate information. For many years this rankled the SEC and quite appropriately. In 1969, the SEC decided to include financial relations consultants in its regulation of disclosure. A major national firm, The Financial Relations Board, Inc., was chosen to be the test case, presumably on the basis of its size and scope of operation in behalf of many clients.

The Financial Relations Board had, for a period of three or four months, served as counsel to a company called Pig n' Whistle. During the course of that period, FRB issued several releases following the procedures standard at that time. It merely took information supplied by the company and released it. Pig n' Whistle was cited for, among other things, disseminating incorrect information. The citation occurred well after FRB had resigned the account on the basis of Pig n' Whistle's refusal to allow FRB access to material and information that it felt to be pertinent. The SEC cited FRB, noting that it should have independently verified information authorized for public release.

Despite the fact that FRB had followed procedures standard almost without exception at that time, it entered into a consent decree under which it was determined that if certain prescribed systems are duly followed for information verification, a financial relations agency has fulfilled its public responsibility and is not compelled to insure the total validity of the information.

These procedures, developed by The Financial Relations Board, now serve as the standard for financial relations consultants. They take into consideration the fact that financial relations consultants are not in the same position to verify information as are auditors and attorneys. The procedures prescribe, however, steps that can be taken to assure, within the limits of any financial relations firm, the most feasible precautions against dissemination of misleading or inaccurate information.

For the corporation intent upon disseminating false or misleading information, very little can be done by anybody to prevent it. Nevertheless, as has been noted before, the acoustics of Wall Street are magnificent. The value to any corporation of issuing false information is remarkably short-lived, and the penalty, in terms of both the law and investor reaction, is swift and intense.

Prior to the Securities Acts of 1933 and 1934, corporate disclosure was minimal. George Benston, Professor of Finance and Accounting at the University of Rochester's Graduate School of Management, notes in an article in *The New York Times* on March 17, 1974, that in 1926 all corporations whose stocks were listed on the New York Stock Exchange published balance sheets showing current assets and current liabilities. In these statements only 71% showed depreciation, 45% showed the cost of goods sold, and 55% showed sales. Today, it would be unthinkable for any published report of a public corporation not to include this and a great deal of other information, where pertinent. And even so, it's only within the past few years, with the growth of conglomerates and diversified companies, that corporate annual reports break down performance by division or product line. Until the SEC made it mandatory to do so, in 1975, there were still relatively few companies that included in their annual reports information that covers the range of material demanded by law in the Corporate Annual Report Form 10K—despite the fact that the Form 10K of any public corporation is available to the public.

To the company that recognizes that it must compete for capital over the long run, the problem of disclosure should be viewed not only as one of regulation, but as the opportunity to display every aspect of the company that can contribute to a rounded picture for the prospective investor or lender.

INSIDER INFORMATION

Nor should the danger inherent in insider information be overlooked. In 1964, the problem of inside information dramatically came to the public's attention with the Texas Gulf Sulphur case. Several engineers working for Texas Gulf Sulphur came upon a rich mineral body. This discovery was kept within a small group inside the company. Several members of that group, taking advantage of their inside information and with full knowledge that the value of the company stock would be greatly enhanced when that information was generally known, purchased Texas Gulf Sulphur stock for their own accounts. This resulted in criminal charges against not only the offenders, but those who merely knew and did not disclose. It also strengthened and further clarified regulations concerning insider information. These regulations were increasingly used as other cases came to light.

A few years ago, several Merrill Lynch, Pierce, Fenner & Smith staff members were given reason to believe that a forthcoming financial statement for the McDonnell Douglas Company would show a sharp decline in earnings. Before this information was made generally public, advice to sell their stock was given to selected institutional clients, at the same time that other Merrill Lynch customers were being given a buy recommendation. When the information was ultimately made public, the price of the stock declined sharply. The SEC took a dim view of the fact that there had been specific benefit from inside information to a selected few, and once again penalties were imposed.

As the economy has become more complex, SEC regulation has demanded more and more in terms of disclosure. The SEC, as a case in point, has moved more intensively than ever before into areas such as accounting. For example, in its Accounting Series Release No. 142, dated March 15, 1973, the SEC notes an increasing use of cash flow per share data in the narrative sections of prospectuses and annual reports. It points out that the term is used in too many variations to allow for clarity, and that it creates confusion. It states, "While the Commission recognizes that there are problems of income measurement for some industries, the unilateral development and presentation on an unaudited basis of various measures of performance by different companies which constitute departures from the generally understood accounting model has led to conflicting results and confusion to investors. Additionally, it is not clear that the simple omission of depreciation and other noncash charges deducted in the computation of that income provides an appropriate alternative measure of performance for any industry, either in theory or in practice."

It concludes, "Accordingly, per share data other than that relating to net income, net assets and dividends, should be avoided in reporting financial results." The effect of this regulation was profound, especially for real estate development companies, real estate trusts, and many others.

Subsequent regulation recognizes that alternative sophisticated accounting methods can alter the measure of a company's performance. Thus companies are now required to indicate, in corporate reports, the accounting principles used in that company's report.

In further drives to intensify disclosure regulation, the SEC now requires annual reporting of a five-year financial history, including a minimum two-year history and discussion of the price of the company's stock and dividend payments, full presentation of company performance broken down by line of business, biographies of officers, and text devoted to management's analysis of year-end financial position and competitive position.

The Exchanges, while they control only listed companies, have been no less lax or intensive in their own drives for disclosure regulation. The

New York Stock Exchange, recognizing the value of credibility in obtaining investor confidence, has proposed a number of guidelines to be developed to increase corporate financial disclosure. These include mailing quarterly reports to all stockholders every quarter, a section of the annual report covering "variance analysis," which would detail the reasons for material changes in the year-to-year operations of the company, consistency in reviewing company performance throughout the president's letter and in graphs, charts and financial statements, based upon identical performance yardsticks, and information regarding the market for the company securities, including common price range, price/earnings ratio, and dividends and book value for the period covered by the company's historical earnings summary table. In other words, every regulatory body concerned with the publicly held company is not only deadly earnest about full disclosure, but is accelerating its drive to accomplish it and to increase those aspects of a company's operation to be disclosed.

DISCLOSURE VEHICLES

The vehicles for disclosure are basically these:

1. The prospectus.
2. The proxy statement.
3. The annual and quarterly reports.
4. The news release.
5. The direct letter to shareholders.
6. The annual meeting.

The Prospectus

The prospectus, issued when stock or a public debt offering is sold, is basically a legal document. It is almost invariably written by attorneys, to legal prescription, and is written in legalistic terms. Therein lies the problem. In the attempt to fulfill every legal requirement of disclosure, prospectuses are meticulously prepared, and therefore read like contracts. Unfortunately, it is virtually impossible for any but the most sophisticated nonlawyer to be expected to have the patience to read all of the information contained in a prospectus, much less to understand it. The SEC has recognized this in recent years, and as a result, it is encouraging companies to be somewhat more readable and graphic in prospectuses. The change is coming slowly, but it's coming. The SEC wants a prospectus to be understood by the average prospective investor. The general belief is that a prospectus can be concise without being obtuse. Furthermore, the SEC believes that while a prospectus should not be a marketing brochure, and should be objective, there is no reason why a prospectus cannot be illustrated, especially if the illustrations increase the understanding of the company. Little by little, this feeling is having its effect, and more and more prospectuses now include illustrations, color, and a more narrative style. While the subject of prospectuses is primarily the province of attorneys, there is no reason why a company president should not recognize that the prospectus is the basic document for reaching into the public segment of the capital market, and therefore should be understandable and readable.

The Proxy Statement

The proxy statement is the legal document sent prior to an annual meeting to shareholders, who must understand and vote on the business to be presented at that meeting. While proxies contain the basic and routine agenda of items upon which the shareholders must vote, such as the election of the board of directors, the election of auditors, the approval of pension plans, and so forth, here, too, there is no reason why a proxy should not be readable and understandable.

More than just a simple basic document, in many cases the proxy is a crucial means of communication for a company involved in an out-of-the-ordinary situation. In the case of mergers requiring shareholder approval, for example, it must contain considerable detail, sufficient to allow the shareholder to understand every aspect of the merger—not only the financial arrangements, but the reasons for it, a description of the other company, the structure of the company after the merger, and so on.

In proxy fights, it is a major document that must present management's point of view to shareholders it is trying to win to its side. By law, in some states, it must also report any proposal by a predetermined percentage of shareholders.

In other words, there are times when the proxy is much more than a routine document. And, as in the case of prospectuses, new formats are emerging for clarity, including illustration and pictures of officers and directors. Clarity and readability need not subvert disclosure.

The Annual and Quarterly Reports

The annual report is the basic document in which the company attempts to tell its story to shareholders, the financial community, and the investing public. Annual and quarterly reports are increasingly becoming the concern of the SEC and the Exchanges. The annual report must be mailed to shareholders with or preceding the proxy statement.

An annual report is a financial document and not a graphics device. Historically, it has been used by an overwhelming number of companies as a cosmetic vehicle to show the company's good side, to make the company appear to be in better shape than it is. Each year, the SEC and the Exchanges increase their demands for greater and greater disclosure in reports. While this has put an increasing burden on companies for more elaborate disclosure and inclusion of a greater number of facts, the ultimate result has been salutary. No company, even one performing badly at any given moment, has ever suffered as mightily from full disclosure in an annual report as it has from the confusion and uncertainty that arises from incomplete disclosure.

Letters to Shareholders

The letter to shareholders is sometimes a useful device to advise shareholders of major events that affect the company between reporting periods. It is prescribed in those circumstances where special action must be taken, such as a merger that will ultimately require the approval of shareholders, and for which a proxy for a special meeting is forthcoming. It is also useful to amplify a news report.

The News Release

The news release, which was treated in the last chapter, is the basic tool of disclosure. Not only are news releases prescribed for routine reporting, such as earnings, but they are essential for announcing any event that might affect the evaluation of the company, whether it be a major contract, the development of a new product, the resignation of a senior officer, or a potential merger or acquisition.

The Annual Meeting

The annual meeting is the official gathering of all shareholders and is the appropriate time to report on the year's activities. As will be discussed in Chapter 5, it must be realistically recognized that the annual meeting is rarely attended by any but the smallest portion of shareholders. It cannot be assumed that any announcement made solely at the annual meeting is proper dissemination of information. Any such announcement should be followed immediately by a news release.

There are two areas of information that are the province of disclosure—detailed financial data and news of significant company activity.

Generally speaking, detailed financial data should include any information that can be construed as useful in understanding the performance of a company. In the first instance, this includes balance sheet and operational information. In appropriate vehicles such as the prospectus or the annual report, this material goes much beyond basic operational information to include material that gives both historical perspective to the information and, increasingly, consideration of the market value of the company's stock. The latter is relatively new and a matter of much concern and discussion. No company, for example, particularly wants to dwell on the performance of its stock in a bear market.

A delineation of the material to be disclosed in annual reports and other documents to the financial community is given in greater detail in Chapters 2 and 5. What should be noted here, however, is that the basic intent is to make every effort to give the fullest possible picture of a company's financial structure, and to include every bit of information that will reasonably contribute to that picture.

INFORMING THE EXCHANGES

It is important that copies of all material—releases, proxies, and so on—be filed with any exchange on which the company is listed as soon as possible after they are issued. This includes both the company's listing representative on the exchange and its specialist. At the same time, it is important that the specialist *never* be made privy to any information about the company before it is made public. His posture must always be one of objectivity, and he could be seriously compromised by any inside information.

A basic problem in disclosure is the inherent conflict that frequently arises between attorneys and financial relations consultants, and others involved with disclosure. This is a conflict that is legitimate in its foundations and difficult to resolve. The financial relations consultant is concerned with the dissemination of as much information as possible. The attorney, inherently cautious, is charged not only with seeing that his client complies with the law, but also with anticipating prospective legal problems. The lawyer feels that anything you say in print may ultimately be held against you. The concerns of both parties are legitimate, but each must recognize the other's responsibilities. The financial relations consultant must recognize that only the lawyer has the experience and training to support his point of view that the company must be protected against future attack. The attorney, on the other hand, must recognize that the company must compete in the capital markets, must compete for the attention of the financial community, and must compete for the attention of the financial press. If each party recognizes the other's needs, these conflicts can be resolved. The attorney must protect and the financial relations consultant must communicate. Both purposes serve the company.

DISCLOSURE BY NEWS RELEASE

The subject of disclosure by news release is a much more difficult one simply because what is material information defies definition. This is where judgment plays so great a part. It is also difficult because not every event that in hindsight may be deemed material can be anticipated.

Perhaps the nearest the SEC has ever come to defining the term "material" is in a consent decree against Investors Diversified Service, Inc., containing the following language, "Material inside information is any information about a company, or the market for the company's securities, which has come directly or indirectly from the company, and which has not been disclosed generally to the marketplace, the dissemination of which is likely to affect the market price of any of the company's securities or is likely to be considered important by reasonable investors, including reasonable speculative investors, in determining whether to trade in such securities."

Any material information by that definition must be disclosed immediately, using the procedures described in the last chapter. While the kind of information that comes under that heading is impossible to list to the fullest extent, there are certainly some obvious activities that should always be reported:

1. Financial results for a period.
2. Changes in corporate structure of any magnitude.
3. Mergers or acquisitions. Here, as in other areas of negotiation, timing becomes sensitive, since premature disclosure can sometimes adversely affect such negotiations. It is generally accepted, however, that such negotiations should be announced at any point at which there is any feeling by both parties that the negotiations will reach a successful conclusion. This can be a verbal agreement or a letter of intent. Certainly, failure to disclose the negotiations at the time a letter of intent is signed is potentially dangerous.
4. Earnings forecasts or estimates.
5. Exchange offer or tender offer.
6. Stock split or stock dividend, or any other significant change in capitalization.

7. Decision to make a public offering.

8. A substantial loan.

9. Listing on an exchange.

10. Major new product introduction.

11. Opening or closing a plant of considerable size.

12. Amendment of corporate charter or bylaws.

13. Any information that legally requires special filing with the SEC. In this context, include any consequential information filed in the 8K report filed with the SEC.

14. Significant environmental or civil rights matters.

15. Decisions of regulatory bodies other than the SEC, such as the Interstate Commerce Commission or the Federal Trade Commission.

16. Litigation.

The list goes on and on, guided only by one's definition of material information for a particular company or industry.

REGISTRATION FOR A PUBLIC ISSUE

One area that has been perhaps the most difficult to understand in terms of disclosure is the regulations that govern a company which has a public issue in registration. A company in registration is severely limited and prohibited from any activity that might be construed as offering, selling, or assisting in the sale of stock. The conflict arises in that the company, even while in registration, is required to conform to other rules of disclosure.

The basis for this regulation is the Securities Act of 1933, which prohibits the offering or sale of a security unless a registration statement has been filed with the SEC, or selling a security unless the registration statement has become effective. There are three periods of registration. There is the time before the registration statement has been filed. There is the period during which the registration statement is on file, but not yet effective. And there is the period after the registration statement has become effective. It is during the second period—when the company is in registration—that it is illegal to issue any material relating to the security, other than the statutory prospectus. That period is clearly defined by the SEC as being "at least from the time an issuer reaches an understanding with a broker-dealer," and it ends with the completion of the dealer's prospectus delivery obligations. Not included are the initial discussions or negotiations between the company and the underwriter. It is only when there is some form of commitment by the underwriter that the period actually begins in which the company is considered to be "in registration."

It is during this period that the corporation may take no action, nor issue any publicity, that can be construed as an effort to sell the stock or enhance the ultimate sale of the stock. And here, in view of other aspects of disclosure regulation, lies the paradox between what can and cannot be publicized.

The SEC recognizes the problem, and further accepts the fact that it is impossible to define in absolute detail those activities which a company may or may not pursue. Each set of circumstances must rest on its own facts. Nevertheless, the SEC has issued seven categories of information which it deems not only acceptable, but which it in fact encourages. They are:

1. Continued advertising of products.
2. Continued distribution of customary reports to stockholders.
3. Continued publication of proxy statements.
4. Continued announcements to the press of "factual business and financial developments."
5. Answering unsolicited inquiries from shareholders and others (if the answers are responsive to the questions and prudently do not go beyond the bounds previously described).
6. Answering unsolicited inquiries from the financial community.
7. Continuing to hold stockholders meetings and answering stockholders inquiries at such meetings.

Obviously, the information disseminated under these seven categories should not include predictions, projections, forecasts, or opinions with respect to value. Nor should it include any attempt to describe the company in ways that might be considered as supportive of a securities sales effort. And so once again we come to the question of judgment. And once again we come into a potential conflict between attorneys and financial relations consultants. Here, too, attorneys and financial relations consultants must consider one another's positions in light of the company's needs and responsibilities.

Without attempting to skirt or stretch the seven categories of information approved by the SEC, it should be recognized that not only is there tremendous latitude in the amount and kind of information that can be disseminated by a company in registration, but that both the need for and the value of such continued dissemination does not diminish.

There is also a value in a financial relations communications program begun well before the company goes into registration, in that such a preregistration program sets the tone for what may be deemed permissible while the company is actually in registration. On the other hand, it can be considered somewhat suspect if a company that has never communicated to the financial community suddenly begins such a program the minute it gets into registration. It is in the exercise of judgment in this area that the experience of the financial relations consultant can be of exceptional value.

In the third stage, when the company is out of registration, all bounds are off for a financial communications program that is otherwise legal under any SEC regulations or sound business requirements.

COMPLIANCE BY FINANCIAL RELATIONS FIRMS

After thorough review with the SEC, The Financial Relations Board has developed a compliance manual for practices by financial relations consultants in issuing information. It protects both the company and the consultant, as well as the investing public. It assures that all issued information is carefully reviewed, and that all sources are clearly identified. FRB goes further by reviewing carefully all available financial and corporate data on each of its prospective clients, to assure that it represents only sound and reputable companies.

A primary factor in compliance procedures for a financial relations consultant is that it know its client. In a proper relationship, the consultant works closely with the chief executive and financial officers. He is well informed about the company's financial and corporate structures, as well as its day-to-day operations. This basic knowledge provides a framework in which to judge new financial and operational information.

Proper compliance procedures require that all issued material must be accompanied by an appropriate form, retained with a copy of the material by the consultant, indicating the source of information, the time it was given for release, the time it is to be released, whether the copy has been or is to be amended, and by whom. Additional comments might indicate who prepared the original material and how the information was transmitted for preparation for release. If additional approval is required or was given by attorneys, accountants, or others, it is indicated. The form is then signed by the company officer responsible, as well as by the consultant responsible. In the case of a release approved by telephone, or supplied by mail or teletype, a variation of the form, designed for that purpose, is used, and signed by the consultant who received it. The Financial Relations Board designates a member of its executive committee as compliance officer for the firm. His job is to oversee all procedures for compliance with SEC and Exchange regulations, and includes a periodic review of all material released by FRB.

There is a keen difference between the requirements of disclosure under the regulations of the SEC and the Exchanges and the need for disclosure for a public company seeking acceptance in the capital markets. The rules of disclosure are requirements, not electives. The *needs* for disclosure are dictated by the attempts of a public company to keep itself visible to the financial community, and at all times clearly understood. One does not preclude the other, and in fact, the values of disclosure far exceed the limitations of the rules of disclosure.

As for conforming to the regulations of the Securities and Exchange Commission and the Exchanges, there is one basic rule—when in doubt, disclose. And fast.

CHAPTER 5

INVESTOR RELATIONS   · · · · ·

One of the great mysteries of financial relations is the subject of investor relations. It is a mystery because so much that is taken for granted is practice and theory that must be seriously questioned. So much that is done in the name of investor relations is done mindlessly; so much is done because that's the way it's always been done. And as in so many other things, the original reasons, which may have been sound at the time, have become lost, obscured, or are no longer applicable.

Furthermore, so much of what is basic to investor relations is really intangible. Aside from the degree to which facts are communicated, it is difficult—sometimes downright impossible—to gauge the effectiveness of any investor relations program with any degree of certainty.

Presumably, an effective investor relations program will result in a warm feeling of loyalty to the company by its shareholders. But how many chief executive officers are now walking around with a glazed look in their eyes because, despite an intensive investor relations program, their loyal and intensively informed shareholders tendered their stock to the other side in a take-over attempt? How many loyal and informed shareholders, subjected to many years of a meticulous investor relations program, have sold their stock when it became apparent that the company was in for a rough year?

On the other hand, how do you gauge the degree to which shareholders held on to their stock when the company anticipated a bad year, because they fully understood that the company was inherently sound and would recover from any short-term problems? How many shareholders increased their holdings when it was made clear that the company was about to enter a particularly favorable period? Even a careful analysis of the stock transfer sheet offers very little measurable evidence, quantitatively, of a sound investor relations program.

There is also the paradox of liquidity. In a company with a relatively small float—the number of shares outstanding that are available for public trading—satisfied shareholders who do not sell their stock can, in a measure, be self-defeating, since if there is no stock available, there is no auction market. And if there is no auction market, the price of a stock tends to stay static or decline.

And yet despite these questions, there is clear evidence that a carefully planned and effectively performed investor relations program is warranted. Certainly, beyond legal obligations, there is an inherent responsibility to keep investors informed of not only current operating data, but of both the general performance and outlook for the company.

Theoretically and legally, management is employed by the shareholders, and therefore the shareholders are entitled to an account of the way their company is being managed. With exceptions, this is, of course, little more than theory. The control of most companies is held by either the management group or a relatively small group of investors close to the management. The theoretical concept of shareholder democracy is, again with exceptions, a pleasant myth. While it is true that minority shareholders, by dint of legal methods or highly visible and publicized activities that pressure the company, are able to effect policies counter to management's original plans, the fact is that companies are run by management. The exceptions are so few as to be notable. Even the efforts of minority shareholder leaders, such as the Gilbert brothers, are successful only by attrition, and then only over a very long time. It is to the credit of the Gilbert brothers that they have accomplished a great deal in the field of shareholder democracy, and to a large extent their efforts have been salutary. But these efforts have taken a very long time, many years in fact. Even after several decades, they have barely made a dent in achieving their own stated objectives.

In fact, in a great number of companies, boards of directors, charged with the responsibility of developing and supervising management and policy, have very little power over management actions.

Yet investors must be viewed for what they are—a source of capital. And as such they must be as assiduously wooed as any other group. The fact that they are already shareholders is a twofold advantage. They have already made a decision favorable to the company, and management usually knows who they are. This doesn't mean that the selling aspect of financial relations in any way diminishes—a shareholder can become an ex-shareholder with relative ease. It merely means that the job of reaching him is simpler. It also means that, as a legal owner of the company, he has a claim to the management's ear. A dissatisfied shareholder has a right to make his opinions known to management and he has many ways to do it. He can ask embarrassing questions at an annual meeting, and be highly visible while doing it. He can write letters to management. He can telephone or call on management in person. And then, of course, he has that ultimate weapon—he can become an ex-shareholder.

If the shareholder is satisfied he can use these weapons in management's behalf. He can get up at that same annual meeting and publicly praise management. He can write letters of praise. He can be an effective spokesman for the company and its stock to his friends and to brokers. And since shareholders are sometimes effective management people themselves, he can sometimes contribute useful ideas. As for that ultimate effective weapon, he can hold his stock during the company's trying periods and he can buy more stock if the company's outlook is good.

And so on balance an effective shareholders' program is warranted and has tremendous value, unquantifiable as the results of such a program might be.

Aside from keeping shareholders informed, the ultimate objective of an investor relations program is to engender understanding and a favorable attitude toward the company on the part of investors.

TOOLS OF SHAREHOLDER RELATIONS

While the normal functions of a financial relations program will ultimately reach and serve shareholders as well as prospective investors, there are some quite specific devices used as tools in an investor relations program. These are:

1. The annual report.
2. Interim reports.
3. The annual meeting.
4. Letters to shareholders, or a periodic newsletter.
5. Distribution of product literature or internal house organs.
6. Distribution of press reports.
7. Phone contact with shareholders.

These are the tools—but the tools are not a program. Certainly, every public company issues an annual report and many companies issue interim reports. All public companies hold annual meetings. Many companies frequently write letters to shareholders to inform them of special events or activities, and many even write welcoming letters to new shareholders. But not only must each of these devices be looked at separately and used artfully, it must be recognized that each functions best when it is part of an overall plan or program. They must not only interrelate and reinforce one another, but they are all judged in terms of specific objectives.

INVESTOR RELATIONS POLICY

For an investor relations program to be effective, there must first of all be a clear-cut decision by management that commits the company to such a program. Internally, a specific officer must be charged with investor relations responsibility. If the program is considered important enough to do in the first place, it should be considered a serious responsibility. Too often, left-handed recognition of the need for such a program results in a half-hearted attempt from which the chief executive divorces himself, assigning the responsibility to a low-ranking officer, and allotting the performance of the program either to inexperienced personnel or to an advertising manager clearly not qualified to deal with it. In order for an investor relations program to succeed, it should ultimately fall under the personal aegis of the chief executive officer, no matter who is assigned to perform the actual task. Of course, for the company with outside financial relations counsel, the professionalism of the program is enhanced. But here, too, the financial relations counsel is thwarted unless the chief executive officer is not only dedicated to the success of the program, but understands the necessity of keeping the financial relations counsel keenly attuned to all aspects of the company's operation, as well as to current corporate policy. While the day-by-day activities of such a program—or any financial relations program for that matter—may be supervised by a designated executive, there must be clear access to the chief executive officer.

The program itself must have clearly stated, and perhaps even written, objectives. Basically, the ultimate objective is to keep shareholders informed, and to do so in ways that engender a favorable attitude towards the company. But aside from the basic rules and requirements of disclosure, how far does that go? The basic requirements of disclosure for even the largest company can be fulfilled with a mimeograph machine. The degree to which the company goes beyond the rules in the elaborateness of its disclosure, as well as the graphic devices used as a medium, must be predetermined. What is the basic attitude of the company toward its shareholders? Are they a cherished group to be assiduously wooed and won, or are they to be considered as transitory, with the obligation to them minimal and limited only to basic information? Are they to be accepted merely as a necessary evil attendant to a public corporation, or is each new shareholder to be greeted with a personal letter from the president welcoming him to the family?

Are they to be seen as a distant group to be dealt with only as the occasion arises, or shall the program include a careful and regular analysis of transfer sheets to keep informed of changes in shareholders? This, incidentally, is a basic and important device not only in investor relations, but in any financial relations program. It not only indicates changes in share-holders, but changes in geographical distribution, the entry or exit of participation by brokerage houses, unusual purchasing or selling patterns that might indicate the necessity for specific action or alterations in the financial relations program, or warn of prospective take-over attempts. Transfer sheets should be reviewed regularly, and each week a summary should be prepared for the chief executive officer indicating changes in shareholding of large blocks. Specific patterns should be watched for such factors as regular purchases of small lots by one buyer, or selling patterns in a particular geographic area.

Only when the investor relations program is carefully planned can specific decisions be made on such questions as, how elaborate should the annual report be? Should interim reports be simple statements or exten-sively illustrated descriptions of company business? Should an audiovisual or film presentation be developed for the annual meeting, or should it con-sist solely of a president's message? Without a clear-cut overall policy regarding investor relations, decisions and answers to these questions and myriad others are arbitrary.

THE ANNUAL REPORT

There is probably no subject in the area of financial or investor relations that has commanded more discussion than the annual report. Since every public company issues an annual report in one form or another, it is the one universal device in financial relations even for those companies that do nothing else in the field. Millions of dollars are spent and wasted every year in the production of these documents. Millions more are spent in their distribution, and the dollar value of executive time is incalculable.

Yet very little written seems to deal with the core issue of an annual report—what it really is and should be, and how it really is to be used. An overwhelming number of annual reports are merely imitations of re-ports that have gone before, with the basic reasoning for the predecessor long since forgotten.

Even the basic audience for annual reports is a subject of much discus-sion, most of it based on irrelevant issues. One school of thought believes that the annual report should be written so that it can be understood by the least sophisticated shareholder. At the other extreme there is the feel-ing that the annual report should be simply the company's Form 10K. Others think of the annual report in terms of a peculiar concept called the corporate image—a predetermined view of the company to be engen-dered to the investing or general public, almost with total disregard to facts or realities.

There are two basic points that should be remembered in planning an annual report.

1. An annual report is basically a financial document and a financial relations tool. It is not a graphics device. It is not primarily an advertising medium. It is the basic tool used by every segment of the investment community—the shareholder, the security analyst, the broker, the money manager, the bank, the institutional investor, the institutional lender, and so on—to make the basic evaluation of the company as an investment or lending vehicle. Furthermore, it has an active life of at least one year—until the next annual report is issued. During that period it serves as the primary handbook for evaluating the company, regardless of what other documents or information are used to supplement the information in it.

2. Each annual report should be approached virtually as if it were the first time in corporate history that any annual report has ever been written. The only legal requirements of an annual report are that they report certain prescribed facts about the company. This can be done with a mimeograph machine. Thus any decision to go beyond the bare bones must not only be predicated upon the needs of the company, but may take virtually any form, in any format, that serves to present a clear picture of the company without distorting the truth.

Thus the greatest effort in developing an annual report should take place in the planning stage. A number of clear-cut questions should be raised early, and examined very carefully in all aspects, before any work is done on the report. It is frequently useful to put these questions, and their answers, in writing, as a form of prospectus for the report. The prospectus may even be longer than the report itself. The result of the effort, however, makes it well worthwhile. It become a clear document and statement of policy for everyone who will have to work on the report. It cuts down the almost inevitable rewriting, and it eliminates time-consuming discussions over drafts that must be ultimately discarded because not everyone involved understood the same things about the directions in which the report was to go.

The prospectus should include the following:

1. Outline of problems and unusual circumstances that form a context for this particular annual report.
2. The objectives of this report.
3. The target audiences.
4. The format.
5. Special features.
6. Graphics.

Objectives

It should be recognized that at the time each company prepares its annual report it faces a specific set of problems and circumstances in regard to both its own operations and the capital markets that are pertinent at that moment. These problems may be peculiar to the company, the economy, or the industry. They may pertain to changes within the company, its corporate structure, its products, the markets it serves, or changes in financial structure. The company may be undergoing some unusual and highly visible litigation. The economy may have certain elements in it which particularly color a view of the company, such as the energy crisis, inflation, or devaluation. The industry may be undergoing significant changes or material shortages. The company may be appreciably outperforming its industry. This kind of problem may be short range, but it is the annual report that serves as the prime vehicle for management to address itself to the company's position relative to these problems. Or the problem may be long range, such as a change in the direction of the company's operations or growth plans. The point is that these problems pose the context against which the company's story is to be told in its annual report. All planning for the report must keep these problems very much in the forefront.

These problems also form the basis for developing the objectives of the report. Obviously its primary objective is to inform. But beyond that, each report each year not only faces a different set of corporate problems, but a different set of objectives. The objectives are determined as the answers to the question, "What is it we want our readers to know and think about our company after they have read the report?" Certain of the objectives are basic. For example:

1. To define the essential nature of the company and its business within a context that augurs well for the future.

2. To demonstrate that management has a firm grasp on all aspects of the company's business; that it not only understands but controls all aspects of the business. This includes a full understanding of the company's markets and market potential, both currently and in the foreseeable future.

3. To demonstrate that the company is internally sound and strong—both fiscally and in depth of management—or is aware of those areas in which this is not the case, and is taking steps to make corrections.

4. To demonstrate that the avenues of the future for the company are to a large degree clearly identifiable; that the company understands them and is attempting to build the kind of flexibility that allows it to move readily into them.

Beyond these general objectives, the company must develop additional goals predicated on specific problems the company faces at the time the report is to be prepared. This may include clarification of industry, economic, or specific corporate activities, or specific corporate problems peculiar to the company. This might include the nature of an offshore tax situation, or the relationship of the company to the energy or monetary crises, or the ways in which inflation affects the company's operations.

The stated objectives should be clearly developed for the annual report, and should not be a broader statement of corporate philosophy or corporate objectives.

Target Audiences

The target audiences for an annual report must be clearly delineated. Without a clear understanding of who is to read the report, it is virtually impossible to determine intelligently how it is to be prepared. Each company must decide for itself the prime targets and their order of importance. For any public company there is no one specific audience to the exclusion of the others. Nor are the audience priorities the same from one company to the other.

There are partisans for every point of view on the subject of audiences for annual reports, ranging from the unsophisticated holder of a hundred shares to the highly sophisticated analyst for a major institution. While no single statement can be expected to resolve that question once and for all, there are some basic considerations.

For example, if an annual report is properly done, with a clear delineation of all aspects of the company's financial and other operations, it must necessarily be infinitely more sophisticated than if the report is written for the casual shareholder. This does not mean it should be more difficult to read and understand, however.

Furthermore, the question must be viewed in terms of how investment decisions are made. The manager of a large fund makes his decision based not only on the annual report, but upon extensive analysis of other factors as well. The individual investor, on the other hand, rarely makes an investment decision on his own. He may read the annual report, or any other document, and draw a conclusion. The number of such investors who will make investment decisions based on that conclusion, and without further consultation, is so small that this kind of investor must be excluded from any serious consideration as a target audience for an annual report. When the widow who inherited a few hundred shares of stock reads a report and makes an investment decision, she is most likely going to consult her broker. He will then presumably contribute his knowledge and sophistication, backed by appropriate research reports, to enforce or amend that decision. Thus, as a practical matter, the primary target audience is rarely the individual investor.

This is not to say that the individual investor does not constitute an important part of the audience for an annual report. The report is ostensibly a report to shareholders. Nor should this be construed to mean that any report should be obscure for the average investor. The point is that the target audiences are determined by more than a responsibility to keep shareholders informed. As the company's annual statement, it is a document that clarifies the company to a much broader financial community.

In the final analysis, and keeping in mind the shareholders, the primary target audience is almost invariably the financial community. The essential prospective audiences break down as follows:

1. *The financial community.* This means the analysts, brokerage houses, money managers, and institutions whose knowledge of the company must be maintained in as great detail as possible, and whose support the company must foster over both the short and long range if the company is to compete successfully in the capital markets. Included are banks, insurance companies, and other lending institutions. This target is particularly vital for the smaller company, where access to other means of communications is limited. For them, the annual report takes on an even greater value as a source of information about the company. It is the annual report that is frequently the first point of contact between the financial community and the company—the first opportunity the prospective investor has to become acquainted with it. There is no question that for the annual report of most companies, the financial community is the primary target.

2. *Shareholders.* The basic legal purpose of the annual report is to report the company's position to shareholders. Therefore, while they are not deemed a primary target, they are still an essential target. The objective in reaching shareholders, beyond the normal reporting requirements, is to demonstrate that their company is well managed and sound.

3. *The broader business community.* For many companies the report can be an annual demonstration to the business community at large of their structure, strength, and capability. Companies do business with one another. It demonstrates the soundness of the company to suppliers, potential merger partners, and others with whom a relationship of one kind or another is valuable.

4. *Prospective customers.* While an annual report is not a sales brochure, a certain amount of display of capability makes it useful as a sales tool by demonstrating not only the range of service, but the substance of the company behind it. In the case of consumer companies, the report has a certain advertising value, in that shareholders and prospective investors are also consumers.

5. *Internal.* For some companies there is a value in considering internal staff as a target audience. The report offers an opportunity to enhance morale and engender pride. Not to be overlooked is the fact that employees are sometimes potential investors as well.

In this area, there occasionally arises a question of the place of the annual report in labor relations. Some companies feel that there is a danger in displaying profitability in ways that might incite trade unions to demand a greater portion of it. This is an unfortunate and negative view. It is unlikely that any labor union of consequence is not already keenly aware of the company's performance, virtually in as great detail as is the management. To consider labor relations as a reason for not fully reporting performance is not only a delusion, but uses a smaller negative factor to override a larger advantage. (The same is true in considering flaunting high margins to the business community as dangerous in that customers might look askance at prices in relation to profit margins or that potential competitors might be attracted by highly profitable market opportunities.)

Format

The format of an annual report is a function of objectives and target audiences. The financials aside, certain traditional practices have sprung up which pervade an overwhelming number of reports. In some cases these formats are followed simply because they are traditional, and not because they bear any relation to the particular needs of a company. There is usually the president's letter, followed by some text and illustrative material describing the company and its products in glowing terms. The standard president's letter starts out with either a statement of how good the year has been or an apologetic note for the company's poor performance. This is followed by several paragraphs recapping sales and earnings, and some brief cosmetic explanation of why earnings were not up to par, or a description of the several factors that resulted in superior performance. If the bored reader continues on, he will find a few paragraphs describing some of the year's outstanding events, followed by a paragraph or two projecting the problems or opportunities that lie ahead, and a statement that the company intends to face the problems squarely or seize the opportunities effectively. The letter ends on an optimistic note for the future, with a bow of thanks to the loyal officers and employees without whom the company's success would not be possible.

The descriptive text, including pictures of the company's plant—which looks like every other plant—describes the company's products, processes, or services.

This format and approach to an annual report virtually guarantees that the report will not be read, nor will it be understood, nor will it be appreciated. Even if the company is performing magnificently and has great potential for the future, this performance or potential will be submerged and hidden in a deluge of words and cliches. The chances are that anybody in the investment community who reads one report will read many. It all begins to dissolve into one shapeless blur.

This need not be. Aside from reporting certain basic required information, the option of format lies entirely with the company. Hearken back to a point noted earlier—each report can and should be written as if it were the first time in corporate history that an annual report has ever been written. The number of legitimate and exciting variations is limited only by the imagination of the company or financial relations consultant who prepares the report.

For the 1972 *Playboy* annual report, The Financial Relations Board put the company's chief executive officer in a room with half a dozen leading security analysts and recorded the interview. The interview was then edited for style only, and printed in lieu of a traditional president's letter.

For its 1973 report, Creative Management Associates, a publicly held theatrical talent agency, printed its report in the form of the publication, *Daily Variety*. All of the pertinent financial information was included, and the company's activities were reported as news or feature stories.

In its first report as a public company, Jones and Vining, a manufacturer of shoe lasts, recognized that few of the people it wanted to reach would understand the shoe last industry, and devoted a full page to a discussion of the shoe last and its role in shoe manufacturing. It also recognized that the company could be judged properly only in the context of the total shoe industry, and devoted another full page to a discussion of the economics of the industry, its structure, and its current status.

In its 1973 annual report, Saunders Leasing Systems, Inc., recognized that a description of its services in behalf of its leasing customers could be considered routine and mundane to those outside the industry. Its financial relations counsel suggested that these services be reported pictorially in the style used by the late *Life* magazine. The report took a Saunders branch manager and pictorially followed him through a day of his activities—a fresh and effective approach to describing services that would otherwise have been of no interest to readers.

Some larger companies have included articles discussing international economics written by prominent economists outside the company. Others, functioning in several countries, have printed their reports in several languages.

In other words, the effectiveness of the report can be enhanced by shifting wherever possible from traditional approaches. No corporate annual report can or should be an imitation of any other corporate annual report, since no two corporations are the same.

From many surveys and interviews it has been determined that professionals who read annual reports tend to follow the same procedure. This becomes necessary, since they read so many of them in the course of a year and must determine very quickly whether the company offers any basis for further interest.

Most analysts turn to the first page for a quick look at the two-year summary of revenues and earnings. They then turn to the back of the book to review the financials—profit and loss statement, balance sheet, and so forth. If they are still interested after having read thus far, they turn to the president's letter in the hope of finding an intelligent explanation of the financial condition of the company and its operating results. If they are still interested, they will go on to read the text describing the company's operations.

No investment professional is ever impressed by the physical format of a report. Many, in fact, indicate a negative reaction to an expensive four-color report for any company that does not show a significant gain in earnings. One of the most exquisite reports ever produced some years ago was for a multinational company. The graphics were extraordinary. The photography could have won prizes. It was obviously an expensive production. It reported an $8 million loss for that year. The reaction of shareholders upon receiving so expensive a booklet when the company lost $8 million was explosive.

The purpose of an annual report is to impart information, and its format should be designed to do just that. Moreover, the SEC and the Exchanges are insisting upon the disclosure of a greater number of factors. The SEC is moving very strongly in the direction of increased disclosure by making a greater amount of information mandatory (see Appendix II). Certainly, the report should include virtually every piece of pertinent information reported in the Form 10K. In fact, the SEC now requires that companies conspicuously offer the 10K to shareholders in the annual reports, and at no charge. But making the 10K available is no substitute for full-scale reporting in the annual report itself.

The President's Message

Readers of annual reports look to the president's message for a rounded picture of the company's performance. This does not mean a rehash of information delineated more succinctly in other parts of the report. Regardless of the format used, the chief executive's message should be simple, concise, free from cliches, and loaded with information. It should not merely state financial data reported elsewhere. It should explain. It should point to significant changes in performance or financial factors and give sound reasons as to why those changes took place and what they mean. It should take note of critical variables—those elements in a business that are crucial to success or failure. It should dwell heavily on balance sheet factors, such as changes in inventory, accounts receivable, important ratios, return on investment, and so forth.

It should outline the framework in which the business functions in terms of both the general economy and the industry.

It should describe the major changes in financial structure that have taken place in the prior year, drawn from the 10K, although not necessarily in its formal language. The SEC has specifically indicated that annual reports be readable by nonprofessionals as well as professionals, that annual report text not be in the same legal language as the 10K. Other information required includes changes in accounting principles or practices, product mix, relative profitability of lines of business, advertising, research and development, acquisition or disposition of material assets, assumptions underlying deferred costs and plans for amortization of such costs, the closing of facilities, business interruption, and significant new contracts. The SEC staff has defined a material change as one in which any item of receivables or expenses changes by 10% and/or affects net income by more than 2% at any time during the prior three years. They are quite clear that this be included in the text, even though these items may be covered in notes to the financial statement. If a projection of the coming year's performance is to be made, it need not contain specific earnings projections, but it should certainly clarify specific reasons for optimism. It should clarify the debt picture as well as forthcoming plans for capital expenditures and how they are expected to contribute to the company's growth and future profitability. The SEC now insists that management comment not only on the year-end financial picture, but on the company's competitive position within its field.

It should clarify uncertainties that may affect future earnings. It should clarify special problems such as international operations, and special situations, such as an unusual tax structure.

In other words, the president's message should be as complete and detailed a report as he might give in summary to his own board of directors. When one has read a president's letter one should have a clear picture of not only where the company has been and where the company is, but where it's going.

There is an increasing tendency to discuss various aspects of corporate responsibility in reports. In some cases, such as environmental control, this is an essential part of a company's business, and would naturally be included. However, some companies, as a matter of corporate philosophy, recognize a larger role of the corporation in the total society. Some companies, such as Xerox and Mobil, have gone to great lengths to define what they see as an obligation to society, and devote a good deal of their corporate effort toward that end. Monogram Industries' chief executive officer, Martin Stone, is an excellent example of a corporate leader of a smaller company who believes that corporate responsibility to the community has a place in the total corporate function and reports extensively on it. The move toward recognizing corporate responsibility in society is, in many cases, a function of the individual consciousness of corporate officers. In other cases, companies are responding to criticism from consumer groups, including activists in civil rights and equal rights for women. On the one hand, it is argued that this kind of corporate activity is irrelevant to the corporation's profit-making function. On the other hand, it is argued that not only does this activity increase a company's favorable visibility, but it contributes to profitability in the long run, since by guaranteeing the quality of life in the future of the nation, a corporation also guarantees its profitability. Certainly in those companies with a position or with activity in this area, reports of the activities are valid and preferred in the annual report. Moreover, there is an immediately tangible aspect in view of the costs and their effect upon earnings.

There is also a growing movement toward the corporate social audit, in which attempts are made to quantify the actual costs, commitments, and values of all facets of corporate responsibility, from environmental controls to minority training programs. The American Institute of Certified Public Accountants has even appointed a committee to develop standards and techniques for measuring, recording, reporting, and auditing social performance. For the company involved in this kind of activity, exploration into techniques or reporting it on an economic basis should certainly be explored.

Financial Information

Elsewhere in the report, the largest possible number of economic factors should be clearly given, in addition to basic financial information. This includes:

1. Sales and earnings by product line and division. This has been a subject of considerable contention. It is now mandatory under SEC regulation. It has long been felt, for example, that reporting this information gives away competitive information. The fact remains that this information is publicly available to competitors in the Form 10K. It is inconceivable

that any competitor interested in the information will not have availed himself of it the instant the 10K is filed. On the other hand, reporting by line gives a clearer picture of the company. And as with all financial disclosure, the greater the amount of information disclosed, the greater the credibility awarded to nonfinancial statements made by corporate executives.

2. Financial statistics for 10 years or more. This is in addition to the two-year summary given on the first page of the report. Granted that historical information contributes only partially to predicting the future growth of the company; it gives a rounded picture of progress over a reasonable period of time. It also demonstrates the effectiveness of management in moving the company through several financial periods. At least the following factors broken down by 10K lines of business, where applicable, identical to the 10K, should be included in the summary, with percentage increases over the prior year for each figure:

   A. Revenues.
   B. Costs and expenses.
   C. Income before provision for income taxes.
   D. Provisions for income taxes, both current and deferred.
   E. Net income.
   F. Net income per common share (pre- and post-dilution).
   G. Number of shares outstanding.
   H. Stockholders' equity.
   I. Stockholders' equity per share.
   J. Return on revenues.
   K. Return on stockholders' equity.
   L. Key ratios.
 3. Research and development expenditures.
 4. Inventory profits.
 5. Compensating bank balances.
 6. Effective tax rates.
 7. Sales and earnings from foreign operations.
 8. Breakdown of order backlogs.
 9. Data on employee pension obligations.
10. Information on the exchange or market where the stock is traded, including market price ranges and dividends paid—for at least the most recent two years.

An increasing number of companies are reporting this kind of information in detail, even as the SEC and the Exchanges drive to make these disclosures mandatory. In addition, the SEC now requires brief biographical information on all officers and directors, including outside affiliations.

In other words, in reporting financial information the rule should be greater rather than lesser exposure. Nor should any company have to wait until disclosure of any kind of information becomes mandatory. For any company competing in the capital markets, the needs for full disclosure are overwhelming. Even for the company performing less than magnificently, the values of full disclosure far exceed the potential harm.

Descriptive Text

The primary purpose of descriptive material in an annual report is not merely to demonstrate the company's business or products, but to do so in a way that demonstrates the viability of the company's business. It must support representations made by the chief executive officer of the company's potential for success. Thus it becomes important to describe the company's business, plants, equipment, or services (this, too, is now required by the SEC) in the context of potential profitability. Simply to describe the company's product is insufficient. It must be done in terms of the product's value to the public and industry, as well as its market potential. It must be shown how that product or service contributes to overall corporate profitability. It becomes too simple a matter for a company to take pride in its capital holdings—its magnificent new 500,000 square-foot plant, or its new process that produces four times as many widgets with half as many people. But while this pride is justifiable within the corporate family, if it is not clear why the new plant will cut costs, facilitate distribution, and increase the ability to meet growing market needs, the report becomes a hollow exercise in self-aggrandizement.

The technique used to describe a company's operations is irrelevant, except as it is dictated by the overall format of the report. It can be broken down by divisions, product line, markets, or service. It can be a separate section or part of a long narrative included in the president's letter. The decision as to the way to go is a function of ease of communication and clarity. Whichever technique works best to communicate clearly, in keeping with the objectives of the report, is the technique to use.

In describing the company's operations, a careful and objective view should be taken to avoid reporting the commonplace as if it were unique. Every manufacturing company has plants and machines. It is expected that every annual report for every manufacturing company will report that its plants are the most efficent, its machinery more modern and productive, its service superior, and its employees the most clean-cut and clear-eyed. But if no way can be found to demonstrate these things in terms of their genuine uniqueness and superiority, then there is a virtual guarantee that the space will be wasted and the report will be unread outside the industry.

In describing a company's operations, every effort must be made to demonstrate uniqueness and clear-cut superiority. If any statement in the description of a company's operations does not clearly demonstrate a contribution to cost cutting or profitability, it serves no purpose and should be left out.

Special Features

Every effort should be made to determine special features that might be included to enhance the value of the report. Certainly, basic to every report should be a one- or two-sentence description of the company's operation on the very first page, or inside the front cover. It should be unnecessary for anyone to have to thumb through 16 or 24 pages to find out what business a company is in. It is also an opportunity to sum up and clarify a description of a company as it sees itself and wants to be seen by others. This simple one- or two-sentence description is sometimes harder to do than it would appear at first glance, particularly if the company is a multiproduct operation or functions in some tangential area of an industry.

Special problems should be dealt with in special sections. A company that is complex in its operations should not hesitate to devote a section of the book, whether it's a few paragraphs boxed off or a full page, to describe itself. It should not have to be necessary to read an entire report to fathom what the company is about. A company with special tax considerations should take a separate section of the book to describe its tax picture. A company that is ancillary to an industry and dependent upon it should take a section or page to describe the economics of the industry it serves. In fact, a context for any unusual aspect of the company should be included, and, where feasible, set apart from the body of the text.

A table of contents is sometimes warranted if the book is large and has sections. It certainly isn't necessary for a brief and concise report.

Graphics

The question of graphics is confused by the conflict between reporting needs and esthetics. As long as a report is complete, neat, and readable, its graphic presentation need not be elaborate. There are several factors to consider:

1. *Graphs.* The purpose of graphs is to give a quick view of the direction in which a company is moving in several of its operational functions. Graphs are helpful if they are well done. They are confusing if they are irrelevant and designed only for looks. The decision whether to use a bar graph of one form or another or a line graph is a function of the informa-

tion to be reported, not the esthetics. The decision is predicated on whichever form best demonstrates the information. Among the material which should be graphed are:

    A. Revenues, net earnings and earnings per share. If you are going to use graphs you must graph all three—or use no graphs at all.

    B. Any other significant factor that shows historical progress, such as return on equity, divisional sales and earnings as a proportion of total sales and earnings (this is frequently useful to demonstrate the growth of one division or product line as an increasing portion of total revenues and earnings), contribution to revenue and earnings by divisions, sources of revenue, stockholders' equity, and so on.

The location of graphs in a book should be determined by where they are most pertinent. Sometimes it's useful to put the graphs on the same page as the 10-year summary. Sometimes it's even more useful to intersperse them with the president's letter, in proximity to paragraphs describing the graphed information.

2. *Illustrations.* There is frequently a battle between ego and value to the report in determining whose pictures are to be included in the book. It's very difficult to include the picture of one vice-president and not another. If the members of the executive team are attractive, clear-eyed, and exude charm and intelligence, by all means include their pictures. On the other hand, if it is known that there is a general feeling that the management team is considered too old and that there is no middle management being primed for succession, it seems rather foolhardy to lace the report with pictures of the management team.

There is nothing duller than looking at pictures of people doing nothing. If executives are to be pictured in the report they should be shown working, and not just behind a desk. The vice-president of manufacturing should be shown in a plant. The vice-president of finance should be shown preparing his budget. Straightforward head shots, or posed pictures of people sitting at desks, belong in college yearbooks—not in annual reports designed to demonstrate the excellence of a company's performance.

Product illustrations that support the text are useful, but they must be adequately captioned. Pictures of plants and machines that look like other plants and machines are not. Sometimes innovative ways can be found to illustrate a particular point. For example, Saunders Leasing System has a service—called FAST—that computerizes a broad spectrum of state and local fuel taxes to give the customer a single printed report, where in the past he had to deal with many individual reports for each locality in which he operated. The company wanted to demonstrate the wide variety of information that went into the single report. The photograph used to illustrate it showed 35 people, each holding a form, a phone, and a computer tape—all standing in a triangle at the apex of which was one person holding the single completed form. The caption—all pictures should be captioned—read, "Behind the single piece of paper, on which is reduced an entire spectrum of details and services on fuel costs and state taxations, is FAST's large staff of experts."

The basic question of design of the report should be predicated on the contents of the report itself. First of all, the design of annual reports is a specialty that differs from the design of brochures or any other printed material. The designer should have at least a modicum of understanding of the financial nature of the report. Secondly, an annual report is a financial tool—it is not a graphics device. The designer should be the last person to be consulted—not the first. At the same time, the designer should be made privy to the objectives and all other aspects of the report's prospectus.

The decision as to whether the report should be in one, two, or four colors, or simply black and white, also depends upon the objectives of the report rather than on abstract design factors. It should be reiterated that no investment decision is ever made on the basis of color or graphic beauty, and, in fact, if the performance reported is not equal to the apparent cost of the report, the effect may be adverse.

There are times when color is clearly prescribed by the nature of the product or services illustrated. There are times when crisp black and white is clearly dictated in order to give a dignified impression of the company. To use color merely because it is colorful is wasteful if its use does not enhance the content and improve the clarity of presentation.

An increasing number of companies are separating the financial section from the text of the annual report and printing the financials as a separate supplement. This is a useful technique in larger companies where the financial and statistical information is extensive. Another use of the separate textual and statistical sections is the flexibility it allows in giving the report additional uses. The textual section, for example, separated from the financial section, can be a valuable sales brochure.

The SEC regulations require that all financial statements and notes to financial statements be printed in a modern, legible type face. This means that no smaller than 10-point type may be used for body text. Eight-point type, properly leaded, is acceptable.

Several companies are simply putting a cover on their Form 10K's and using that as an annual report. Certainly this is an extreme recognition of the annual report as a financial document. If there is no valid or legal reason to supply the reader information beyond that which appears in the 10K, which is rare, this is, at least technically, the ultimate fulfillment of every requirement of an annual report.

TIMETABLE

The timetable for an annual report is a matter of serious consideration. The timing of the annual report is predominently dictated by the annual meeting, as well as by certain aspects of SEC regulation. The SEC requires that the Form 10K, which is the legal annual report to the SEC, be filed no later than 90 days from the closing of the fiscal year. The annual report to shareholders should be mailed no later than 30 days prior to the annual meeting. The problem is that there is almost invariably a tight squeeze because the auditors require a certain amount of time to do their work, and their report is an essential part of the annual report. Only when the annual meeting is set set well ahead—and there is rarely a reason why annual meetings cannot be set with a consideration of the timetable for the annual report in mind—can an annual report be completed at a leisurely pace, without frantic last minute rushes and expensive overtime charges at the printers.

The best time to begin planning an annual report is three to six months before the end of the fiscal year, depending upon the size of the company and the scope of the report. Very large companies begin planning their annual reports six months before the end of the fiscal year. The report is planned in much the same way as described earlier, and individuals within the corporation or the financial relations firm are assigned specific responsibilities. Considerable time must be allowed for researching the various elements of the report, and for photography and writing. Since most annual reports are carefully scrutinized by several officers of a company as well as attorneys and accountants, the best plan is for every aspect of the report except the financials—the text, the photography, and the layout—to be completed by the end of the fiscal year. The next 45 to 60 days will be consumed with the tremendous pressures of editing the text, including the president's letter, to coincide with the financial figures, as well as supervising the production of the book.

Production schedules should be carefully and realistically developed and adhered to. A timetable should be prepared—on paper—with a copy to every individual who has anything to do with the report. It should begin with deadline dates for research, photography, layout, and first draft. Approval dates for each aspect of the report should be scheduled. Deadlines should be set for delivery of text to the art director, as well as delivery of final mechanicals, printing, binding, and mailing. Arrangements should be made well beforehand with the transfer agent and others who are responsible for the mailing.

It should be remembered that in the production of an annual report, if anything can go wrong it will. An attorney or an accountant will object to a statement on the grounds that it is potentially misleading. An operation will be altered after the text describing that operation is completed. A photograph will turn out to be inadequate. The best answer to contingencies is to anticipate as many variables as possible, and to plan as carefully as possible.

INTERIM REPORTS

Unlike annual reports interim reports to shareholders are not a legal requirement of the SEC, although both the New York Stock Exchange and the American Stock Exchange require them of their listed companies. There is no question, however, of their value in keeping the financial community informed of a company's operations and performance on a timely basis. The problem with all financial reporting is that it freezes an ongoing process as of the moment of the report; it seizes only one moment of an operation that is in vigorous motion. It's like a still picture taken at high noon of a crowded downtown square in a busy city. It is a photo of the instant. Minutes after the picture has been taken everyone in it has gone off in different directions, and the scene has entirely changed. So it is with annual reporting. The interim report, usually issued quarterly, updates the picture.

The interim report serves several purposes:

1. It indicates the company's progress and financial performance since the end of the last reported quarter, and since the end of the last fiscal year.

2. It compares the performance of the current interim period with that of the comparable period in the prior year. This is valuable since very few businesses are level in their performance throughout a single year. Some quarters are traditionally stronger or weaker than others, and a comparison on a quarter-by-quarter basis with the same quarter in the prior year gives a valuable measure of a company's performance. For most companies it's a more valid measure of performance than comparison with the immediately prior quarter.

3. Textually, it reports significant corporate activities since the annual report.

4. It indicates the degree to which projections made or implied in the annual report are being fulfilled.

5. It reports short-term changes in the company's direction.

For the company attempting to compete in the capital markets, the notion of not issuing interim reports is unthinkable. In at least one respect, the interim report is even more important than the annual report, because it shows a commitment to keep information flowing. In the competition for attention, success is a function of an ongoing effort. As in any form of marketing, competing in the capital markets is successful only as a cumulative effort.

In fact, so significant is the interim report that Ted Pincus, president of FRB and one of the financial relations industry's leading innovators, has suggested that instead of an annual report and three quarterly reports, there should be four equal reports during the course of the year, with only the year-end report audited. Each of the four reports should be equal in importance in terms of the presentation of the company in all its aspects. The SEC, moreover, favors an auditor's review of the quarterly, even though the report itself is not audited.

As in the case of annual reports, interim reports have fallen prey to a kind of mindless repetition of everything that's gone before, without any consideration of whether the principles behind doing them in the first place still apply. And yet the interim report offers the opportunity for some of the most creative work to be done in financial relations.

In its simplest form, the interm report can be merely a copy of a release reporting the quarterly results. At the other extreme, it can be in an elaborate newspaper style, with articles covering virtually every aspect of the company's business, as well as the basic financial data. The variety of formats between the two extremes seems endless.

As in the case of the annual report, the format for the interim report is dictated by objectives. The shape and format of the report are determined in precisely the same way as for the annual report. The same questions about objectives and target audiences are asked, and, except where there is a significant change in the circumstances under which the company functions, the answers should be essentially the same as those for the annual. Naturally, in any fast-moving company these objectives will alter slightly from report to report as different problems arise. Nevertheless, there should be some measure of consistency springing from the last annual report.

Considering the fact that for most corporations the interim report represents one of the few opportunities during the year to demonstrate the company's condition in print, and to reach shareholders and prospective shareholders with current information, it seems sensible to include as much as is feasible. The report should include at least the following:

1. The unaudited quarterly results. This includes not only sales, earnings, and earnings per share, but any other financial information that is available at that point. This may include changes in cash position, changes in inventory, income before taxes, average number of shares outstanding— in fact, any pertinent financial information that is meaningful in an unaudited statement. Figures should be given both for the current quarter and the comparable quarter for the prior year. Percentage differences should be shown.

2. Sales and earnings should be broken down line by line or division by division. Stanray Corporation, a leading exponent of full disclosure in its quarterly reports, shows its results by group using a bar graph. Stanray also reports backlog by group for the quarter.

3. Second and third quarter reports should include both the current quarter and the six- and nine-month totals, both current and previous year.

4. More and more companies are including the balance sheet as of the close of the quarter.

5. Because it is proving to be of such great value in analysis, an increasing number of companies are reporting, in addition to quarterly figures, figures for the trailing 12 months—the full four quarters ending in the current quarter. This serves to put operations in proper perspective, instead of freezing the view of the company at just its last full fiscal year plus the quarters of the current year. Many companies also include the figures for the last full fiscal year.

6. The president's message should be as well thought out and as inclusive as it was in the annual report. In an active company, the events of any three-month period should be extensive and worthy of full reporting. It should also be remembered that the quarterly report should represent a full view of the company, without the necessity of having to refer back to the annual report, except for greater detail. The interim report will, for many of its readers, be the first document seen on the company. It should be sufficiently detailed and interesting to encourage them to want to investigate further.

7. If the use of graphs is appropriate for the annual report, it is just as appropriate for the interim report.

8. The interim report is a useful vehicle for focusing on a single aspect of the company's operations with the kind of detail not normally found in the annual report. For example, some companies devote each issue to

a discussion of a particular aspect of its business. Other companies devote each issue to a biography of each of the key officers and operating divisional heads, with a description of his responsibilities, and a report on his performance since he assumed his position. Some companies use each issue of the interim report to describe a product, its markets, its performance, and its potential.

In addition to favoring an auditor's review of the quarterly report, the SEC is pressing for additional information, which may ultimately be mandatory. While the SEC's immediate concern is with the quarterly Form 10Q, it seems reasonable to go beyond that to include the same information in the report to shareholders. They are also proposing that the annual 10K reconcile significant differences between performance reported quarterly and annually.

Typical of the problems these proposals seek to avoid is seen in the case of CNA Financial Corp. CNA reported, in 1973, that its first six months' earnings were the second highest in its history. It then showed a loss in the third quarter. At year end, it showed a 12-month loss of $79 million. It seems that in the first half of the year they had neglected to report to shareholders that a subsidiary was in deep trouble.

While the elements described seem to be profuse they can be included in a well-planned interim report without its becoming elaborate and expensive. Physically, it should be designed to fit in a standard letter-sized No. 10 envelope. Unusual shapes and formats are not only expensive to produce, but require specially designed and expensive envelopes.

Some reports include summaries of presentations before security analysts groups. Others include a summary of the presentation before the annual shareholders meeting, with significant questions and answers.

Some companies, to maintain consistency with the annual report, use the same cover photograph from the annual report for each of that year's interim reports.

One other interesting use of an interim report, particularly one filled with facts and reporting excellent results, is as a prospecting piece to broaden the base of interest in a company in the financial community. The interim report, which is infinitely less expensive than the annual report, can be mailed, with a self-addressed return postcard, to a larger, carefully selected list of analysts, brokers, money managers, and so on, than are normally included on the company's mailing list. This group can be all the analysts in a geographical area, or all the analysts covering a particular industry or financial interest. The postcard indicates that the report is being mailed to them for their information, and the card should be returned if the recipient has any interest in receiving further material about the company. This invariably develops pockets of interest not formerly identified.

THE ANNUAL MEETING

The annual meeting of shareholders is a legal requirement rarely looked upon by corporate executives with pleasant anticipation. Even if a company is performing beautifully, and management expects that the event will be a display of mutual pride, it requires a great deal of anticipation and preparation that seems to most corporate officers to be irrelevant to the specific business of running a company. They may be right, but they cannot avoid the annual chore.

In smaller companies, meetings are rarely well attended unless the company is facing some specific problems. In even the largest companies, only the smallest portion of outstanding shares is represented in person, and most matters on the agenda have been predetermined by the mail proxy vote, combined with the votes of the shares held by management groups.

In smaller companies with problems, the president anticipates being roasted by dissident shareholders who are more vocal and visible than usually seems warranted by the number of shares they represent. In recent years, larger companies' meetings have been beseiged not only by legitimate representatives of minority shareholders, but by publicity seekers who seize the opportunity to be difficult in public; to use the meeting as a vehicle for their own personal publicity and aggrandizement.

The date of the meeting, usually prescribed by corporate charter, further serves to put pressure on the production of the annual report, which must be mailed 30 to 45 days prior to the meeting.

And so it is not difficult to understand why few chief executive officers look forward to an annual meeting as anything but an unpleasant but necessary chore.

Yet, properly run, an annual meeting can go beyond its basic legal requirements to be a useful communications tool. It can be a focal point for presenting a company point of view not only to shareholders, but to the entire financial community. For listed or NASDAQ companies, it can be publicized. It can serve as a sounding board to allow management to fathom the reactions of its shareholders to its activities. And there is no question that shareholders have frequently come up with useful suggestions at annual meetings.

The secret of success of an annual meeting is in its preparation. Its basic elements are prescribed by state corporate law. The meeting is generally run under Roberts' Rules of Order, follows the agenda prepared well beforehand by the attorneys, and covers specific items which have been outlined in the proxy statement. Predetermined motions and seconding are usually assigned to executives so that the meeting runs smoothly. These usually cover the motion to dispense with the reading of the minutes, motions to cover the business of the agenda, such as elections of the board of directors and auditors, and any other business that must be legally covered. Proxies are collected and officers are appointed to tally both proxies and votes made in person. This formal part of the meeting is usually scripted by the attorneys to assure that the format protects the company under legal requirements.

These activities are formalized and cut and dried. The potential problems come in three areas—the president's message, the questions and answers, and new business.

Every meeting, even those where minimal attendance is anticipated, should be prepared meticulously and with every detail covered. The president's message should be either written, with ultimate publication in mind, or outlined in great detail.

Every question that might be asked should be anticipated in writing and, in a rehearsal, the appropriate answer carefully worked out. It is important for the success of an annual meeting that every likelihood be anticipated. There should be no surprises.

The key to the meeting, of course, is the president's message. The annual meeting is the president's report to his shareholders—to his ultimate employers. He is expected to report on the condition of the company, its progress, and the directions in which it is going. It is easy to assume that the message will be essentially the same as the message in the annual report, which presumably all shareholders will have read. The fact is that most shareholders will not have read it, or if they have will still appreciate hearing the report in person. The message will also differ from the report in several ways. The company will have several months' progress to report since the time the annual report was written. In all probability the first quarter figures will be available, and if the timing is right, the annual meeting will be used as the medium to report the quarter's results. Since the target audience is quite specifically the shareholders, the kinds of information and the format in which they are presented will be much more focused for them, even though it is anticipated that the speech will be either reported by the financial press or will subsequently be mailed to shareholders and the financial community in a post-meeting report.

Furthermore, if the speech is well prepared, it should tend to anticipate —and therefore forestall—some of the thornier questions that are likely to be raised in the question and answer period.

The message should be as short and as concise as possible and still cover the material to be presented. Following the initial greeting and welcome to shareholders, it should contain the following elements:

1. A summary of operating results, including, if appropriate, the first quarter's results.

2. The operational condition of the company in terms of its products, services, markets, and finances.

3. Special events during the course of the year that are significant to the company's past, present, and future activities.

4. The economic climate in which the company is now operating, or will be during the coming year.

5. A general prognosis for the future. Here, great care must be taken to be realistic and cautious. Better to err on the side of caution than to forget that external economic events can alter the best laid plans, and to say something that will put the company on the defensive at the next annual meeting. It is well to remember here, too, that any significant projections made for the first time must be reported as soon as possible to the general public under the rules of disclosure.

Following the president's message come the questions and answers. It is at this point that many meetings which might otherwise be successful turn into a shambles. The importance of anticipating questions cannot be overemphasized. And if the company is large enough for press coverage, it must be anticipated that questions and answers reported out of context can sometimes be distorted. Some years ago, the chairman of the board of Hotel Corporation of America had anticipated announcing that since he was gradually withdrawing from active participation in the business, he was taking a reduction in salary. Prior to the meeting he was advised to include that statement in his presentation. He waited instead for what he deemed to be an appropriate moment during the question and answer period. As it turned out, questions were somewhat hostile. His announcement of a pay cut was reported in the context of the hostility, and appeared in the press to have been a decision forced by the attacks made during the course of the meeting. The report was wholly inaccurate, but arose naturally from a failure to anticipate the effect of bad timing upon the announcement.

Aside from anticipating questions, the basic rule for every chief executive officer presiding over an annual meeting is to keep cool at all costs. Failure to do so, even in the face of the most hostile and irrelevant question, tends to inflame shareholders and to evoke even more hostile questions. Any appearance of being evasive has the same effect. Patience is of the essence.

Even for a company in deep trouble, most questions are cursory and honest, reflecting the legitimate interest of shareholders in their company. Some questions, on the other hand, are flagrantly designed to attack and to antagonize management. Dissident shareholders, dissatisfied with anything from the stock action to the dividend policy to the company's environmental practices, come well prepared and armed with their own research data.

Lewis and John Gilbert run a nonprofit organization called Corporate Democracy, Inc. The organization consists, in addition to the Gilberts, of a large number of individuals located throughout the United States who are dedicated to increasing the voice of minority shareholders in corporate activities. The Gilberts themselves attend a great many meetings each year of corporations in which they hold shares of stock. They have devoted themselves to achieving quite specific aims in the name of corporate democracy. They strongly advocate such corporate practices as cumulative voting, locating meetings at places convenient to the majority of stockholders, the distribution of post-meeting reports, the use of more effective and informative annual reports, the presence of all directors at annual meetings, improved accounting procedures, audit committees, opposition to stagger systems in which only a portion of the board is subject to election each year, and executive compensation programs that are responsive to the company's losses as well as profitability. While considered a thorn in the side of many an executive officer, they have, through attrition and constant public exposure, achieved remarkable success over the years in moving corporations toward accepting their points of view. Rarely do the Gilberts succeed in any motion on the floor that is not expressly the wish of management. However, the publicity they have garnered has resulted in exposing management practices which they oppose. This has been an effective device in making them successful over a period of time because most shareholders were unaware of the issues involved until the Gilberts spotlighted them.

Other special interest groups have also become prevalent in recent years. These include environmental and women's rights groups. The participation of these groups has become increasingly forceful, and must be recognized as a fact of corporate life.

The executive who does not allow any such dissident shareholder his full measure of public voice will almost invariably find himself in trouble, not only during the course of the meeting, but in the press. For the press, most annual meetings are dull and not particularly newsworthy. A dissident stockholder is the most exciting thing, and therefore the most reportable thing, that happens at most meetings.

The dissident shareholder is best disarmed by being given the fullest and most polite audience possible. He must be recognized and his point of view given full consideration, even if the outcome is predetermined and his views are inconsistent with corporate realities. There is no better answer, in situations such as these, than, "I want to thank you for your suggestion. We will certainly take it under advisement."

There are times when the complaints of the Gilberts and others are particularly pertinent. For example, the Gilberts have always defended the rights of a successful corporation to make legitimate charitable contributions. However, some time ago, Eastern Airlines made a $500,000 five-year pledge to pay for a new production of a Wagnerian opera by the Metropolitan Opera Company. Particularly in view of the company's profit picture at the time, Mr. Gilbert's statement at the annual meeting was quoted in *The New York Times* as follows: " 'I defy anyone to prove one extra benefit to the company from that gift. It is for the social benefit of one man so he can sit at the opera,' said Mr. Gilbert." Whether Gilbert was right or wrong did not matter quite so much as the fact that his highly damaging statement was widely broadcast in the public press.

The environmental and women's interest groups are functioning on a rising tide of favorable public sentiment. They both deal with issues of national concern that quite naturally focus on many aspects of a corporation. This is particularly true of any corporation that functions in areas that might in some way contribute to pollution, and in companies in which women are not represented as executives or members of the board of directors. Larger companies, such as AT&T, have been through some highly publicized and expensive problems in affording equal employment opportunities for women, and naturally the subject has been a matter of concern to shareholders.

Comparable action has come from consumer groups, a subject also very much in the realm of general public awareness. In fact, a most successful attack was made on General Motors in this area, with the annual meeting used as the focal point. Public interest groups even went beyond that to approach universities and other institutions that were holders of large blocks of General Motors stock, in an attempt to pressure them to vote their stock in behalf of specific measures proposed by the groups. Among the responses made by General Motors was the inclusion of individuals on the board of directors who specifically represented public interest viewpoints.

For companies potentially subject to shareholders' discussion on these topics, not only is careful planning necessary for the annual meeting, but if appropriate, the questions should be anticipated by covering the subjects in the president's message.

In physically setting up a room for a shareholders' meeting, seating should be arranged for the convenience of shareholders and particularly for those who wish to ask questions. A sufficient number of microphones should be located on the floor, strategically placed in the aisles, or should be of the hand-held type that can be passed to a shareholder in place.

If the meeting is orderly, as it should be if the chief executive officer is calm and patient, the question and answer period should be allowed to last as long as is necessary for all shareholders to have a fair chance to participate. Any attempt to rush a meeting, or to cut off the questions, will only serve to inflame the shareholders and turn the meeting into a fracas.

The chief executive officer should not allow himself to be goaded into anger, or to allow the meeting to get out of hand. There are some shareholders who make a practice of disrupting meetings, apparently for publicity purposes. Their questions are antagonistic and irrelevant. A meeting should be run strictly under Roberts' Rules of Order, and in some cases it may be necessary to advise a questioner politely that his question is out of order or irrelevant. There are even times, when shareholders become unnecessarily abusive and may have to be physically ejected. The judgment resides with the meeting's chairman. A good rule of thumb, however, is to visualize tomorrow's headlines before taking any extreme action. In some cases where chairmen have had to physically eject obstreperous shareholders, it has been done so appropriately as to garner sympathy for the chairman rather than for the shareholders.

It is frequently a good idea to decorate the meeting room with a display of the company's products and services. There are times when meetings are further enhanced by supplementing the president's message with either a film or a slide presentation. Care must be taken that the audiovisual devices are supplements, and not a substitute for the president's report.

In some larger companies, where meetings may be expected to take several hours, refreshments are sometimes in order. This should consist of coffee and pastry, or perhaps a light snack if the meeting runs through lunchtime and the circumstances seem appropriate.

Meetings held on a plant's premises can sometimes be enhanced by a post-meeting plant tour. This, too, should be carefully planned.

Press coverage for a meeting, aside from the company's own desire for it, depends on the size of the company, the prospective newsworthiness of the information to be imparted, and the availability of a reporter to cover the meeting. Certainly, the press should be invited beforehand by letter and phone. It is pointless to believe that the press can be excluded from a meeting that might prove to be unfavorable to management. If the company is important enough, any attempt to exclude the press will not only fail, but will result in hostility and a negative report.

The presence of any representative of the press will, of course, be known, since all shareholders check in at the door. If a member of the press does come to the meeting, a representative of the company, and preferably the financial relations counsel, should sit with him for the purpose of answering questions as they occur to the reporter during the course of the meeting. Prior to the meeting, a press release should be prepared for immediate distribution, either during its course or immediately following it. Complete press kits, including the release, should be on hand for any member of the press who attends. The kit should contain not only the release but, if possible, a copy of the president's speech and material on the company including a background report, an annual report, product information, and any other printed material that may be available.

Frequently it is advisable to invite important analysts, brokers, money managers, and other representatives of the financial community. The meeting affords them a good opportunity to see management in action at first hand, as well as to gather more information about the company. The same kind of material prepared for the press should be made available to any representative of the financial community who attends.

Following the meeting, the officers of the company should make themselves available to meet shareholders, reporters, and analysts. Frequently they have questions that they prefer not to ask from the floor. These questions should be answered in the same responsive, forthright manner as the questions from the floor.

It is sometimes appropriate to use the occasion of the annual meeting to arrange for a specific interview by the press wtih the company's officers. This should be done beforehand, with an opportunity to sit down in a separate room or a quiet corner where the interview can proceed undisturbed.

In answering questions, the chairman of the meeting should attempt to call upon other executives to participate. The purpose is to demonstrate the depth of company management; that the company is run by others beside the chief executive officer. Properly prepared, it can also be expected that the vice-president of finance will give a more detailed answer to financial questions, or that the vice-president of marketing will give a more specific explanation of marketing programs.

THE POST-MEETING REPORT

The post-meeting report is an extremely useful device to multiply the value of the annual meeting for the financial community at large. It can be a simple printed version of the president's message, including an edited selection of questions and answers from the floor. In a more elaborate report, photographs of the meeting can be included. This report is facilitated by taping the entire meeting, even though the president is speaking from a prepared text. Some companies include a summary of the meeting in their quarterly report, although this is not quite as effective as issuing a special post-meeting report. The post-meeting report is then mailed to both shareholders and segments of the financial community that have expressed interest in the company.

Through careful planning, then, the annual meeting can be turned from a legal chore and unwanted responsibility into a favorable investor relations device.

LETTERS TO SHAREHOLDERS

There are times during the course of the year when special events warrant a letter to shareholders to keep them advised. For the company that issues interim reports, these occasions should arise infrequently. A letter is particularly useful in announcing an impending merger, or a major change in business direction, or to dispel a serious rumor. Some companies use a letter to shareholders to introduce a new product by making it available as a sample or at a discount to shareholders.

A letter to new shareholders is sometimes effective. This is a standard form, signed by the president, welcoming the new shareholder and describing the company, its products, and its aims in a few short paragraphs. Unfortunately, for most companies there seems to be no evidence that the letter to new shareholders contributes to a sufficient sense of loyalty to overcome bad performance. It comes under the heading of general public relations—an attempt to engender a warm feeling. There is no question that it contributes to the overall goodwill that is so useful in shareholder relations. As to whether the expense is warranted by the results is open to some question. As part of a large and full-scale investor relations program it is certainly useful. An an isolated activity unsupported by other activities it is questionable.

The use of the publicity reprint as part of regular or special shareholder mailings is especially effective. It focuses attention on favorable articles that the shareholder is not likely to have seen. With a little covering note attached, it puts the article in its proper context. Since press coverage is presumably objective, a news or feature article adds a kind of editorial third-person endorsement to the company's story, which has an effect of giving added credibility. Also included in this category are reprints of favorable research reports by brokerage houses. One word of caution in the use of reprints of either articles or research reports. Such material is copyrighted and may not be reproduced without written permission of the publisher. This is usually easy to obtain, and there is no excuse for distribution of such material without prior permission.

Many companies publish internal house organs for employees or external house organs for customers. Shareholders, too, are interested in this information, unless the internal house organ is too completely taken with purely personal information such as bowling scores or engagement announcements. If the house organ contains useful information about the company, it should certainly be considered as part of a regular mailing to shareholders.

INQUIRIES FROM SHAREHOLDERS

There is nothing more startling—although legitimate—than the unexpected phone call from a shareholder to the chief executive officer of the company. The shareholder may own 50 shares, but he feels he is entitled to information and to get it directly from the president. The chief executive officer should deal with him in exactly the same way he would handle an inquiry from a security analyst. No matter how busy or inopportune the call, the shareholder must be dealt with politely and given the information he requires. Perhaps the best way to handle these inquiries is to be simply responsive to the question and to volunteer no more information than is asked for. Going beyond that leads to more questions. Naturally, a measure of judgment must be exercised. A shareholder with a block of 5000 shares will certainly want more intensive information than a generalization of the company's progress. In any event, patience, courtesy, and being solicitous wins the day. A written record of such communications should be kept to offset any questions about inside information.

Shareholders frequently write the chief executive either to complain or to inquire. These letters should be answered politely and promptly. The answers should be specifically responsive to the question and should be brief.

As part of a full-scale investor relations program it is sometimes useful to plan plant tours and visits for shareholders. Plant tours, too, come under the category of shareholder activities that are meaningless as isolated practices. They work best only as part of a total program. Certainly it's out of the question if it means disrupting operations. A plant tour is also useful in dealing with environmental groups, to demonstrate at first hand the measures the company is taking to deal effectively with the problem.

CORPORATE ADVERTISING

As in all financial relations, one of the most controversial aspects of investor relations is corporate advertising. Corporate advertising, in this context, takes many forms, ranging from a full-page ad in *The Wall Street Journal* extolling the virtues of the company to participation in special editions of newspapers or magazines to advertise the availability of the annual report. Larger companies sometimes use television and radio.

Corporate advertising is expensive, and should be viewed very carefully in terms of effectiveness. The overall effectiveness of any kind of advertising is not the question here, except that there are very few publications in which everyone who sees the ad is a prospective customer. In corporate advertising the same problem exists. The ad will be seen by many more people than will be affected by it. If the purpose of corporate advertising is to engender a favorable attitude on the part of shareholders or potential investors, a very narrow view of that purpose must prevail.

In advertising to the financial community it must be recognized that, first of all, there is a kind of inherent cynicism with which the company is viewed, predicated on some tangible facts about the company's performance. No company that is performing poorly is going to be loved by shareholders no matter how adorable is the advertising program. In fact, there will be quite a contrary effect, since shareholders can calculate how much advertising costs.

While it's true that the overall psychological effect of large-scale advertising will still serve to focus attention on the company, a judgment must be made as to whether the contribution the advertising makes is sufficient to warrant the cost. In some cases the answer is favorable. It is difficult to imagine, though, that a small or medium-sized company with stock that is not performing well, even if it is undervalued, will accomplish a great deal in proportion to the cost of advertising. The same amount of money put into other aspects of financial relations will be infinitely more effective.

The same kind of judgment must be applied to annual report advertising. Sometimes it is useful for a larger company to summarize a favorable annual report in an ad. But again, the judgment must be made on the basis of cost versus results. Unfortunately, corporate advertising seems to be an easy way to tell the company's story. But this is deceptive. Very little corporate advertising is effective on a one-time basis, since in all advertising repetition is a major requirement. Certainly no small or medium-sized company should expect miracles from a one-time ad.

Advertising the availability of an annual report, either alone or as part of a large cooperative arrangement in a special section of a publication, is sometimes useful in developing broader interest—if care is taken in the selection of the medium. But there is a hidden cost in this kind of advertising which advertising space salesmen frequently neglect to mention. That is the cost of the reports themselves in the quantity usually necessary for distribution in response to ads. Annual reports can cost as much as $1 per copy or more, including mailing. A successful ad in a major business publication can produce requests for thousands of annual reports. And if the people who make these requests are added to the mailing list, this can become tremendously expensive, since each name on a mailing list can cost the company as much as $15 a year in material and postage. Certainly, any report mailed out in response to an advertising request should include a self-addressed, return postcard that attempts to ascertain the continuing interest of the inquirer. Unfortunately, cooperative ads make it remarkably easy to request reports for a company in which one has only a casual interest. If it were possible to make an analysis of the names of those who request copies of an annual report in response to an ad against transfer sheets, to determine the number of inquirers who ultimately become shareholders, the likelihood is that the company will conclude that the cost is not equal to the result. And since so many shareholders make their purchase in Street name, this kind of research is virtually impossible to do accurately.

On the other hand, there are cases where it makes good sense. In highly specialized publications, such as *Barron's*, the readership is much more clearly identifiable than it is for the general business publications, and requests for reports are more likely to come from serious prospective investors. It is also useful, at times, for companies whose service is sold to other businesses. In this case, the annual report is being read not only by prospective investors but by prospective customers as well.

The rule, then, in corporate advertising, is not to do it unless there is a clear and realistic picture of potential return on the advertising dollar.

SPECIAL PROBLEMS

There are special problems that sometimes arise in shareholder relations that require specific attention. There is the problem, for example, of the company that is potentially subject to a take-over attempt because management holds too few shares of stock outstanding. This will be discussed in Chapter 8. There is the problem of geographic distribution of stock where too many shares are concentrated in too few geographic areas. There is the problem of the company whose stock price is being buffeted by large block trading by institutions over which the company has no control. These problems will be dealt with in Chapter 10.

Effective investor relations is a function of management and financial relations skill. Since it is so difficult to measure results on a day-to-day basis, the program must always be viewed with perspective, and constantly monitored. It rarely works if it is treated as an isolated jumble of irrelevant activities. It almost invariably works if it is planned, programmed, and executed by sensitive management and experienced financial relations counsel.

CHAPTER 6

GOING PUBLIC

There have been times in American economic history when the simplest—if not necessarily the best—means of acquiring capital for a corporation was to go public. Most recently, this has included the late 1960s and a part of 1971 and 1972—periods of extraordinary economic growth in America. Corporate profits for most companies were high and the economic boom showed no signs of abating.

During these periods, the psychology that fueled the stock market was predicated on confident anticipation of consistent and sustained growth, which could only mean to the investor a consistent and sustained increase in dividends and the price of stocks. Price/earnings ratios for some stocks reached astronomical multiples of 20, 30, and even 60. The price/earnings ratio of the Dow Jones stocks reached an average as high as 17.3. Heaven only knows what the market and investors were anticipating in the way of corporate profits in the ensuing years to justify those multiples.

In this economic climate not only did companies go public with impunity, but there seemed to be almost no way in which a new issue, no matter how unlikely the company behind it, would fail to sell and then be traded up to many times its original offering price. Companies with no substance, no production, no sales, and even little hope of succeeding had virtually no trouble fulfilling their desires for capital—never mind their needs. It was obvious that many companies were going public not for capital needs, but for many irrelevant reasons. Among these reasons were to spread the risk of capitalizing new ventures so that corporate management was virtually immune from the dangers inherent in a new venture, to bail out to the public when no other firm would buy or merge, and to solve estate problems for family-owned businesses. Needless to say, many of these ventures ultimately failed, leaving a gullible public not only with a feeling of having been bilked, despite all the safeguards of the regulatory bodies, but more significantly, in the long run, with a feeling of disenchantment about the stock market in general.

But it is not so much that the individual investor deserted the market—a cause for much keening and wailing on the part of the securities industry—but that industry has been deprived of a significant source of capital.

And herein lies the core of a great problem.

The securities industry is predicated upon the fact that it is a prime source of capital for industry. The success of industry is reflected in a rise in the price of stocks, in anticipation of vast earnings. It is the dream of continued economic and stock market boom that has brought the individual investor into the market in droves. In fact, this dream amounts to pure speculation.

The securities industry, during the several decades following World War II, began to change in nature and structured itself to cater to the speculative bent of investors. When, for various reasons, the stock market failed to fulfill its implied speculative promises, the investors pulled out, leaving the securities industry a hollow shell. The structure, designed predominantly for the marketing of securities which were no longer being purchased, found itself bypassed like a vast hotel preempted by a super highway that diverts traffic to another part of town. It is geared for business that no longer exists. This as much as anything has resulted in the disappearance, through either merger or bankruptcy, of literally hundreds of securities firms. It seems obvious that the only hope for the securities industry lies not in increased hawking of its wares to a disenchanted public, but rather in returning to first principles—providing capital to industry.

In the meantime, there still remains the problem of the viability of equity as a source of capital. For the sound and growing company, properly managed and properly structured, selling equity is still an extremely important and necessary way to form an appropriate capital structure. And this despite the fact that only 15% of capital is supplied by the equity market. For psychological reasons, if for no other, other sources of capital still view a company's stock performance as one measure of a company's ability to function. For the right company, under the right circumstances, going public is still a necessary business function.

For the company choosing to go public, there is a vast area of concern in terms of relations with the financial community. Activities begin well before the public offering, and continue well afterwards.

Financial relations enters into the selection of the underwriter, includes structuring and dispersing information about the company to the financial community, follows through the period of registration, and enters yet another phase with the sale of the issue and the after-market (the period following the initial sale of the issue). And in view of SEC regulations regarding dissemination of information while a stock is in registration, a financial relations pattern must be established well before that, so that any such activities during the course of registration cannot be construed as having been developed solely for the purpose of selling stock.

CHOOSING AN UNDERWRITER

While this is not meant to be a primer on going public, the choice of an underwriter readily comes under the heading of financial relations because the underwriter will serve as a significant conduit to the financial community.

Most companies choose the wrong underwriter for the wrong reason. Before the Wall Street debacles of 1973–1974, there was a great proliferation of underwriters. These were predominantly brokerage houses who did underwriting. They were not investment bankers. An investment banker may also sell securities, but his job is primarily to understand the nature of all capital markets. He must help his client to structure his company for the intelligent use of capital as well as to acquire it, to supply information on not only the capital markets and alternative sources of capital, but the total economic picture as well. In an underwriting, he must guide the company through its many tortuous steps before, during, and after the underwriting. This is very different from merely putting out a public issue that serves as merchandise for the stockbroker to peddle. Fortunately, most of the old-style and questionable underwriters are now gone from the scene. Those companies that survived are predominantly investment bankers who predicated their own operations on long-range financial structures that served companies in so many ways that they were able to withstand the assault of sustained bear markets.

Back in the halcyon days, when virtually any company could go public, underwriters were wooing privately held companies not only to solicit their underwriting business, but to convince them to go public even in cases where it wasn't warranted. Smaller unstable companies, eager to go public and take advantage of the rising stock market, frequently accepted the first offer to do an underwriting that came along, often with disastrous results. Frequently, an underwriter was selected simply because somebody knew somebody. Many smaller underwriters calculated that if only a small percentage of their underwritings succeeded, the profits would offset the many that didn't make it. Playing these kinds of odds, the trick was to do as many underwritings as possible, regardless of the quality of the companies being taken public. Another device, particularly with speculative ventures, was for the underwriter to take exceptionally large blocks of stock options as a kind of auxiliary fee for doing the underwriting. Here, too, the odds game was being played. If just a portion of the issues succeeded and the stock price went high enough, the underwriter made enough money to cover those issues which did not succeed. Forgotten in this whole procedure was the company—and certainly the shareholder. This wreaked particular havoc on the better companies that survived and thrived, only to find themselves saddled with a poorly devised equities program that hurt the company in the long run. There are now hundreds of companies originally taken public by underwriting firms that are no longer in existence, or for which there is no longer a market at any price for their stock. The poor structure of the original issue left the company inadequately capitalized for its growth, which forced early demands of other sources of capital, such as banks. Many of these companies now find themselves in the position of being unable to split their stock because the price is too low, unable to issue new stock because they gave away too large a percentage of the company in the original underwriting, and too highly leveraged because they had to go to banks to finance growth that should have been paid for by a proper equity issue.

Properly done, the company that feels it should consider going public must begin by doing a great deal of homework. This should include taking a realistic view of its long-term capital needs, and assessing alternate sources of capital. A complete financial analysis should be done including pro forma operating statements and balance sheets for at least five years ahead. This program should be done with the assistance of the company's own internal financial staff, and with the help of its accounting firm and attorneys.

The company should review its decision to go public not only in the light of opportunities, but obstacles as well. The costs of going public are tremendous. Legal fees are astronomical. Printing costs for prospectuses are high. Most underwriters insist that a company going public use one of the larger accounting firms—one of the so-called "big eight"—and this almost invariably means an increase in accounting fees. Furthermore, most company presidents don't discover until it's too late that when they go public, they are suddenly in two full-time businesses—their own and the public corporation business. There is a tremendous difference between running one's own business and running a public corporation. There is a whole raft of new regulations and reporting requirements to conform to. Suddenly there are shareholders to deal with, annual meetings, annual reports, and so forth. These are all factors that somehow don't get calculated until it's too late.

The company should select and approach no more than three or four investment banking firms. With the aid of the accountant and the attorney, the firms can be readily identified on the strength of reputation, limitations of size of companies they will accept as clients, the number of comparable client companies they have in terms of size, industry, and capitalization, and the history of the issues they have taken public. Even more significantly, the investment banking firms selected should be precisely that—investment banking firms. They should be at least reasonably large and well established. They should offer a full range of services that include departments for acquisitions and mergers, fixed income securities, syndication, research, financial consulting, and all other aspects of the financial spectrum. The size of the retail operation is of lesser importance than would appear at first glance. Some of the most successful underwritings are achieved not by the firm's own retail operations, but by the ability to syndicate. The firms normally included in an investment banking syndicate are more important in the distribution of stock than the number of retail branches the underwriter has. The size and quality of its research department are better gauges of the investment banker's operation than is the number of registered representatives on the company's roster. The investment banker's trading operation is more important to the aftermarket than is the length of the list of underwritings it has done. In other words, the measure of the investment banker's capabilities lies not in its obvious first capability to do an underwriting so much as in its ability to help the company over the long range.

THE SYNDICATE

In any underwriting syndicate, as seen in the "tombstone" ad placed in a newspaper to announce the new issue, the firms in the listing are not in alphabetical order. They are in pecking order—the order of importance.

At the head of the list, standing apart, is the managing firm—or underwriting partners and co-managers if there are more than one. Next come the major firms, listed in order of the size of the portion of the issue each has agreed to market. This is followed by the secondary firms—smaller national firms taking a smaller portion of the issue. Last come the regional houses and smallest firms.

REGIONAL FIRMS

In most major cities, there are investment banking and brokerage firms whose operations are generally limited to serve the geographic areas in which they are centered. Many of these regional firms are excellent, both in marketing securities in their areas and in serving investment banking needs for smaller companies in their territories. Properly structured and staffed, a regional firm can frequently offer the smaller company better service than can a major national banker. They are more likely to give attention to a small company in their area than will a New York-based national firm. A good regional firm that is generally included in a good syndicate also has access to that syndicate, which means that a regional underwriting can be distributed as broadly as can a national underwriting.

There is a growing trend away from the traditional investment banking fee predicated on a portion of an underwriting, and toward the straight fee structure for investment bankers. A good relationship with an investment banker is extremely important for a growing company, and particularly a public one. To expect any kind of service from an investment banker whose total source of income from a company is the underwriting fee is a peculiar form of self-deception that almost invariably costs the company more in the long run.

When the company has gone as far as it can go in identifying at least three good investment banking firms, it should then invite representatives of each of them to meet separately with the company executives for discussions of a potential relationship. The evaluation should be based not on some ancillary issue, such as the pricing of the stock—that's a problem to be faced further down the line—but on the ability of the investment banking firm to serve the company's total financial and financial service needs. Another value of these interviews is to further review the company's total capital needs, including its decision to go public. On the strength of these interviews the investment banker should be selected.

THE NONPUBLIC COMPANY

It is normally believed that the financial community will not concern itself with information about a privately held company. In an overwhelming number of cases, fortunately, this is not true—assuming that the program is properly handled. In skilled hands, a certain amount of premarket conditioning can be done. A proper program has two advantages—it serves to inform the financial community, as well as the general public, of the facts about a company and its industry, and second, it establishes a pattern of public relations activities which, if it does not flagrantly function to sell stock, serves as a pattern and precedent for allowable public relations while a company is in registration.

Under skillful examination, any company can be found to have aspects about it that should be of interest to the general business press, even though the company is not public. It can be an unusual facet of the company, it can be an unusual relationship to its industry, or it can be an unusual approach to routine problems in an industry. Following the procedures outlined in the chapter discussing press relations, a nonpublic company can expect a measure of publicity in the financial and business press. Granted that it takes considerably more skill to develop newsworthy material for a nonpublic company than for a public company, but a review of the business press will show that it is done with regularity.

In many cases, and in selected industries, a nonpublic company can be a valuable source of general information about that industry to the financial community. Analysts specializing in any industry are always eager to receive fresh and pertinent information from any valid source. There is no reason why a nonpublic company cannot take the initiative to supply the information to the very analysts they will ultimately be dealing with when they go public.

Certain kinds of product or service publicity to the nonfinancial press can also be useful to the financial community in contributing to their knowledge of a particular industry. There is nothing untoward in sending reprints of such publicity to selected analysts specializing in that industry.

The objective, of course, is to precede the public offering, much before registration, with a program that engenders recognition of the company name and understanding of the company's activities and position in the field, even while it enhances the view of the industry in which the company serves.

As for establishing a pattern of public communications that will be acceptable while in registration, the basic rules of disclosure apply. Nothing is acceptable that can be construed as offering to sell stock or conditioning the market for the sale of stock. Nevertheless, the SEC says that, barring those specific exceptions, the company may continue its normal pattern of publicity. The point is to establish a normal pattern of publicity.

Prior to registration, and as part of putting the company's story together for presentation to prospective underwriters, the company should orient its material. This should be done not only in the legalistic terms of a prospectus, but in ways that are acceptable to the financial community in general. One approach developed by FRB's Ted Pincus and used with some measure of success is the financial annual report for the nonpublic company. The report need not be expensive or elaborate, but it can follow the same general procedure as used for an annual report for a public company. This kind of report can also be used for customers, employees, suppliers, and, of course, the financial community, as part of a program to acquaint them with the company and its position in the industry.

It may also be worth considering the preparation of a background report similar to that recommended for distribution to the financial community by a public company.

At all costs, in any prepublic publicity, or representations by a prepublic company to the financial community, all SEC regulations pertaining to a company in registration should be kept clearly in mind. Nothing will defeat an ultimate public issue so much as misrepresentation of the facts about a company even before it has gone public. And certainly, if the program is to succeed, it must be done in such a way that the prepublic material will be remembered well after the company has gone public. Any significant discrepancies in the information given in the two periods will seriously and adversely affect the financial community's view of the ultimate issue.

REGISTRATION

When a company is in registration for a public stock offering it enters a period of silence. That is, it may do nothing in the way of disseminating information about itself that can under any circumstances be construed as marketing the stock, promoting it, or conditioning the market for the sale of the stock.

This does not mean that the company must go into hiding from the public or the financial community.

First of all, the SEC requires that the normal rules of disclosure for a public company be maintained even for a company in registration. Any basic information about activities that alter the nature of the company, such as a merger, an acquisition, or a major contract, must be disclosed. Certainly, periodic earnings reports must be disclosed. The basic rule remains, however, that no activity must be undertaken, nor new public relations effort initiated, which can in any way be construed as selling stock or conditioning the market. This particularly includes any form of projections, any subjective material that implies growth potential for either the company or the industry, or any material that interprets any information being disseminated. The exception, perhaps, is product information which is consistent with an historical pattern of marketing established well before registration.

THE NEW ISSUE

Once the company is out of registration it can begin to pursue the normal financial relations activities described throughout this book. The first step is a press release which simply announces the new issue, made available by prospectus. It should include the underwriter, the size and details of the issue, and a brief description of the company's business. This release and the tombstone ad in the financial press is usually taken care of by the underwriter.

THE DUE DILIGENCE MEETING

Immediately prior to the effective date of the registration, the underwriter usually holds a meeting for representatives of all the underwriting firms who will participate in the syndicate to distribute the stock. The purpose of this meeting is to assure that all participants understand the nature of the issue. Its larger purpose, however, is to assure the participants in the syndicate that they haven't made a mistake in their participation, as well as to develop some enthusiasm on their part about the company. Legally, the purpose of the meeting is to demonstrate that due diligence has been exercised in the preparation of the issue and in the presentation and up-dating of facts about the company, and so it is referred to as the "due diligence meeting."

Due diligence meetings are usually cut-and-dried affairs, attended re-luctantly by people who have already decided to help sell the issue. For this reason, it is the better part of wisdom to put on a thoroughly profes-sional performance in explaining the company in order to engender the kind of enthusiasm necessary to make the issue a success.

The presentation should be carefully prepared so that the material is presented in an orderly fashion, and that it is succinct, precise, and to the point. The objective of the meeting is to have each participant understand the company's current financial structure and, in the case of analysts, to demonstrate the company's ability to appreciate the invested dollar. And, as with analyst meetings, questions should be anticipated and the answers rehearsed. Management should appear confident, open, and willing to answer all questions.

In beginning the financial relations activities, the syndicate is a key to developing the geographic aspect of the program. Since the location of the syndicate members is a basis for the geographic distribution of the stock, there is a first inkling of those cities that might be targets for analyst meet-ings and press attention. Moreover, a representative of a syndicate mem-ber can usually be depended upon to assist in identifying the key people in the local financial community.

THE AFTERMARKET

The aftermarket is what happens to the stock after the public issue. In too many cases, a company is led to believe that the underwriter will take and maintain a proprietary interest in the stock issue after the company has gone public. This is rarely the case, even for companies that do well in the stock market following the original issue. There are several reasons for this.

Maintaining a sound aftermarket beyond the period legally required is arduous and time-consuming, and demands skills and facilities that are frequently beyond the capabilities of even the larger underwriters. In order for the price of a stock—and particularly a new and untested one—to reflect consistently the company's earnings and earnings potential, there must not only be market-makers, but quality sponsors. Presumably the underwriter will serve as both—but this is a presumption more often honored in the breach. Frequently, the underwriter will issue a research report, primarily to assist its own registered representatives in the sale of the stock, but the report is plainly qualified to indicate that the firm issuing the report maintains a position in the stock, and is therefore not entirely objective. Unfortunately, unless the company is growing at a consistent rate of 30% a year and expects to do it for the next five years, and its stock price reflects this growth, the underwriter has very little time to spend on any one stock—and that amount of time diminishes the farther away from the date of issue.

There is a realistic aspect to the problem, too, in that the underwriter has probably earned a fee from just the underwriting. Unless the stock really takes off and sharply increases in value, there is a limit to what the underwriter can profitably do.

He may continue to sponsor and make a market in a stock, but one sponsor and one market-maker are not sufficient for an issue that is not performing superbly on its own. He may call upon friends and associates in other firms to help him, but there is a limit to the time he can profitably spend in pursuing this activity.

There is also the question of exposing a company to a broad spectrum of analysts. This, too, is beyond the capability of most underwriters, both in terms of time they can profitably spend and the overall perspective necessary for developing a strategy tailored to a particular company at any one time in the market's performance. Even the largest and soundest underwriting firm places a strict limit on what it can reasonably do in developing additional sponsors, market-makers, research reports, and exposure to the financial community at large. Underwriters are not geared to support an issue to any degree that might enhance its long-range acceptance by the financial community. This is essentially the purpose of a separate and professionally performed financial relations program.

THE EMPLOYEE STOCK OWNERSHIP TRUST (ESOT)

An increasingly popular and relatively new way to raise capital, particularly for the private or closely held corporation,, is the employee ownership plan and trust.

The company sells stock to a noncontributory trust fund it sets up for its employees. The trust uses the stock as collateral for a loan from a bank. The trust, in turn, gives the money to the company in payment for the stock. The company then pays an expensible maximum of 15% of its payroll annually to the trust. With ESOT, it is paid with pretax dollars. Furthermore, the plan is allowed to function without the margin requirements usually applicable in a stock pledge. Instead, the bank accepts the corporation's guarantee.

In a specific example, a company needs $1 million for five years. It has 300 employees with an annual gross payroll of $3 million and is in the 54% tax bracket. The ESOT borrows $1 million from the bank, which the company guarantees. ESOT then pays the $1 million to the company in exchange for $1 million in company stock. The company pays $300,000 —or 10% of its payroll—annually to the trust. The trust pays the bank $254,976—principal and interest—annually on the debt, leaving it $45,024 for its reserve account. As the loan is paid off, the stock is allocated to the employees' account and is usually vested over a period of 10 years.

The plan has several advantages:

1. For the nonpublic company not in a position to go into the equities market, it allows the company to go public, in a limited sense, without registration.

2. Because pretax dollars are used to finance the debt there is a substantial tax savings.

3. Cash flow is increased substantially.

4. Net worth is increased substantially.

5. It creates liquidity at fair market value, comparable to that of a public company, without SEC registration or underwriting costs or time.

6. It allows for capital gains sales by individual shareholders.

7. The stockholder-employee accumulates values in the ESOT which are not subject to estate taxes.

8. It establishes a definite valuation of shares for estate tax purposes of major shareholders.

9. Buy/sell agreements for the stock of major shareholders may be funded by life insurance, with premiums deductible from pretax income by flowing it through the trust.

10. For the employees, it builds unity and team spirit by allowing them to share in the capital growth of the company, to realize capital gains on income, and to accumulate values that are funded by employer contributions, with no diminution of employee take-home pay.

The ESOT is also useful for the closely held company, or for the company already public, but not in a position to issue additional shares due to existing stock market conditions.

The ESOT is sanctioned by the Internal Revenue Service. An ESOT is best established with the assistance of one of the several firms specializing in such programs, such as Lanton Associates of Los Angeles, California.

GOING PRIVATE

In the chastening cold light of changing economic conditions, an increasing number of companies have come to realize that they are better off as private companies than as public companies. The procedures for going private are relatively—*relatively*—simple, so much so that the SEC is taking a dim view of the process, as are many individual shareholders. When stock prices are very low, and particularly when they are considerably lower than book value, the decision to go private is very tempting. Unfortunately, the shareholder who bought his stock at $20, now sees it at $3, and is being offered $5 for it in a tender offer by a management that wants to go private and will obviously benefit from the transaction, is not likely to be overjoyed at the company's action. In some cases there have been stockholder suits, although considering the high cost to an individual for filing such a suit, these have not been overabundant.

Globe Security Systems, Inc., a subsidiary of Walter Kidde & Company, Inc., is a typical example of a public company going private. It had 335,450 shares of its common stock in the hands of the public. It tendered for that stock at a cash price that was 38% higher than the last sale price on the American Stock Exchange. Globe had once traded as high as 31½, but at the time of the tender it was trading at 3⅞. As a result of the tender offer, Kidde's holdings in Globe went from 81% to 95%. With fewer than 300 shareholders, Globe was exempted from SEC regulations and was delisted by the Exchange. It was, in effect, a private company. Those shareholders who did not tender their stock might just as well have done so, since there was virtually no further public market.

Among those techniques for going private, there are several that are more commonly used.

One of the most popular methods is to offer a new nonconvertible debenture in exchange for the common stock. Another technique is a merger or liquidation, usually using a dummy corporation. Management establishes a dummy corporation into which it merges the original company. The public shareholders don't get shares in the new company, but are instead offered a price for their stock in the original company. The merger is then voted by the shareholders, but invariably the buyers have enough votes to carry their proposal. Another technique is a reverse split, which sharply reduces the number of shares outstanding and leaves each share at a price so high that trading is precluded. The variations on the technique are myriad.

Among the dangers of going private, which are many, is the very strong barrier of antifraud and antimanipulative provisions of the Securities Exchange Act of 1934. This becomes particularly cogent in a deal in which the public shareholder is obviously going to lose out. A great measure of care must be taken in presenting any such arrangement so that there is no misrepresentation and that there is full disclosure of every aspect of it. Naturally, a company in the process of buying in its own stock under any procedure must pay strict attention to SEC regulations.

There is also a question, the answer to which is difficult to anticipate, as to the future of any company going private. Perhaps it should not have gone public in the first place and going private is a proper amendment of that mistake. On the other hand, at some distant future date, the public company going private may need equity money to expand to meet changing conditions. How then will the market view that company, if, in going private, it had not done right by its shareholders?

For the company planning to go public, it's certainly a good exercise to view the experience and reasons of companies who have gone private.

Going public to find a source of capital that is appropriate to a company is fraught with pitfalls and expenses that somehow don't get readily talked about in discussions prior to an underwriting. While it is unlikely that these activities should reach a proportion to preclude a public issue where one is otherwise indicated, it would be foolhardy for any corporate management to plan to go public without being aware of the problems and expenses inherent in doing it.

CHAPTER 7

ACQUISITIONS AND MERGERS

In 1967, there were some 3000 mergers in the United States. By the end of the decade, merger fever had struck the corporate community like a plague. Everything was ripe for it. The economy was growing at a rapid rate and the stock market was at its peak. For companies with price/earnings multiples of 20 or more, stock was a commodity almost more valuable than cash. The smallest and most obscure company, recently gone public and with the price of its stock highly inflated, was constantly on the prowl for other companies with which to combine. They sought to perform a mystical process called synergism, wherein, theoretically, the total was greater than the sum of its parts.

Accounting regulations at the time fed the fertile ground for many such mergers. Under pooling of interest regulations, one company that absorbed another in November could show the combined earnings as its own for the full year.

Family-owned companies that had long resisted going public, or sale to a public company, readily fell prey to the lure of high stock multiples that offered untold wealth in years to come. Companies went public for the sole purpose of leveraging their stock into companies with even higher earnings and a greater basis for higher p/e's by merging and merging again. Emulating the larger conglomerates, companies with sales of under $10 million set out to become mini-conglomerates. With exceptions, there was no apparent reason for these mergers except a kind of legal-financial manipulation.

With the recession of 1970 and the change in accounting regulations that all but eliminated pooling of interests as an acceptable accounting technique for mergers, and substituted restatement of the profit and loss statement, the merger fever ran its course. For the most part, those mergers that have subsequently taken place have had a sound business rationale behind them. This, of course, is as it should be.

During the course of the merger fever, companies were sold for the most irrational and irrelevant reasons. Virtually as many mergers were conceived on the golf course as in the board room, and the shareholders loved it. It meant more earnings per share and the dim promise of a base for continued growth.

Today, the rationale for merger and acquisition finds its roots more readily in legitimate business needs. Companies merge to expand capability, to enhance distribution, to broaden a product line, to assure a source of supply, for increased technology, for diversification to offset the cyclical nature of a business, and ultimately to improve the ability to appreciate the invested dollar.

In the final analysis, the most potentially successful merger is one that is seen ultimately as a solution to a capital problem, either to improve the capital position or to improve the company's overall capabilities in ways that will improve the company's capital position. Naturally, the improved capital position is expected to generate greater profits.

In an article entitled "How to Sell Your Company," in the Harvard Business Review in September 1968, Richard N. Hexter, Executive Vice President of Donaldson, Lufkin & Jenrette, wrote:

Not only is selling a company an investment decision, it is the *ultimate* investment decision. There are at least two reasons for this: 1. No investment decision so totally commits the company's assets, and 2. No investment decision is so irrevocable.

A stockholder group selling its company for $20 million in stock to the PDQ Corporation is making the same decision as would a portfolio manager in considering a $20 million investment in PDQ stock. If a cash sale is planned, the seller is presuming he can reinvest the cash in another portfolio with equal or better prospects. In both cases the same question must be asked: Can an investment be made wisely so that the new holdings will grow faster than would equity ownership in the selling company? Unless viewed in this light any decision to sell must be considered somewhat arbitrary.

While this was written as a guide to the company as a potential seller, it also holds true for the potential buyer. It is an investment decision.

For the company considering merger, for whatever reasons, whether as a buyer or a seller, the financial community will view the transaction in just these investment terms. For the shareholder or the prospective investor, the merger will be looked upon in terms of its value in appreciating the investment. For other segments of the capital markets, and especially those called upon to help finance the merger, the question of how the action will enhance the company as an investment vehicle is no less pertinent.

Traditionally, Wall Street reflects its views of any such action in the stock market. If Wall Street sees the merger as salutary, the price of the stock will go up upon announcement of the merger. If the value of the merger or acquisition is not understood, the price of the stock will go down. Nor is this market activity solely the result of the activities of arbitrageurs—traders who specialize in taking advantage of differences in stock prices in different markets. It is invariably a genuine Wall Street reaction.

Therefore, the financial relations view of a merger or acquisition must be expressed in terms that allow the financial community to view the merger as salutary, and to make clear the ways in which the merger will enhance the company's growth potential.

ATTRACTING CANDIDATES

For the company with a growth pattern that includes acquisition, or for the company that may ultimately want to merge, the process begins well before the identification of merger partners. While most mergers are a result of a formalized search for partners by investment bankers, attorneys, accountants, and others, high visibility remains the key to attracting merger partners. This, of course, is a function of a well-performed financial relations program. What is most important in the total financial relations picture is the annual report. It becomes a kind of brochure—a selling piece for both merger partners. For the company that is merger-minded, certainly this fact should become one of the objectives in planning the annual report.

In a bull market, when high price/earnings ratio stocks are the commodity for purchase of a company, visibility in the financial community is essential to maintain high stock price and volume. Price/earnings ratios are now considerably lower, but are still an essential factor in a merger, even when cash or notes are used instead of stock. Thus the financial relations program becomes even more important in maintaining the p/e ratio at a reasonable level. Companies whose shares are undervalued have a considerably more difficult job in acquisitions and mergers, regardless of the stock price, than do companies whose stock prices more accurately reflect earnings and earnings potential.

In determining those factors that must be projected in a financial relations program designed to enhance merger possibilities, at least the following should be included:

1. *The financial value of the company.* This should be projected as clearly as possible, and with a full understanding that hidden factors remain hidden only for the briefest period of time.

2. *Management.* As in any form of financial relations, management's strengths must be clearly exposed and projected.

3. *Marketing and production strengths.* Both the current structures and the anticipated needs and capabilities should be projected in the growth pattern.

4. *Current and anticipated funding needs.* This is a point to be emphasized in the projection of plans.

5. *Long-range management objectives.*

6. *Attitudes of management toward growth.* How does management see merger in terms of both its own future and the future of the merger partners as well?

Essentially, then, these areas of concentration for projecting the acquisition-minded company differ from other financial relations practices only in emphasis, and in the fact that the financial relations program, while continuing to be concentrated on the financial community, must also include the general business community as well. Further emphasis must be placed on such factors as those directions of growth which delineate the kinds of mergers sought by the company, in terms of the company's needs. This includes growth for diversification, source of supply, management, distribution, and so on.

DIVESTITURE

It is inappropriate to talk about merger without considering, at the same time, divestiture. In many respects, they are opposite sides of the same coin. Frequently, a company will find itself with a segment or a division that no longer serves its corporate needs. It may be a market that the company no longer wishes to serve, or a division that is no longer profitable under the company's structure, or an operation that has not responded to the company's management. It could be a forced divestiture by order of a government regulatory body. In the case of divestiture, there is the added problem of projecting the company's need to sell without diminishing the overall view of the company's abilities or of the unit's potential. There is frequently the added problem of internal morale, during the course of the divestiture program, where management wants to avoid a negative feeling on the part of those responsible for the operations of the unit to be divested. To the extent that operational efforts of the unit to be divested are diminished, this is not only an internal problem, it also tends to undermine the strength of the unit, and therefore makes it harder to sell.

The program for divestiture, then, must be carefully formulated with these factors in mind. The positive aspects of the unit to be divested must be emphasized, as must the positive aspects of the reasons for divestiture. This is not to imply that any misrepresentation is warranted. The key word is *emphasis* in the course of disclosure. It must be recognized by even the most insensitive managements that not every kind of operation functions well or consistently in every management or corporate context. Clopay Corporation, a Cincinnati-based manufacturer of homewares and plastic products, purchased an office products operation at one point in its expansion program. At the time of the purchase, the move was reasonable, both as a diversification move and because the office products industry offered great potential. During the several ensuing years, however, both the nature of the office products industry and Clopay's corporate directions changed. Clopay's otherwise satisfactory earnings were, for a brief period, diminished by the negative results of the office products division, and divestiture seemed in order. Clopay management wisely recognized the fact that the problem was not the office products division so much as the mixture of the division's operations with the company's other operations. The office products industry was still promising, but not necessarily so under the Clopay corporate structure that had emerged over the years. Approaching the problem in this positive way, Clopay managed to divest itself of the division in a reasonable period of time. Furthermore, by properly anticipating the sale and setting up reserves, the divestiture was accomplished at a loss to Clopay that was not too serious. Once the divestiture was completed, the company moved on to increase its success in its remaining operations.

Divestiture is not always as uncomplicated as in the Clopay situation. When it is ordered by federal decree, a number of additional problems are posed. To the challenge of finding a buyer under pressure is added the problem of convincing shareholders and the investment community that the company, after the divestiture, is still a sound investment vehicle. When Work Wear, Inc., a manufacturer and renter of uniforms and working clothes, was ordered to divest its entire rental operation, the problem was further compounded by the extraordinary procedure the company used. First, there was the need to explain to shareholders that the company was still sound despite the fact that the units to be divested represented half the company's earnings. This was done in the annual report, which went to great lengths to analyze the potential market for the company's products, and demonstrated the company's strong position in its field.

Second, Work Wear divested its rental division by splitting it off under its own separate management, and then offering Work Wear shareholders the option of exchanging Work Wear stock for stock in the new company on a proportional basis. This, too, was explained in the annual report, as well as in the proxy statement.

But the annual report came out at about the same time that the split-off company went into registration for the new stock. This meant that the report had to be written so that descriptions of Work Wear's continuing potential did not interfere with the registration by appearing to condition stockholders who might opt to exchange their stock. This was handled by hewing closely to the language of the registration statement. The same approach was used at the annual meeting, which was held during the registration period.

When Maremont Corporation was forced to divest its warehousing division, the problem was quite different. The warehousing division was relatively new, and had not yet reached a point where it was a major contributor to corporate earnings. This was easy to explain in news releases, analyst meetings, and the annual and interim reports. But the division was most likely going to be sold to several buyers, piece by piece. The problem was to develop a divestiture program to sell the several pieces. A written presentation for each unit was prepared, outlining its history, its assets, its operations and performance, its market potential, and so forth. Prospective purchasers were identified and approached. Publicity in the trade press about the units to be divested developed other potential purchasers. Ultimately, and within the deadlines set by the divestiture order, all of the units were sold.

ANNOUNCING THE MERGER

A merger negotiation is a sensitive situation. Under the best of circumstances, many more mergers are seriously discussed than are consummated. There are many stages of discussion, ranging from the first query to the actual consummation of the merger, and at any one of the stages something can happen to upset it. Throughout the discussions secrecy is essential—not for any Machiavellian reason, but to avoid undue speculation, to protect employee morale, or to avoid a counter offer by companies that otherwise might not have known that one of the merger partners was available.

At the same time, there is a point in a merger negotiation at which a number of insiders are aware of the potential of the merger and are therefore in a very precarious position under the SEC rules of disclosure. At this point, the timing of the announcement of merger discussion becomes crucial.

Obviously, the safest time to announce a merger negotiation is at the first sign that it becomes clear to both parties that there is general agreement to merge. Ideally, the signal to disclose would be the signing of the letter of intent. Sometimes, however, the discussions have made considerable progress well before a letter of intent is drawn, or there may even be no letter of intent planned. Whether to wait for a signed agreement or to announce the merger negotiation in the drafting stage is a question of judgment. The timing of the disclosure should be that point at which it is felt that both sides are in general agreement, and that the weight of the inside information on those who hold it, or the number of people in either or both companies that are privy to the information, has reached a dangerous proportion in view of the general principles of the rules of disclosure.

At that point, a simple one-page release should be issued by either party or jointly, announcing that the merger negotiations are taking place. The announcement need not state the specific terms of the merger except generally—for stock, for cash, for notes, and so forth. The press will undoubtedly make further inquiries, but these should be politely put aside by the simple statement of truth that the negotiations have not yet been completed and that the terms have not been set.

If for any reason subsequent to the first announcement the merger is called off, an announcement must be made immediately. If, on the other hand, negotiations continue for several weeks beyond the original announcement, a subsequent release should be issued merely to indicate that further progress has been made in the negotiation. The specific details in subsequent announcements should be limited to those facts which are needed to update the original announcement. The purpose of the second announcement is to maintain an orderly flow of information that precludes undue speculation as to the cause of the time lag since the first announcement.

As soon as the merger is reduced to binding agreement, the announcement must go out immediately. It should include all facts about the merger, including details of terms. There is no reason why the release cannot be prepared beforehand, agreed to by both parties, for distribution within an hour or two after the signing of the agreement. Distribution of the release should follow the normal pattern for news distribution described in Chapter 3.

There are times when, following the announcement of the consummation of a merger, the two parties then decide to disagree. This can happen for any number of reasons, ranging from personality conflicts to the discovery that the facts weren't as represented. The simple announcement of change of agreement then poses some thorny problems, since the required explanation may be embarassing to either party. But explanation there must be, since the speculation as to reasons can be more damaging than the facts. And explanations will demanded of both parties by shareholders, the press, the investment community, and perhaps even the SEC.

SHAREHOLDER APPROVAL

In those mergers in which shareholder approval is necessary, the description of the merger in all its facets is given in a proxy statement. In some cases, the nature and timing of the merger require a special shareholders' meeting.

But the proxy is frequently written in formal, legal terms, which rarely show shareholders the advantages to the action as seen by management. There are two ways to logically reduce the barrier between management and shareholders constructed by legal language. The first way is to be sure to include shareholders on mailings of all releases relating to the merger. The second way is to send a personalized letter from the chief executive officer to each shareholder, describing the merger and its advantages in simplest terms.

This kind of consideration becomes even more necessary for the shareholders of the company being acquired. In many cases, it is the smaller of the two companies. Many of its shareholders are often employees or former employees, or individuals who bought their stock in its earlier days. They want to know that the deal they are getting as individuals is a good one and doesn't subvert the reasons for which they originally bought stock.

Many a merger has been delayed or scuttled by a suit instituted by a dissident shareholder of an acquired company who believes, however falsely, that only the company's management will benefit but that the shareholders will not. This kind of suit is frequently avoided by doing a good job of keeping all shareholders of both companies well informed at every step of the way.

FOLLOW-UP

Once the merger has been consummated, there remains the job of convincing the financial community that the merger is indeed salutary. There is also, frequently, the internal job of communicating to the executives and employees of both companies the nature of the merger and its potential effect on their future.

Following the merger, an intensive financial community and press relations program should be undertaken. A new background report should be prepared describing the newly structured company, and an intensive program of meeting with analysts, brokers, money managers, and so on, should be undertaken, with representatives of both companies involved, if feasible, to explain the reasons behind the merger and the ways in which it will help the new combined company to grow.

A press relations program should include interviews with executives, stories about the company in relation to its industry, and so forth. For the listed company or the OTC company whose quotations are carried by *The Wall Street Journal*, it is a marvelous opportunity for a Dow Joneser— an in-depth interview about the company and its potential, which appears on the Dow Jones tape and frequently in *The Wall Street Journal* in abbreviated form. A similar interview with *Reuters* should also be arranged. Remember, the idea is to establish in the minds of the financial community, as quickly as possible, the favorable nature of the marriage, as well as to reaffirm the growth potential of the company.

INTERNAL COMMUNICATIONS

Employee morale problems arising out of uncertainty in a merger can be devastating to a company's operations during and immediately following a merger. At the earliest feasible moment, even before the consummation of the merger, a meeting should be held for executives and employees of both companies to clarify the nature of the merger and the probable effects it will have on employees of both companies. Frankness is essential, even if it means imparting bad news. Employees whose jobs may be in jeopardy must, of course, be treated diplomatically. On the one hand, key employees shouldn't be lost through uncertainty. On the other hand, it may take some time, subsequent to the merger, to determine who is to be kept and who is not to be kept.

A letter to all employees from the chief executive officer is very much in order. The idea is to encourage calm and a sense of security—as best as possible—in an uncertain situation and in a period of transition. It is also an opportunity for the chief executive officer to convey the spirit of optimism in which the merger was consummated.

CORPORATE IDENTITY PROGRAM

An integral part of a merger or acquisition is establishing the identification of the newly merged company as part of the parent or survivor. Unless carefully planned, this can be a painful and expensive problem.

Some years ago, an old and famous privately held company, Sossner Tap & Die Company, was absorbed by HeliCoil Corporation, along with a number of other small companies. Sossner was a well-established name in the field, and, in fact, better known throughout the world than was Heli-Coil. Merely to have changed the Sossner name to HeliCoil would have eliminated all the marketing goodwill that had been built up over the years. This, combined with the fact that HeliCoil had absorbed a number of other small companies within a short period of time, dictated the need for a new corporate identity program that would bring all the companies under one umbrella without losing the identity and goodwill of the individual companies.

Judgment of the value of corporate identity programs enters a grey area. During the 1960s, they were seriously oversold by zealous designers who seemed to imply that by changing the corporate logo there would be a significant change in something called "the corporate image," and that by changing the corporate image all kinds of miraculous good would accrue to the company. This, of course, is patent nonsense. First of all, the term "corporate image" has been flagrantly perverted since it was first used in a somewhat different context some years ago. The implication seems to be that people have an image of a company that, if favorable, carries with it a public attitude that will help it in all of its dealings with everyone, from the financial community to the consumer. If the corporate image of General Electric, the idea suggests, is that of a company that deals well with consumers, suppliers, the financial community, employees, and society in general, then the public will buy its products regardless of quality, invest in it regardless of sound investment principles, and smile blithely if it pollutes its industrial environment. Moreover, the notion is fostered that this corporate image can be achieved by changing and modernizing the company's logo and graphic appearance, supported by cosmetic public relations. Unfortunately, this ludicrous idea is accepted by a great number of people.

There are times when a company's graphics should be modernized and, in the case of the absorption of another company through merger or acquisition, when its graphics can be used to identify the new subsidiaries as part of the parent company. But no corporate graphics program is going to change a public impression of a company by itself. Only the company's operational factors can do that.

A particularly successful corporate identity program was achieved by Eastern Airlines some years ago. It modernized its logo, its graphics, and the appearance of its outlets and personnel. After a short period of time, there was no aspect of the public appearance of Eastern, from its advertising to its airplanes, that was not readily identifiable as being Eastern Airlines. This graphics program, however, did nothing to improve the quality of the airline's service. Its planes were still maintaining poor on-time schedules, its personnel did not improve their efficiency, nor could all the graphics and advertising improve the quality of its operations. What resulted was an instant and consistent identification of an operation that was considered so generally inferior that its profits were below those of its competitors for many years.

On the other hand, a corporate identity program is useful in unifying, in the minds of all with whom it must deal, the view of a company in its many elements—if certain safeguards are taken in the transition.

A good corporate identity program begins with an analysis of the company and all its operations, including its subsidiaries, divisions, and so on. More than just a view of graphics, the analysis must concern itself with the consistency of not only corporate literature, stationery, and logos, but titles and descriptions as well. For example, too often terms like "divisions" and "subsidiaries" are used interchangeably. These are precise terms in the corporate sense, and no corporate identity program can function without a clear understanding of the difference.

A well-designed graphics program will include a manual that indicates the company's standards for the use of its logo in every aspect, including size, color, and terminology. It should be remembered that no corporate identity program succeeds overnight. It must be promoted and popularized. It takes time for it to sink in.

It is in cases such as a Sossner company that the problem arises.

Logically, the corporate identity program of HeliCoil dictated that the former Sossner company become simply the Tap and Die Division of HeliCoil. But when former Sossner salesmen began calling on their old customers as representatives of some strange new company, called the Tap and Die Division of HeliCoil, the salesmen were greeted with blank stares. This, despite a rather intensive advertising campaign in the trade press announcing the change in name. The solution was to print new double business cards with both names on them, to have the sales manager write letters of explanation to all former Sossner customers, and to be sure that salesmen clearly explained the change on each of their calls. There still remained the problem of new customers who had heard of Sossner but not of HeliCoil. Here, too, the double card was successful.

PROMOTING THE NEW CORPORATE IDENTITY

When the new corporate identity program is completed, it must be made known as quickly and as broadly as possible. The audiences for this campaign are:

1. Customers.
2. Suppliers.
3. The general public.

4. Employees.
5. The financial community.
6. The plant community.

A number of devices are used to reach these audiences. They include:

1. *Publicity.* Press releases with illustrations of the new graphics and a description of how the company is incorporating its subsidiaries and divisions under the new graphics should be sent to every segment of the press that serves the target audiences. This includes the trade press, the business and financial press, local papers in which plants are located, employee publications, and the financial press.

If feasible, public events should be instituted that are themselves publicizable, such as a sign-changing ceremony at a plant, or human interest pictures showing a sign painter facing 50 trucks on which he must paint the new logo. Under some circumstances, the change in logo can be a useful peg for a feature article on how the company has grown since it was first started 25 or 50 years ago.

2. *Advertising.* An appropriate advertising campaign should be developed to announce the change. The obvious media are those publications serving the audiences to be reached.

3. *Announcements by mail.* A letter, a brochure, or a reprint of the announcement advertisement should be sent to every company, customer, and supplier with which the company does business. If there is a case of potential confusion, such as the Sossner situation, a personal letter should go out to every customer served by the old company. This letter can be signed by the company president, by the sales manager, or by the salesman serving that customer—whichever is most appropriate.

The changeover cannot be so abrupt as to lose the values inherent in former names and earlier identifications. It takes time to establish a new identity, particularly if there is a corporate name change.

And, most importantly, it should be remembered that a new graphic identity will not enhance a company's image. Only superior service, product quality, and consistent good management can achieve that.

After the rash of mergers in the late 1960s, and because so many of them were irrational, the financial community is skeptical of mergers and acquisitions. This should be kept foremost in the minds of corporate executives who contemplate merger. The very fact of a merger alone, it should be recognized, will not be accepted with enthusiasm without considerable explanation and an intensive financial relations program to explain most clearly the reasons and hopes for it.

CHAPTER 8

THE PROXY AND THE TENDER OFFER

In the late 1960s, the president of HeliCoil Corporation received a surprise visit from the president of Mite Corporation. Mite's president pleasantly suggested that there were some sound reasons why the two companies might merge. HeliCoil's president, proud of the fact that he had built the company virtually single-handedly from a product designed and perfected in his garage, was horrified at the thought—and rejected it out of hand. The president of Mite then announced that he had been quietly buying shares of HeliCoil in the open market, and that he owned enough shares to form the base for mounting a tender offer for sufficient HeliCoil shares to take over the company.

Thus began a classic proxy fight of the period. Unlike many of the highly publicized and spectacular tender offers and proxy fights that made huge headlines, this one was more typical of those that took place. Both companies were under $100 million sales. HeliCoil, moreover, had heretofore resided in a sense of security that it was impervious to such a raid.

Despite Herculean efforts by management and sound reasons why the deal was not a particularly good one for HeliCoil shareholders, Mite nevertheless won the proxy fight and HeliCoil became part of the Mite family.

Could this have been anticipated and avoided? Could HeliCoil have prevented the take-over? In the answers to these questions lie some measure of guidance for today's companies. While those swashbuckling days of proxy fights and tender offers appear to be over, they still take place and will continue to, especially where book value greatly exceeds market value of shares. Moreover, we now face the danger of take-over of American companies by foreign companies, as a result of massive international shifts of capital. If rumors in 1974 of an Arab take-over of IBM could gain credence, as they did, what company can consider itself immune?

The HeliCoil situation was not only predictable, but was actually predicted by some consultants to the company. Management owned only some 20% of the stock, with the rest in the hands of the public and several large investors. The company, which had grown nicely both internally and through acquisitions made with stock selling at reasonably high multiples, had an exceptionally strong cash position. It was a successful and attractive company, with a sound competitive position in its field and a generally good management team.

The company's answer to warnings about its attractiveness as a take-over candidate was to point with pride to its excellent relationships with several holders of large blocks of stock. This, plus good relationships in several quarters in Wall Street, constituted to the company an early warning system. They felt that any unusual buying in the stock would be readily noted and reported to management, and that the loyalty of the holders of the large blocks was inalienable.

When the vulnerability of the company to take-over was noted by the company's financial relations counsel, a program was instituted—too late, unfortunately—to build whatever barriers could be built for some measure of protection for the company. The investor relations program was strengthened. Noting that a good deal of the stock was concentrated in just a few geographic areas, a program of analyst meetings in cities throughout the United States was begun in the attempt to broaden the geographic base of smaller investors. The feeling was that it would be even more difficult for a raider to buy up the stock if much of it was held by small investors scattered throughout the United States. There was some feeling, not unwarranted, that shareholders outside of major financial centers tend to invest for the longer term than do shareholders in major cities.

A program was established to monitor the transfer sheets on a weekly basis, both to anticipate a take-over attempt and as a sound measure to keep abreast of buying patterns as a guide for focus for the total financial relations program.

Unfortunately, the entire program was instituted too late. Buying by representatives and allies of Mite had been taking place over a long period of time, and a large amount of the stock had already fallen into the hands of investors sympathetic to Mite.

By the time Mite was ready to start its take-over attempt, it was well along in its accumulation.

HeliCoil's first steps were sensible, and constituted a pattern that is sound even today in fighting a take-over attempt.

A major investment banking firm was retained to analyze and scrutinize the Mite offer in its every detail. Detailed projections were made of the meaning of the Mite offer in terms of the ultimate value of the stock and the company, should the take-over attempt succeed. Despite the fact that the tender offer was at a premium over the current market value of the HeliCoil stock, the analysis showed that the shareholder would be better off if he did not tender his stock to Mite.

As part of the analysis of the offer, an examination was made of Mite Corporation, in order to project the value of Mite stock and Mite as a corporation as compared to HeliCoil stock and HeliCoil as a corporation.

The results of this analysis were then broadcast to HeliCoil shareholders. Mite's advertising for the tender offer was countered by HeliCoil's advertising, delineating reasons why HeliCoil management felt that the tender offer was not a good deal for the shareholders. Letters to shareholders were sent, describing reasons why management felt that the offer was not good for HeliCoil shareholders.

The most difficult part of the job is, of course, reaching those shareholders whose stock is held in trust or in Street name. These shareholders, as well as others known to the company, had to be reached both to tell the HeliCoil story and, ultimately, to gather proxies for the shareholder vote on the merger.

At the same time, the financial relations program was intensified. Analysts and brokers were reached, both individually and through meetings. They were told the company's story not merely in terms of the offer, but also to demonstrate its strength and growth potential, so that existing shareholders, and those who advise them, might be further assured of the company's continued strength. Emphasis was placed on those analysts and brokerage houses that might be in a position to issue written reports separately or as part of their regular publications for shareholders.

The publicity campaign to both the business and financial press was intensified, with every effort made to tell the company's side of the story in the tender offer, and to demonstrate every facet of the company's strength in its total operation.

Shareholders of large blocks were directly approached to solicit their support.

Management also tried to find its own choice of merger partners in the attempt to preclude the take-over by selling the company to another more sympathetic one—a company with whom HeliCoil felt they could live more happily. While several such candidates were identified and negotiations begun, they could not be completed in time to solve the problem.

Behind-the-scene maneuvers by management included attempts to convince those brokerage houses and others working in Mite's behalf that the offer was not sound, that it was being vigorously opposed, and that the time and effort spent in behalf of Mite would not be warranted in terms of the results.

Internally, HeliCoil took the routine steps, such as changing the terms of service of the members of the board of directors, that might make a take-over more difficult.

And with all this, and despite the apparent validity of its point of view, Mite won.

Not only did many of the smaller shareholders tender their stock to Mite, but many of the holders of large blocks—thought to be allies of HeliCoil management—also caved in and tendered their shares.

There were two reasons for this. One, aside from personality problems peculiar to this particular case, which arose in the heat and anxiety of the battle, was that management second-guessed experienced professionals in too many instances.

The second and more pertinent reason is that although the take-over attempt was foreseeable, it was not taken seriously until it was too late. In fact, when a take-over attempt reaches a point at which it is known to management, it is most often too late.

PREVENTING A TAKE-OVER

Other than the steps outlined thus far, and the obvious one of not allowing management holdings to fall too deeply into too great a minority position, what could have been done to prevent this take-over?

First of all, the company should have audited itself for its vulnerability as a take-over candidate. The fact that management had a minority position in its own stock was clear right along. Unfortunately, even with this it had no sense of its own vulnerability, but was blinded instead by its own success without realizing that the very success contributed to its attractiveness.

Second, it read the wrong things in its own balance sheet. The exceptionally strong cash position was a point in pride for management. To the prospective raider that cash position was a beacon light, as is often the case in these kinds of situations. It was that cash that ultimately paid for the cost of the take-over.

Third, the company began its investor relations program too late, even though that program, both internally and externally, was well executed. It was a sound one, but only for a normal, well-run company—not for a company that had reason to be defensive.

Fourth, the company did not know enough about its own shareholders until it was forced to find out under fire. The transfer sheets were not sufficiently nor frequently analyzed to determine a normal buying and selling pattern for the stock, so that it could recognize an abnormal one.

Furthermore, the company, as do most companies, made only cursory efforts to reach shareholders in Street name or trusts, nor was there any monitoring of the degree to which the proxy departments of the various brokerage firms holding shares in Street names were doing an effective job of distributing company material. When the attempt to reach these shareholders was made during the proxy fight, the number of proxy departments found to be doing a haphazard job was appalling. Presumably a good many of these brokerage houses are now out of business or merged, and those that remain are responsible ones. But, it never hurts to find out beforehand, when there really isn't any urgent reason to know.

Fifth, management in its anxiety did not rely on its professionals—its financial relations counsel, the proxy firm it hired, and its attorneys. It second-guessed, ignoring the fact that the professional not only has the technical ability and the experience to deal with these matters, but can do so dispassionately and objectively.

And last—peculiar to this particular fight—management panicked, which was uncharacteristic of a leadership that had otherwise done a tremendously effective job in building the company. Because the chief executive officer of the company had been its founder and had seen it through some extraordinarily difficult times, he was emotionally involved in the struggle. Quite understandably, this emotional reaction precluded clear cold thought and the ability to rely on professionals when it was needed most.

The moral of the story is that take-over attempts, perhaps more than any other business conditions, are predictable, foreseeable, and therefore frequently preventable.

In recent years, take-over attempts have been considerably curbed by more than just economics. New laws, as well as accounting changes, have restrained at least some of the excesses of the raiders of the 1960s.

In 1969, the Mills Acts was passed into law. It limits the amount of debt that can be exchanged for equity in a take-over, while still permitting interest payments to qualify as a cost for tax purposes. The Williams Act requires that any individual or corporation making a tender offer must file a variety of facts with the SEC, if after the termination of the tender offer the tendering corporation would directly or indirectly be the beneficial owner of more than 5% of the class of stock for which it is tendering. The advantage to the corporation being raided is that the necessity to file this information makes it more difficult for the raider to function by surprise—an important factor in any take-over attempt. Furthermore, should the raider fail to file, the tender offer—and even the take-over, if it's gone that far—may be voided. At the same time, the Williams Act places a restriction on both parties against false and misleading statements to shareholders. As a result of the Williams Act, many recent take-over attempts have failed, either by virtue of having lost the element of surprise, or as a result of subsequent law suits.

Another defense against take-overs is antitrust law. Since the Justice Department and the Federal Trade Commission positions on antitrust vary from one administration to the next, it's always a good idea, when defending against a take-over, to run to the FTC and the Justice Department, on the possibility that the attempt can be aborted.

The changes in the accounting rules make many take-over attempts much less appetizing. Pooling of interests, where the combined earnings of two companies are reported as one, regardless of the length of time the two companies have been combined, is no longer acceptable in most cases. Goodwill must now be shown on the balance sheet and written off through annual charges against income over a maximum of 40 years.

Nevertheless, these stringent regulations, both legal and accounting, have not entirely precluded take-over attempts. The best defense still lies in preparation before the fact.

TAKE-OVER DEFENSES

Experience tells us that by the time a company knows of an attempt to take it over, it's often too late. The wise company takes steps to defend itself against take-overs well in advance of any threat. It will have a carefully devised defensive plan—frequently updated—much before the need for it. This becomes increasingly important at times when stock prices and price/earnings ratios are very low. In June 1974, Chrysler Corporation's book value was $49 per share. The market price of Chrysler stock was below $12. An outsider might have bought more than 50% of the stock for $425 million by offering shareholders a $3 premium on market price, or $15 a share. Moreover, it would have cost the buyer practically nothing if, upon purchase of controlling interest, he liquidated Chrysler Realty Corporation, a wholly owned subsidiary with total assets in excess of $535 million.

Low stock prices have created this kind of vulnerability in hundreds of companies in the United States. At the same time, there is increasing concern over how the Arabs will use their very large sums of newly acquired petrodollars. In an economic climate in which stocks are selling at a fraction of their book values, preventive measures should be very much the concern of any potentially vulnerable corporation. In fact, this concern has reached such proportions that many members of Congress, anxious that no defense contractors be subject to foreign take-over, have at the time of this writing begun to explore new legislation to make foreign control of American companies increasingly difficult.

The defensive plan should analyze every possible reason why the company might be attractive or vulnerable to take-over, determine what protective measures can be taken immediately, and, in the event of an actual take-over attempt, what must be done—step-by-step and day-by-day—to defend the company. Every possible action should be anticipated, including timetable, assignment of responsibilities, and all legal and other steps that might be taken. It should be designed for effective action on a moment's notice.

There are many anticipatory steps that can be taken well in advance, other than those already described:

1. Maintaining the best possible liaison with shareholders is still the best defense. The battle can be won or lost in the first 48 hours of a take-over attempt, solely on the ability to reach shareholders before they have a chance to take action simply on the basis of a small premium on their stock. And shareholders whose loyalty has been nurtured are more receptive than those who rarely hear from management.

2. Bylaws should be reviewed defensively. Many companies change their bylaws to divide boards of directors into three groups, each of whose term of office expires in different years. Bylaws can also be changed to prevent removal of directors except for cause and, as an even stronger measure in some states that legally allow it, to require 80% shareholder approval of any merger.

3. Many companies, recognizing the necessity for fast action in preventing a take-over, have strengthened the executive committee to build a stronger and faster acting fighting body, and a few have even restructured their boards to include only members who live close enough to the company to get to a meeting on a moment's notice.

4. In a tender offer, the enemy in the first instance is not the tendering company, but the arbitrageur. An arbitrageur is a stock trader who profits by taking advantage of different prices in different markets. In a tender offer, a fast-acting arbitrageur can buy a tremendous amount of stock at trading price before the market is fully affected by the offer, and then resell it to the tendering company at the higher price of the offer. Since the arbitrageur deals in very large quantities of stock, he is willing to work for a very small spread in the stock price. This is one of the major reasons why it is essential to reach stockholders in the first 24 to 48 hours following the announcement of the tender offer—to prevent selling to arbitrageurs.

5. A listed company, particularly one with good relations with its

listing officer, can sometimes arrange to have trading halted in its stock for a day or two in order to allow time to prepare a defensive statement. For an unlisted company, the SEC can sometimes be prevailed upon to do it. This serves not only to allow time to develop the defensive position, but to put the defensive plan into action as well. It also puts a severe crimp in the activities of the arbitrageurs.

6. The defensive plan should also anticipate all the legal defenses that might be available, such as an antitrust suit. When Standard Oil of Indiana announced its intention to take over Occidental Petroleum, this was Occidental's first defense.

Still the best defense of all is for a company to recognize both its attractiveness to others and its vulnerability before that attractive and vulnerable position is forced to become a defensive one.

HOLDERS IN STREET NAME

Inherent in this whole situation is an area of stock market operation, the details of which seem to be a mystery to an extraordinary number of corporate executives. This is the holder in Street name or trusteeship.

Many shareholders, for a wide variety of reasons such as the ease of stock transfer, choose to have their stock held by their brokers. Other shareholders maintain their stock in trust portfolios, such as those administered by banks, or under discretionary management, where the manager has the legal power of attorney to buy and sell shares in its own name without consulting with the actual owner of the stock. The number of shares of stock held in these ways is vast. It constitutes a large body of shareholders that can be reached, often most unsatisfactorily, only through a third party. It is very difficult to build shareholder loyalty when you don't know who your shareholders are.

When a broker holds shares of stock for an investor in Street name, it is the broker who is the holder of record for those shares, even though the shares are legally owned by the investor. The investor is the beneficial holder.

The beneficial holder may vote his shares only through the holder of record. Thus when a broker's name appears on the transfer sheets as the holder of a number of shares of stock, there is no way of knowing how many shareholders actually own the shares, or even how many of those shares are owned by the brokerage house itself in its own account.

When a proxy statement is sent to shareholders, the proxy department of a brokerage firm will request a quantity of proxy statements and proxy material to be sent to the beneficial shareholders. Since the request for this material is frequently made several weeks in advance of the time of mailing, the number is approximate because shareholdings can change overnight. The brokerage house then forwards this material to the beneficial holders. Since brokerage houses cannot always be relied upon to make this request sufficiently in advance, it is a good idea to anticipate the request by sending a questionnaire to each broker on the transfer sheets. It can be a two-part business reply postcard, requesting information on the size of their holdings and the exact amount of proxy material they will need. This goes a long way to assure the distribution of this material to shareholders in Street name.

When the proxy material is received by the brokerage firm, its proxy department then sends it on to the beneficial shareholder. At least 30 to 45 days should be allowed for this procedure prior to the meeting at which the proxies are to be used.

The beneficial holder then designates the way his proxies are to be voted and returns the information not to the corporation, but to the broker. *Only the broker, as shareholder of record, may vote.* However, he votes on the instructions of the beneficial shareholder, combining his votes in one total number for, and another against. Traditionally, brokers assume that any proxy unreturned by the beneficial holder is a vote in favor of management's proposals, and usually votes accordingly. Moreover, a traditional 10-day "rule" applies. The broker, at his option, may vote all proxies if he has not had any instructions from the beneficial shareholder 10 days prior to the meeting. This is a general practice rather than a hard and fast rule, and normally does not apply in cases of proxy fights, where votes may be held until the last minute.

It is important to note that brokers, trustees, or any other individual or organization who holds shares of stock for someone else is under strict obligation to maintain the privacy of the beneficial holder. Under no circumstances will any holder of record reveal the name or identity of any beneficial holder, and any attempt to discover the identity of the beneficial holder through any but his own volition will be strictly rebuffed. He can be reached only through the holder of record. The exception is that, under a law passed in 1970, the identity of any holder of more than 5% of any one class of stock in a company must be disclosed.

This is sometimes even further complicated by smaller brokerage firms that use a second firm as their clearing house. This is usually the case in the smaller out-of-town firms which use a New York correspondent. The holder of record may be the beneficial holder's stockbroker, but the link between the beneficial holder and the stockbroker is the clearing firm. This is one more step between the corporation and the true owner.

CEDE & CO.

Cede & Co. is a name that appears frequently on the transfer sheets of listed companies and the more heavily traded over-the-counter companies. It is an unusual operation.

Cede & Co. is the name—the nominee—for Depository Trust Company. This is an operation established by the securities industry to facilitate interbroker transactions. When stock is bought or sold, it is deposited with Cede & Co., which then appears on the transfer sheets as the shareholder of record until the stock is transferred by Cede to the new shareholder or broker.

To reach the beneficial shareholder listed through Cede, then, the corporation must go to the broker who is the shareholder of record, then through the correspondent if there is one, and then through Cede.

Cede makes it simpler to some degree. If a corporation's shares are held by Cede, it should be receiving a monthly printout from them showing the names and positions of the brokers or banks which have deposited their shares with Cede. If the corporation does not receive these printouts, they can be arranged for directly with Cede in New York. Their address is 55 Water Street, New York, New York 10041. Since Cede is a transitory operation by its nature, any proxy material to be sent out should be established from a printout from Cede, dated as closely as possible to the mailing date of the material. Cede will supply a fresh printout for the exact record date required, as well as its monthly reports. To determine the exact number of shares held in Street name by any one broker, the number of shares listed by the broker as holder of record must be combined with the number of shares Cede records for that broker on its transfer sheets.

Remember also that when shares are held by Cede, even in behalf of a broker, it is Cede and not the broker who is the holder of record for those shares. For those shares held by Cede, the broker will turn over proxy instructions to Cede for forwarding to the corporation, although the broker may occasionally ask that Cede supply the signed proxy to the broker to be returned with the proxies he already holds.

NOMINEES

Nominees are firms that represent large shareholdings either held in trust, as by banks, or by other institutions. Nominees do not register under their own names; they take an artificially contrived name to designate their identity as shareholders of record. In passing along proxy material, they must be dealt with in exactly the same way as brokers, and they vote the shares they represent in the same way as well. The difference is that since they are predominantly representatives with authority to act for the alternate beneficiary, they do not have to get the approval of the individual beneficial shareholders they represent in order to vote a proxy. They do not accumulate proxies, nor do they have a 10-day rule. The nominee merely passes the proxy material on to the beneficial holder, who can if he wishes, return the proxy directly. This is a matter of agreement between the nominee and the beneficial holder.

Since nominees use names which do not indicate their principal, it is sometimes difficult to distinguish brokers from nominees on the transfer sheets. Brokers can be identified in Standard and Poor's directory, *Security Dealers of North America*. Nominees can be identified from a directory called *The Nominee List*, published by the American Society of Corporate Secretaries, Inc., 1 Rockefeller Plaza, New York, New York 10020. It should be remembered, though, that nominees are also absolutely recalcitrant about identifying the individual shareholders they represent.

From the Street name and nominee structure it should become clear that it is virtually impossible to identify any potential raider who is quietly buying up a stock. Larger companies engaging in a take-over attempt frequently use several brokers or nominees to purchase holdings in smaller quantities. This is why it is extremely important to scrutinize the transfer sheets regularly to determine unusual buying trends. Watch for the sudden and frequent appearance of new brokers as holders of record or for new nominee names. While the attempt to fathom the meaning of unusual buying patterns or unusual stock activity can be tremendously frustrating, it is still worth the effort. It at least supplies a clue that something unusual is happening. And the first clue is sometimes unusual stock activity—a sharp rise or drop in volume or stock price may be a warning sign of something—even if it's only a rumor regarding the company. The corporate management that pays attention to these signs may not sleep better at night, but it retains control of its company.

Since most Street name holders do so for reasons not usually connected with aggressive take-overs, there is nothing untoward—it is even wise— in making an attempt to make contact with them directly. This is done by including a note in the annual report or in any other shareholder material that will reach them through their nominees, suggesting that the company will be delighted to further supply additional copies of shareholder material, or to answer questions directly from any beneficial shareholder. This frequently works well, and in no way subverts the efforts or activities of either brokers or nominees.

Whether it is to win a proxy fight or to garner votes for management on a controversial issue or merely to maintain good shareholder relations, communications with the large body of shareholders that holds stock in Street name is every bit as important to the company as it is with the shareholder of record who can be reached directly. Every feasible effort should be made by the company to reach every one of its shareholders as part of its investor relations program.

CHAPTER 9

THE INVESTMENT BANKER

It is impossible to function in the capital markets without a clear under-standing of the investment banker and the role he plays in them.

Many a corporation—and many an investor, perhaps unknowingly—has been the beneficiary of a brilliant investment banker's structuring of an extraordinary deal, or his imaginative pricing of a new public issue, or his prodigious input or exceptional business acumen.

Many an investor, on the other hand, has lost his shirt because, in the name of investment banking, somebody took a company public in the wrong way for the wrong reasons, or didn't follow through with after-market support, or didn't understand and have access to alternate sources of capital, or was not sophisticated enough to understand the relationship between a corporation and the economy in which it was functioning, or didn't understand the nature of the stock market itself.

To the vast nonfinancial community, ranging from the housewife to the small investor, and sometimes including even the heads of many major companies, Wall Street—the financial world—is regarded with a measure of awe. Virtually no distinction is made among the many categories in a Wall Street firm—the broker, the securities analyst the trader, the research director, the investment banker. They are all Wall Street, they are all financial wizards, they are all a breed apart from ordinary men.

To the man in the street, or the ordinary investor, the people of the financial community are wizards who manipulate millions of dollars daily, functioning with a knowledge and a power both intricate and mysterious. To the heads of most businesses, Wall Street represents a source of vital capital. But even to a great many captains of industry, there is virtually no understanding of how Wall Street really works in supplying capital; no real distinction of the separate and distinct roles played by each specialty, and how each functions in behalf of the businessman. In fact, so lacking in this knowledge are many company presidents that they are ignorant of even the most primitive criteria for selecting one financial institution over another to serve their most vital financial needs.

Little known and little written about, this lack of knowledge about the role of investment banking has given significant friction to the American economy. In fact, the investment banker, a most important practitioner of the financial arts, is the Wall Street figure about whom the least is known and understood.

First, the term is the most loosely used on Wall Street, despite the fact that the ideal role of the investment banker is most precise.

Second, the role the investment banker has played in our economic system has been changing acutely—and will continue to do so in the foreseeable future.

While the role of the intermediary between capital source and business is by no means new in America, the investment banker as we know him today is a relatively recent breed. He is a child of the burgeoning economy of the United States since the turn of the century. He is, at best, an invention of industry whose role is more defined by the demands of the economy than the other way around.

But the economy continues to change; continues to increase in diversity and complexity. Is the investment banker, in his familiar role, keeping pace? As he presently functions, is he able to serve the needs of the new economy and the new corporation? The answer, not clear-cut, is at least rapidly evolving.

As America entered the twentieth century, its business was created and nurtured as a powerful force. New distribution and production methods, and the changing balance from agricultural to an industrial economy, created new markets to be served and new technologies to be exploited. Capital was required in progressively increasing amounts to fuel this growth and expansion. This geometric growth of American industry and its insatiable appetite for capital generated a need for a new kind of functionary—one capable of opening a channel to larger sources of capital. It was to fill this need that the investment banker emerged in the form in which we currently find him.

Today, three-quarters of a century later, the growth of our nation and the world has created an infinitely more complex and demanding economy. The changes in corporate structure to serve this economy have been acute in just the last decade alone. The demands for capital to fuel this new economy have become increasingly pressing.

But economic growth is a moving and constantly evolving force. So, therefore, must be the sources of capital and the techniques for finding and channeling that capital into the economy.

The earlier needs placed upon the investment banker by industry were relatively simple and accommodating. The relationship between the corporation and the investment banker then went from accommodating to comfortable to static and, ultimately, to traditional. Practices and structures froze in form—accepted and unquestioned.

In earlier, simpler times, the investment banker played more of a principal's role. His own capital was often the equity used to begin or to enlarge the enterprise, with small help from institutions, foreign investors, and an elite but small section of the public then in the market place. Because investment bankers and their associates frequently owned controlling portions, they could and did exercise rights of ownership. Many managers routinely came to Wall Street for key decisions. Investment bankers served as directors to represent their ownership, and they even helped to engineer the wave of mergers which created the corporate giants in the 1920s.

This relationship was by and large successful. Gradually, through the 1920s, the public began to find equity investment more interesting, and sought to emulate the financial success of the better known bankers. But by the time the great depression arrived, they were still a relatively small part of the ownership of American business.

The events following the depression, and again following World War II, dramatically altered the role of the investment banker. His appetite and capacity for direct equity ownership decreased markedly. Following World War II, prodigious amounts of new capital were necessary to propel the new economy. But large corporations had become better known to the public, and the investing public's focus was aimed more at the corporation than at the investment banker, upon whom the public had formerly relied as a source of information for investing. Public confidence, enhanced by government regulation, also fostered the concept of direct investing. Close corporate ties became more difficult and less rewarding for the investment banker.

As a result, investment bankers became more agent than principal. Control was now in the hands of a larger and more diffuse ownership—one that was more interested in dividends and stock market performance than in the direct relationship between operations and the increase in asset value. And as the post-World War II economy snowballed at breakneck pace, markets increased and corporations grew bigger to serve those markets. As the economy boomed, it generated even more purchasing power and, obviously, markets increased again. The need for capital to fuel this growth became more acute. New corporate structures were necessary to service this burgeoning market, and new management techniques and controls were necessary to run the growing corporations. There was an increasing need not only for managerial talent, but for more sophisticated input of the kinds of information necessary to help guide the corporation in its growth.

By the 1960s, the rush for infusion of capital was primarily equities oriented, and the role of the investment banker had almost entirely changed from that of the involved investor he had been earlier to that of a kind of commodity broker, simply supplying capital as one of the many necessary elements for modern corporate growth. He was little more than a funnel to move public funds into the corporation. The burden of the increasing need for sophisticated management and financial control now fell readily and almost entirely upon corporate shoulders, where once, in simpler times, it had very much been the bailiwick of the investment banker as an active partner of management.

Both partners prospered in their expanded, newly defined roles. The fees that came from raising huge amounts of capital kept underwriters well fed. A new kind of securities analyst and portfolio manager developed to make after-markets—and investment profits—from a broadened base of the investing public.

With the phenomenal growth of the equities market in the 1960s, investment banking, in many firms and generally, began to take a back seat to the equities-selling aspect of the securities industry. Since it was so easy for companies to go public, little was required of the investment banker beyond the underwriting of a securities issue. Securities firms shifted their emphasis to stock peddling, and vast structures were erected solely for that purpose. Branch offices proliferated, and brokers—registered representatives—were sent out to sell stock as quickly as they could be trained. The industry found itself less concerned with capitalization than with recycling stock at a profit to the brokerage firm. In this climate, there was virtually no opportunity for the investment banker to be much more than an underwriter, since it was believed—erroneously, as it subsequently turned out—that the answer to any corporation's problem was more money from the public.

When the bubble burst in 1970, and again in 1974, and the securities industry was hit with a disastrous wave of bankruptcies and forced mergers, the investment banker in a great many firms, regardless of his capabilities, went down the drain along with the stock peddling arm of his company.

Now, in the mid-1970s, the structures of both the corporation and the investment banking industry have again changed considerably. What is more significant is that the change is far from complete. More than at any other time in the financial history of this country, the relationship between industry and Wall Street is altering in almost a kaleidoscope fashion, and at a breakneck speed. It seems clear that at the other end of the tunnel, two to five years from now, the relationship that emerges will not only be different, but will be predicated upon a different configuration of requirements and abilities. While the precise nature of that relationship is difficult to predict, it becomes increasingly obvious that the partnership between Main Street and Wall Street will continue. But it is also obvious that the nature of the partnership must take some new forms if it is to survive—if it is not to develop into a structure that spells disaster for both the corporation and the investment banker.

It seems unlikely that the securities industry will repeat the mistakes of the 1960s, in building investment banking firms predicated predominantly on stock distribution, at least in the foreseeable future. Not that the industry can be depended upon to have learned a lesson from its past mistakes, so much as that changes in the economy and government-dictated changes in securities practice will substantially alter the nature of the business in the future. The institution of negotiated rates, for example, virtually guarantees substantial alteration of the industry. More important, the increased complexities of a stringent economic climate, where capital is even harder to come by than it has been for many years, place a tremendous burden on investment banking and the need for its services. The changes in securities practice will substantially alter the nature of the new relationship between Wall Street and Main Street is just now beginning to emerge. Like a phoenix arising from the ashes of the holocaust of 1974, the new relationship should be very different from anything that has preceded it.

Of the many avenues through which this emerging relationship can arise, there are several that can be identified and anticipated now, in which the partnership might best function to enhance the corporate economy. There are other alternatives, but they are either not feasible in terms of the economy as it is currently structured, or they will emerge as a result of some elements not immediately predictable.

One new element is the changing role of the commercial banker in corporate finance. Historically, the banker, restrained by his own sense of fiduciary responsibility as well as the Glass-Steagall Act of the 1930s, which removed banks from the securities industry, has played a limited role in corporate finance. Until very recently, banks were little more than simple-interest lenders. But in recent years, many bankers have sensed the vacuum in corporate financial service created by the failure of a very large segment of the investment banking industry to serve contemporary corporate needs. As a result, more and more banks are successfully fulfilling the investment banking function for many corporations, short of transgressing the Glass-Steagall Act and selling securities. Some of the most sophisticated financial advice and service now being supplied to corporations are coming from the friendly neighborhood banker, instead of the investment banker.

The shifting pools of capital are another element that is altering the role of the investment banker. Insurance companies, for example, have become a major capital pool.

While capital from insurance companies has always been simply funds available for investment, these funds have become so large that many major insurance companies have gradually shifted their focus from the insurance business to the investment business, and have done so to such a degree that questions are now arising as to whether insurance reserves are being too heavily invested, to the degree that they are no longer adequate for insurance needs.

The growth of pension funds has created another large pool of capital for investment—and opened new areas and opportunities for serving capital needs. Even under the new Employee Retirement Income Security Act of 1974, which places great stringency on pension fund investing, the funds still represent a vast source of investment capital.

Another significant shift in capital is the petrodollar—the vast funds now in the hands of the oil-rich Arab countries. As of this writing, the uncertainty as to how this capital will be used nags at every segment of the American economic community.

It is from this amorphous base that the changing role of the investment banker will emerge. There are a number of possibilities that begin to become clear.

One of the feasible avenues for change is for the investment banker to remain in his present role as an agent representing sources of capital for the corporation, but with expanded ancillary services and a new perspective on his role, predicated upon both the changing economy and the changing needs of the corporation. Another is for the investment banker to revert to his former role as part-time principal by virtue of not only his ability to assist in capitalization, but to contribute the kind of expertise and sophisticated input that industry now demands.

The changing relationship will probably be brought about in several ways:

1. An extension of current and traditional relationships, where the investment banker has demonstrated his ability to serve the corporation with not only capital, but with expertise and service.

2. Changing structures of both the corporation and investment banking practice resulting from external factors such as regulations, taxation, shifting capital pools, competition from commercial banks, and so on.

3. The rapidly expanding economy, which requires a very much more complex and sophisticated configuration of input, service, and skills that none but the very largest companies can supply internally.

4. The emergence of other sources of corporate financial service, such as the commercial bank and consultants.

The new relationship—and the new investment banker—will focus more readily on planning than on merely supplying capital. Corporate planning, after all, is predicated upon capitalization, and is the architectural structure that both applies capital and dictates the need for further capitalization.

However, corporate planning, as the term is normally used, is really far too comprehensive to adequately describe the full range of operational, marketing, and financing needs of a growing company in the next 10 years. In the past, much of corporate planning was too short range, both for lack of ability to judge the factors involved and/or lack of input.

For the medium-sized company and smaller, there is also the lack of ability to control much of its own destiny. On the other hand (and except when there is a profound shift in the economy), doesn't a General Electric, for example, virtually command its sources of growth capital, as compared to, say, the $100 million XYZ company? And isn't it generally true that the greater the command of sources of capital, the greater the potential to reduce the cost of capital? And therefore the greater likelihood of improving, also, return on investment?

Not that each follows naturally one to the other, so much as that size and success mean factors that support the likelihood of each of these things. General Electric's ability to alter the size of its market almost at will, for example, or to improve its productivity, as compared to an emerging company, gives it a capability not readily available to the smaller company. And so in the burgeoning economy of the past decade or so, emerging companies tended to be at least inept, to a large degree, in planning. But now other things are happening.

1. The total economy is getting larger, placing greater demands on companies, but also offering greater opportunities.

2. The economy is changing drastically. Not only shifts in capital pools and the petrodollar, but an economy that will undoubtedly be constricted in many years into the foreseeable future by material shortages, inadequate fuel reserves, overcapacity in some industries, and undercapacity in others —all against a backdrop of inflationary expectations which have proven self-fulfilling.

3. The markets for goods and services are getting bigger and so are the

capital needs. But then, viewing the changing international picture, the capital *sources* are changing too.

4. Corporate elements are getting more sophisticated. Today's mergers and acquisitions—and even divestitures—make the earlier wheeling and dealing look almost primitive. Marketing and distribution techniques are more complex. Inflation and shortages must be dealt with—and on an international scale for even domestic companies. There are also new factors, such as real estate as a portfolio element for corporations. And not as ancillary investment, either. Real estate is one way of controlling capital intelligently until it's needed for specific aspects of corporate growth.

5. Changes in accounting and government regulations are having an increasingly significant effect on not only ways of doing business, but on profitability and therefore the ability to capitalize. Once accounting was relatively static and straightforward in reporting those aspects of company operations that management arbitrarily deemed itself willing to disclose. Accounting is no longer passive; it's changing rapidly in the attempt to increase disclosure as well as to put it into contemporary perspective. Accounting for inventory versus accounting for real profits during inflation, for example.

6. Management is getting sharper. Better educated, better able to use new tools, better able to function easily in the larger milieu.

7. New social concepts are emerging that have very real consequences for the corporation. Health, safety, and environmental controls by government fiat move the concept of corporate social responsibility from the abstract of morality to the profit and loss statement that measures the cost of health, safety, and antipollution equipment.

In other words—new kinds of corporations functioning in new ways in a new and larger economic context. And a context that moves at a continually accelerated pace.

With this increasingly complex corporate/economic structure, there will be, obviously, a need for vastly superior input and support (financial, marketing, etc.). Granted the increasing superior structure of the corporation and the corporate manager, where is all this input and wisdom and service capability supposed to come from?

The corporation itself? Only the smallest percentage of very large companies will have even a part of all the facility needed. Obviously, an external source—and force—is imperative.

The investment banker? Not as he has been in the past, to any large degree. Historically, the investment banker has been a product of accident, rather than design. A finder of capital, but with a small measure of imagination. A diverse operator—a loose federation, in fact, of services in various stages of development. As a market maker in equity securities, he's been only as good as his weakest trader or registered representative. In fixed income securities, he's been a victim of his market. In ancillary services, such as mergers and acquisitions, real estate, asset management, discretionary investment, and even corporate financial structuring, he's been functioning within the limitations of isolated flashes of talent and initiative, acting more as an opportunist than as a professional. Until now, most investment bankers have been both the beneficiaries and victims of their own virtuosity.

But now this changes. As the new kind of corporation emerges in the 1970s, so does the new kind of investment banker.

1. As a financial institution itself, the investment banker wears a new cloak. Now his firm may be a public institution, with new sources of capital of its own, new regulation (as well as the self-discipline that is the best defense against regulation) and new relationships with exchanges, etc.

2. Changing security market structures alter the nature of the firms that function in them—and vice versa.

3. Competition among investment bankers is keener. The old school tie isn't good enough for the emerging corporation in the growing economy. You've got to *know* something if you're going to compete.

4. Experience in all of those ancillary services is now being *managed*. No more loose federations of vague semiexperts. Tightly run corporations will be served only by tightly run investment banking firms. And only tightly run investment banking firms will survive competitively.

5. With the growth of competition in investment banking expertise coming from the commercial banker and the consultant, the investment banking firms are going to have to think differently about their industry than ever before. The kind of investment banker that is needed is rare enough now. If the investment banker is going to have to compete with elements outside his own industry he will have to find ways to broaden his base of intelligence, skills, and service.

But most significantly, the investment banking firm is becoming a carefully directed fountain of expertise. And not just in consulting, either, like the management consultants whose reports reside, unacted upon, in myriad executive desk drawers. This is expertise in

1. *Input.* Not just undigested intelligence, but integrated fact, projectable experience, crosshatch of information from many industries and disciplines, and so on.

2. *Action.* Asset management. Capital supply. Merger and divestiture finding and negotiation. Market-making, in not only the company's securi-

ties, but its portfolio as well. Moving a corporation into new markets—both goods and services, and capital. International entree. And on and on.

3. *Projection.* An interplay of information and action means the ability to control, to a larger degree, the factors of a corporation's own destiny. And now we come back to the advantages of a General Electric mentioned earlier. *The greater the ability to control the factors of one's economic environment, the farther and more realistically one can project and plan.*

Now, with the input and action of the modern investment banker, corporate planning takes on a different meaning. Now it can work—and work effectively over the longer range.

And if the new investment banking firm will serve the corporation in these ways in all aspects of corporate planning, it will serve in any of the aspects of financial management.

INVESTMENT BANKING SERVICES

What exactly should the corporation expect in the way of investment banking services?

Essentially, it adds up to not only the supply of capital, but intelligence necessary to maximize the profits on that capital. It's a total range of financial services that embraces every aspect of corporate operation as it relates to capital.

Currently, there are really very few investment banking firms that are qualified to meet the needs of the growing corporation, although the number may be increasing. A typical example of one such firm is Donaldson, Lufkin & Jenrette, Inc. DLJ see its role in relation to its clients as one that begins with a thorough understanding of the corporation and its needs, to which it brings

1. Business and industrial analysis.
2. Economic, social, and political research.
3. Knowledge of financial markets and timing.
4. Tax accounting and legal skills.
5. Investment judgments.

Its list of services brings to bear on any of its clients' problems an extraordinary range of capabilities in the areas of capital raising, capital management, professional advisory services, and market-making. It delineates at least the following services in each of these four areas:

Capital Raising
    Public underwriting

Equity
Fixed income
Private placement
    Equity
    Fixed income
Lease/project financing
    Corporate equipment
    Real assets
Public finance
    Health care
    Pollution control
Mortgage brokerage
Divestitures
Creating companies
Venture capital
Real property development
Natural resource financing
Capital Management
    Portfolio management equities
        Pension funds
        Profit sharing plans
        Endowments
        Corporate
        Individual
        Public funds
    Fixed income
        Corporate funds
        Institutional funds
        Public funds
    Real estate
        Pension funds
        Public partnerships
    REIT management
    Real property management
    Personal asset management
    Venture management
Professional Advisory
    Securities—equity, fixed income, options
        Research
        Portfolio strategy
        Economic analysis
        Opinion research

Corporate development
  Merger
  Acquisition
  Corporate strategy
  Financial planning
  Communications
  Market studies
Investment advisory
  Personal assets
  Tax shelter
  Real estate
  Financial planning
Market-Making
  Stock brokerage
    Common stocks
    Preferred stocks
    Convertible securities
  Bond trading
    Government
    Corporate
    Municipal
  Block Placement
  OTC Trading
  Arbitrage
    Domestic
    Foreign
  Options
  Stock clearing services
  Real estate brokerage
  Special corporate transactions

Goldman, Sachs & Co., another major investment banking firm, offers essentially the same range of services, but with perhaps somewhat stronger capabilities in areas such as international financing and commercial paper.

It should be clearly noted that the services of these two firms are delineated as examples of the several outstanding firms in the field. Nor does size imply superiority. What is most important is intelligence and the ability to grasp the full range of a corporation's needs, and the investment banker's ability to serve that range of needs. There are several smaller investment banking firms in which the focus of talent is so intensified or so specialized that they serve the needs of the smaller corporation or the specialized needs of the larger corporation. One such very small firm,

Harlan, Betke & Myers, for example, is unexcelled in its knowledge and facility in real estate investment and financing. Its size has not precluded its contribution to the very largest corporations.

Obviously, this kind of service will not be compensated for in the old way. The fee from an occasional underwriting cannot supply the investment banker the wherewithal to pay for the kind of talent, and to run the kind of integrated organization, necessary to serve the corporation. More and more, then, investment banking firms are moving to a straight fee structure. More and more corporations, recognizing the value of a full range of services, are happily accepting the fee structure.

As a result of a recent suit, a new element has entered into the picture. Shareholders of a company that ran into difficulty—Tidal Marine International Corp.—successfully sued Shearson Hammill & Co. Inc., on the basis that as investment banker for Tiday, Shearson should have informed its brokerage clients of problems to which the investment banking side was privy. Shearson claimed that to have done so would have violated the confidential client–investment banker relationship. Paradox. The Judge ruled that Shearson Hammill should either have made the information known to its brokers and brokerage customers, or refrained from handling orders or recommending Tidal stock.

Assuming the further development of the investment banking firm as outlined here, how is the difference between the investment banker–corporation relationship ' and the broker–customer relationship reconciled? The courts gave no answer. What remains from that decision, however, is the spectre of the severance of the brokerage function from the investment banking function. A knot yet untied.

This spectre is neither intangible nor necessarily bad. More and more investment bankers are coming to recognize that the recycling of stock is not the major function of investment banking, and that it must never again be allowed to overwhelm the role of investment banking in capitalizing industry. This spectre is beginning to take shape very rapidly and may become quite tangible in the foreseeable future.

Thus the emerging investment banking firm is just that—emerging. As of the moment there are all too few investment bankers who function—or who are capable of functioning—in ways that serve the needs of the corporation. A talent here—a capability there—but very little total capacity. The answer has not yet caught up with the need, and the need is proliferating.

For the emerging corporation in need of sophisticated investment banking services, the search for it becomes arduous. As the competition for capital becomes keener, the spectrum of expertise needed to find and intelligently use the capital has not kept pace. It behooves the corporation, then, to search it out assiduously. Corporate management can no longer afford to be cavalier in accepting an investment banker relationship on superficial criteria—such as the number of retail outlets or even the prestige of the names found in its syndicate structure. Every aspect of investment banking must be reviewed, in the judgment of capability, including those for which a need is not immediately foreseen. Circumstances change. The corporation not interested at the moment in an effective real estate capability may suddenly find itself, as a result of a merger, in possession of several million dollars worth of real estate. That's hardly the time to go looking for outside real estate expertise.

CHOOSING AN INVESTMENT BANKER

In choosing an investment banker, there is always a subjective element in the judgment of intelligence, personality, and the evaluation of skills as they will be applied to the wide range of corporate problems. Nevertheless, there are a few basic points that can be considered beforehand:

1. Get the best quality available. The smaller company need not feel it must settle for second best. Very few investment banking firms will refuse to discuss a relationship with any company of any size that can demonstrate real growth potential. Don't be put off by awe for the name of a Donaldson, Lufkin & Jenrette, a Goldman Sachs, a Lazard, a Morgan Stanley, a Lehman Brothers, or a First Boston. An investment banker is interested in the future as well as the past or present. But don't be unduly flattered, either, by being approached by a name firm.

2. On the other hand, don't be overimpressed by reputation. A lot of history has gone into building that reputation, but it may be just history. Or the reputation may have been built on elements irrelevant to a corporation's particular needs. A firm's present investment banking skills may not be sufficiently broad and innovative to deal effectively with today's capital markets and corporate needs.

3. The really supurb firms will dazzle you not with their history or reputations or private dining rooms, but with their people. At the point of day-to-day contact, it is an individual with whom management must work, and not a firm's history. Nor are one or two superstars an indication of depth of capability and service.

4. In this context, some newer and smaller firms have more capability to offer than do many of the older giants. Size and age are sparse measures of investment banking skill.

5. The number and size of deals a firm has done are less a measure of capability then the *kinds* of deals they have put together, and the imagination with which they have been formulated in times when a more traditional approach to financing has not been possible. Aggregate amounts of private placements they have done will not help a corporation if it needs $2 million in a tight market, and the investment banker can only boast of $25 million placements for blue chip companies.

6. Ask questions. Lots of them. Simple and broad questions are the best, the better to gauge the investment banker's ability to grasp and understand a company, its industry, companies of comparable size, and the company's specific problems. See how thoughtful are the answers—or how glib and evasive.

7. Ask to speak to their clients, especially those in comparable positions. Was performance as promised? Did the investment banker understand at all times the dimensions and difficulties of all the problems? Was the range of service broad and intensive? Was the strategy functioning as planned? Did initiative come consistantly from the investment banker, or was prodding necessary?

8. Don't go to an investment banker for the wrong reasons. Don't hire an investment banker because he promises to support your ailing stock price with research reports you might not otherwise get from the Street, and certainly don't retain one that promises shallow short-term solutions when you have long-range problems.

These are the basic points to consider and basic approaches to use. And one more thing—don't be romanced by an investment banker. That's how so many companies got taken public in the 1960s—companies that are now either out of business, or undercapitalized or looking to go private again.

It is most important to remember, in choosing an investment banker, that times and the economy have changed. This is now the time of full service, the time for the broadest possible understanding of the full range of corporate needs and how to serve them, and the time for greater sophistication than ever before. The investment banking hero of the vast debt placement for the giant company is not necessarily the man capable of the hybrid deal so important today for the smaller or medium-sized company—nor is he always right to serve the full range of corporate needs for the emerging company. The investment banker of the past is clearly not the investment banker of the future.

A thorny point. Many companies have on their boards a representative of the underwriter who first did the public offering. Too often, this board member sees the investment banking function subjectively, in terms of the limitations of his own firm. His presence on the board should not preclude objectivity in the search for sound investment banking relationships.

The point has been made that the securities industry is in the greatest state of flux it has seen in the financial history of our country. The facts are too commonly known to review here. However, one thing becomes crystal clear. In whatever form the industry ultimately evolves, it must be predicated on its primary purpose—to finance industry, not merely to sell securities. No matter what else happens to alter the structure of the securities industry, that remains primary.

More than just a conduit to the capital markets, the investment banker is a primary factor in any corporation's operations. No company begins without capital, and no company functions without capital. Not to understand the investment banking structure and its relation to the capital markets is a weakness that no company can allow itself in today's economy.

CHAPTER 10

STRATEGY

During the bull market of the late 1960s, when merely the availability of stock in virtually any company was sufficient to warrant its rise in price, financial relations firms simply had to perform their mechanical routines, and then scratch their bellies with self-satisfied glee as their client's stock prices rose. Today, after two severe bear markets and a couple of recessions, the market no longer responds so readily to just mechanics.

It is said that a head cold, carefully treated, will get better in seven days. Untreated, the cure takes a week. By the same token it can be difficult to gauge the effectiveness of financial relations efforts in a bull market. Something is working and, as noted in the first chapter, undoubtedly financial relations is making its mark. But whether these same activities, in the same configuration, will have the same effect in a bear market is yet another question.

Two things seem abundantly clear, however. One is that as the nature of the stock market and the other capital markets has changed, so has the degree of effectiveness of each of the devices used in financial relations. Secondly, as the financial community becomes increasingly insensitive to certain financial relations activities—if for no other reason than that the financial community is sharply altered—then it becomes clear that things must be done differently.

This is not to say that the mechanics of a financial relations program are of themselves not sound. Every technique delineated in this book continues, in its own way, to be effective. What is significant, though, is that the strategy for using these devices changes as the structure of the financial community changes. That strategy consists of priority, degree, and timing.

Priority is a function of the changing value of each technique relative to the others. There are times when an intensive program of security analyst meetings has a greater potential for effectiveness, relatively, than a full-blown press relations programs. There are times when it is the other way around. The one activity takes priority in the program over the other.

The degree to which emphasis is placed on each activity is yet another function of the nature of both the market and the company. There is only so much time and so much budget available for any corporate program. The allocation of effort depends upon the structure and receptivity of the various aspects of the financial community, as well as the structure and performance of the company at any given moment.

Timing is that sensitive element that not only dictates the exact point at which something should be done, but whether a particular activity should be undertaken at all at any given moment, in terms of the structure of the financial community.

Unfortunately, financial relations is not a science, and it can hardly be called an art form. It is a skill and a perspective. Planning a program calls for a strong measure of understanding of reality, along with a knowledge of the structure of the capital markets at any given moment, as well as of the company in all its aspects. To be insensitive to the structure of the market and to rely merely on mechanical techniques mindlessly performed, simply because that is the way they have always been performed, is foolish, wasteful, and expensive. It is also frustrating, since the results can be relied upon to be negative in relation to the effort. There is no such thing as a standard financial relations program that will work effectively for every company. There is no such thing as reaching into a drawer to pull out Plan A as a program to meet the needs of all companies. Each company has its own needs, its own problems, its own strong points to sell to the financial community, and its own weak points to overcome.

In that sense, there is no single financial community. Throughout this book we have talked of the financial community as a unified body. Realistically, it exists and is defined only in terms of a company's trying to establish a liaison with it. Obviously, the financial community for a petroleum company showing a fantastic increase in profits as a result of an energy crisis is very different from that of a capital intensive public utility trying to find funds when it is already highly leveraged, the prime rate is hovering around 12%, and there is virtually no viable equities market. The financial community is very different for a company with a float of 300,000 shares than it is for a company with a float of more than a million shares. The company with a five-year annual growth rate of 27%, virtually no debt, and a strong market for its products deals with a very different financial community than a company, no matter how sound, that has just come through several very bad years and yet has a potential for ultimate success and growth.

And so the strategy for a financial relations program for every company must be specifically tailored to it. Some rather specific factors must be taken into consideration, catalyzed by a large dose of intelligence—perhaps wisdom—perspective, foresight, and basic knowledge of both the capital markets and the company. Among the elements to be considered are:

1. The nature of the capital markets.
2. The company itself.
   a. The nature of its business.
   b. Its strengths and weaknesses.
   c. Its size.
   d. The size of its float.
   e. Its particular problems.
   f. Special factors or activities.
3. The state of the economy, including special problems such as an energy crisis, material shortages, or ecology.
4. The nature of its industry.
5. Credibility.

One thing is certain—the nature of the market will change. Perhaps some day the economists will develop the formula for tuning the economy so that it will be absolutely controllable. But it won't be this week. In the meantime, it can be said with some measure of certainty that if the market is up it will ultimately go down, and if the market is down it will ultimately go up. This is small consolation for the corporate president whose stock is selling at four times earnings while plans for a necessary expansion sit, unable to be financed, on his desk. But whatever the nature of the market, at any given moment, two things are clear. First, any public company must continue to function within the framework of that market. And second, no company can expect the market to react immediately to its efforts in the normal course of events. And so the financial relations program must be an ongoing effort in bad times if it is to be successful in good times. When there is an upward market shift, the first companies to come back are those that are best known and understood by the financial community.

Another point. There is no such thing as a normal market. When the Dow Jones average is in the six or seven hundreds, there is a tendency to speak of the "current market" as if the roaring bull markets of the late 1960s were the normal market. As Richard Hexter of Donaldson, Lufkin & Jenrette, the investment banking firm, put it in discussing a bull market, "*This* is the once and future market."

When the market is on the rise, and there is a great deal of buying power, and the economy is strong, and the banks and institutions have lots of money to lend, the emphasis is on reaching as many analysts as can be interested in the company. If the company is performing well, and the economy is sound, and there is a favorable future foreseen for the company's industry, the task is relatively simple. The focus is on analysts specializing in the industry, and if the company's float is large enough, it is on the institutional analysts and analysts at brokerage houses servicing institutional customers.

If, on the other hand, the market is down then the strategy must be more acute.

In the fall of 1970 the market was thoroughly depressed. The individual investors had left in force, and those mutual funds that had survived had turned practically everything into cash to prevent further losses. There was virtually no buying power. At that time Northwest Industries, a Chicago-based conglomerate, was an essentially sound company with a stock that was grossly undervalued. The company had recently come through an unsuccessful attempt to take over another large company, and for this and various other reasons, Northwest's potential was not readily seen. And yet the potential was there.

It was determined that the only buying power in the market at the time rested with the pension funds. Since the pension funds, unlike the mutual funds, are long-term investors, day-by-day performance does not matter quite so much, and therefore there is no great urgency to pull out of the market on its down side. Pension funds, with a steady influx of contributions, tend to stay fully invested.

The problem was reaching the pension funds quickly and effectively. The most obvious answer was a nationwide series of meetings with pension fund managers and analysts. It was determined, though, that this would take too long and be too time consuming for Northwest executives.

The strategy used was to identify the three largest sources of research information for the pension funds. Just three meetings were set up, one with each of the three sources. Thus the information about the company's soundness and potential was quickly disseminated to the pension funds and buying began relatively quickly. As the stock started to rise, it was then a simple matter to begin talking to the analysts for the larger retail houses. Northwest Industries' stock recovered well before the market itself did.

There was once a time when traders were totally ignored by financial relations practitioners. The trader is a mysterious man who functions in the back office, executing buy and sell orders at the instructions of others. He is considered to be a mechanic with nerves of steel, the ability to make split-second decisions, to work under enormous pressure, and to negotiate shrewdly. With the exception of a few prominent people, such as the extraordinary Gus Levy of Goldman, Sachs, traders were viewed in some dim, dark context that seemed only ancillary to the glamorous end of the brokerage business and corporate finance.

But as the bear market entered 1974 and the so-called "two-tier" market idea emerged, there began to be a subtle shift in the buying and selling activities of Wall Street. The two-tier market was a concept derived from the fact that most analysts viewed as safe only a select number of blue-chip stocks. This was the first tier. Everything else was ignored and placed in a second tier. For a considerable period, the bulk of trading activity was in the first-tier stocks. The trouble with the concept was that, first of all, it fell apart when some of the larger companies in the first tier began to respond to the same economic ills that affected the total economy. Secondly, despite the concept's popularity, the two-tier market existed only on a relative level. It seemed to imply that no trading was being done in second-tier stocks, which of course was not the case. The market opened every day at 10:00 and closed every day at 3:30. And if volume was not what it had been a year or two earlier, trading was still being done.

It was at this point that the formerly uncourted trader began to emerge as a figure of importance, particularly for the smaller over-the-counter company. Many of the traders were actually trading in 100- or 200-share lots of stocks not otherwise heavily traded. They were taking positions—buying for their own account for resale later at a profit. To an increasing degree the over-the-counter market was—and still is—being made by traders.

When this little known fact was perceived, it was also discovered that the traders were dealing in stocks in which they had only a minimal amount of information. In those firms that had research departments, there was some information about companies being traded, but not much. In large segments of the Street, where this kind of activity was taking place, information was sparse. A trader is required to know some basics about the company he trades, but these are just bare facts. Until several financial relations consultants discovered this new and growing phenomenon, most traders were simply ignored.

In early 1974, when volume was down, brokerage houses were falling like leaves from trees in October, and purchasing power was sharply diminished. But if fewer shares of stock were traded in any one financial center, if the buying power at any geographic point became sparse, then that volume had to be made up by going abroad geographically. If each apple tree is producing fewer apples, then you have to gather apples from more trees in order to fill a bushel basket. To maintain liquidity and volume in any stock whose volume has fallen off, more houses have to become involved and the geographic base of trading must be expanded.

The point is that while the nature of the market may change, there is still a market. It must be discerned and fathomed and the strategy directed accordingly.

* If interest, attention, and maintaining the flow of information are essential, the answer to a diminished market is frequently an increased financial publicity campaign. In such cases, greater emphasis must be placed on assiduously pursuing attention in the financial and business press. If visibility cannot be achieved to a satisfactory degree by direct contact with the financial community, then it must be done indirectly through the press. For the eligible company, the Dow Joneser—the Dow Jones interview— and the Reuters interview must be sought as frequently as possible, twice or four times a year if feasible. Every aspect of the company's operation must be scouted to determine those activities which may be deemed newsworthy, and these must be energetically projected. The emphasis must shift, and shift in force. Articles must be developed for the financial and business press and interviews must be arranged.

Strategy is also dictated by the nature of the company at any given moment. A growing company is a constantly changing company. It grows internally and it grows externally to meet the changing needs of its markets and its sources of supply. As this happens, so does its relationship to the capital markets change.

It must also be recognized that the market is slow to accept a change in a corporation. When a company has been seen in one configuration, the job of changing the view of that company is enormous, unless there is some drastic and dramatic activity. It is almost as if the entire financial relations program must be started from the beginning, except that most companies change slowly and do not make a clear-cut transition. This change must be constantly monitored and communicated.

Recently, Monterey Life Systems, a successful company in the nursing home field, underwent such a change. While the greater part of its revenue came from the operation of nursing homes, it held strong positions in both medical technology and hospital operation. Two things happened to cause the company to reevaluate itself. The first was a severe attack on the nursing home industry for shoddy practices, both in operations and in finance. Of course, the failure of Four Seasons, a nursing home company, was well known. As a result, any company in the nursing home field, no matter how well run or successful, was tarred by the brush of the Four Seasons fiasco.

Second, management recognized that the industry itself had reached a plateau—and perhaps saturation in the near and intermediate term. Growth potential, while it still existed, was decelerating. While existing operations were still profitable and producing an excellent cash flow, the future of the company did not lie in continued emphasis on the nursing home field.

At the same time, the company recognized the tremendous growth potential in its medical technology operations, as well as in hospital management. As quickly as possible the company shifted its emphasis, its management, and its resources to medical technology and hospitals. It restructured management, increased its research and development activities, refocused its capital, and expanded its marketing structure. In a relatively short period of time the company emerged as an entirely different business. And yet until these activities were communicated through a carefully developed and executed financial relations program, the financial community was relatively ignorant of this marvelous secret.

At the time it happened, not only was the market depressed, but analysts following the nursing home industry were themselves depressed and negative. Even the superior performance of any company in that industry failed to impress anyone. The financial relations program shifted its strategy, then, from attempts to deal directly with analysts to a strong financial publicity program. The changed company was clearly described in the annual report. Press features were developed to discuss the changes in the company, to review the opportunities it saw in the industries it now emphasized, and to discuss management's point of view on all aspects of its operations. When, shortly after the financial publicity program took hold, the decision was made to go back to direct Street contact, emphasis was not on the analysts specializing in nursing homes, but on generalists, special situations people, and those following medical instrumentation and technology. To most of these analysts, the company was virtually new, and was freshly viewed, without the prejudices of the industry it formerly emphasized. Its nursing home operations were seen in a different light as well—from the point of view of their profitability.

As may be seen from this case history, the nature of the industry in which a company functions frequently plays an unduly large role in how the financial community views the company. At a time when the apparel industry was depressed, industry analysts were sour on all apparel companies, including those that were substantially out-performing the industry. When the failure of several major toy companies made industry analysts wary of Milton Bradley, a company that was well and profitably managed, the well-managed company suffered the same low multiple as the rest of its industry. When Dayco, a fairly large midwestern company had not effectively communicated the fact that only the smallest part of its profits came from the automotive industry rather than from plastic and other products, the company was awarded the same low multiples during and following the energy crisis as were the automotive companies. In each of these cases a shift in strategy was dictated. Ways had to be found to separate the company from its industry; to refocus attention on the company's performance as a company rather than as a segment of an industry.

Granted, this is difficult to do. When a company is out-performing its industry, either the management of that company is superior, or the managements of other companies in the industry are inferior, or there is something basically wrong with the industry. It can be argued that the best managed company in the buggy whip industry had no great future when the automobile was invented. On the other hand, it can be argued that if management was really that good it would have anticipated the shift in its market and taken steps to alter the nature of its business. This is what good management is about, after all. A case in point is the Ethyl Corporation. When in the mid-1960s lead in gasoline was recognized as a major source of air pollution, everyone pronounced Ethyl as good as dead, since it was a major supplier of lead additives. The company shifted its business to include industrial chemicals and other products and is still very much alive.

Changing to meet shifting economic needs is not only a function of good management, but it is precisely what must be communicated. A company is, after all, more than just a structure for producing and marketing products. It is a vehicle for making a profit—for appreciating the invested dollar. The ability of a company to appreciate the invested dollar rests not merely in its production, marketing, or distribution capacities, but also in its management—and carrying a company successfully through a negative period is precisely the role of a good management. The question is, how is this very difficult fact to be projected?

Primary, of course, is the clear-cut orientation of the facts—the way the story is presented, supplemented by a good financial publicity program.

But more important is to identify those segments of the financial community that are willing to look at a company as a successful entity rather than solely as a representative of its industry. Strictly to be avoided, in this context, are the industry specialists. They know all the reasons why not. This is a time for the generalists and the special situations analysts, for the brokers, and the traders. They are interested in success and the reasons for it, and in the potential for future success. They tend to be generally more free of prejudices regarding a particular industry than are the industry specialists. This is the time for the pension fund, with its greater emphasis on long-range investment potential, and for the institution that invests for the long term and is the kind not dependent upon the exigencies of the tape. The analysts for these groups must be identified and exposed to the company as forcefully and effectively as possible. This is not to say that the industry analysts and others in the financial community are to be ignored in terms of the normal dissemination of information, but certainly they are not the prime target. At the same time, the concept of increasing the size of the total audience applies as well. By broadening the geographic base of coverage, more potential investors can be reached.

The size of the company and particularly the size of its float—the number of shares available for purchase on the open market—are also important. Obviously, a major fund, used to buying 5000- or 10,000-share blocks of a stock, is not going to be interested in a company with a float of 250,000 shares. A purchase of 5000 shares in a company with a float that size can of itself increase the price of the stock by a substantial percentage. But that purchase also adversely affects liquidity. During the late 1960s, many smaller companies found themselves in positions where mutual funds, anticipating rapid growth and therefore a rapid increase in the price of the stock, bought large blocks, trading the price upward. At the first sign of trouble these blocks were unloaded, rapidly driving the price not only downward, but lower than it should have been in relation to the companies' real growth potential. Focusing attention on the funds, for the smaller company, then, has its dangers.

Concentration on institutions as a financial relations target must therefore be done with caution. True, there is nothing to prevent an institution from discovering the potential of a smaller company and buying a large portion of the stock, but that doesn't mean that this attention has to be sought, either.

On the other hand, for the smaller company certain kinds of institutional buying can be useful to develop a stability in the stock. There are smaller funds, smaller pension funds, private funds, and some of the more solid but less glamorous mutual funds. One of the most effective of these funds is the Over-The-Counter Fund run by Ralph Coleman in Jenkintown, Pennsylvania. Mr. Coleman, who is also publisher of *Over-The-Counter Securities Review*, has quietly and carefully built a portfolio that is not only well-balanced, but that has also tended to out-perform the market. There are special situation funds and special industry funds, many of which deal in smaller companies as well as large, and are of a size that does not consume a small float in one bite.

Special problems, or special factors or activities, frequently require a shift in strategy, not only in that they frequently need special explanation, but in that sometimes the nature of the company is altered. A company forced to divest itself of a large segment of its business by order of the Federal Trade Commission or, in an antitrust situation, by the Justice Department, must reevaluate the kind of company it has now become, and shift its financial relations strategy accordingly. It may find itself having to deal with an entirely new group of analysts and a very different segment of the financial community.

This, of course, also applies when there is a merger or acquisition.

A case in point is Maremont Corporation, a well-run Chicago-based supplier to the automotive after-market.

Some years ago, Maremont found itself under the shadow of an FTC order to divest itself of a segment of its business. Under the consent decree, it appeared that the company was to lose a substantial portion of a source of revenue, although, in fact, this was not the case. The division to be divested was comparatively new in its structure at the time, and was not yet the major contributor to profits that it might ultimately have become. As a result of the long drawn out FTC proceedings, the stock of the company was appreciably undervalued. At the time of the consent decree it was selling at around $10 a share.

The start of the program for Maremont was devoted to explaining and clarifying the exact effect of the decree on the company. This was done with a press release, which was also distributed to analysts, and through newspaper interviews and direct communications to shareholders.

Starting from a base of an undervalued stock, it was determined that the quickest way for the company to reach a price/earnings ratio appropriate to the market at the time was to focus on special situations analysts. These analysts, who concern themselves with companies that seem to be undervalued for one reason or another, were identified and a series of meetings were held with management. The story came across very effectively and the stock started to rise. As it went past $18, it became apparent that the stock would soon no longer be a special situation—that it would be appropriately priced. What was needed, it was determined, was some price stability. Groups of analysts representing or dealing with smaller and medium-sized institutions were then identified, and the emphasis of the program shifted to meetings with them. As institutional buying began, the price of the stock headed toward $30. All of this happened in the unusually short time of about one year.

With the advent of institutional buying, concern began to develop about possible liquidity problems, with large blocks of stock being held by institutions. And so the emphasis shifted once again, this time to the large retail houses such as Merrill Lynch and Bache. With the successful record in earnings to back the company, and with the sound support of institutional purchasing, the stock was readily accepted by the retail analysts, and the desired liquidity was developed. Within less than two years the stock had gone from $10 to $60, and volume was well up.

All of this adds up to the fact that the effectiveness of a financial relations program is a function of not merely the performance of its mechanics, but the intelligent and imaginative use of these mechanics in different configurations to meet changing needs. What works for one company will not necessarily work for another. What works under one set of market conditions or in one economic structure will not necessarily work in another. What worked once will not necessarily work at a different time.

Strategy has its cautions, too. In a declining market, for example, it is very easy for the company to take defensive action to try to revitalize its stock. It might declare a larger dividend, or it might try to buy blocks of its own stock.

But actions like these not only have a short term effect, they can sometimes subvert the company. Decisions to declare dividends or to repurchase stock must be viewed primarily in terms of the company's operational needs. Patience, in a down market, is sometimes a better solution than short-term action. Can that money be put to better use internally? Then the dividend or stock purchase is a poor investment. And what must be done to follow the act, to keep the stock at its new price, if the action should work? When the market goes up again, will that cash be easily reclaimed so that it could be put to better use? Short-term strategy is sometimes poor strategy.

One thing is certain, however. For any reasonably sound company, under any economic conditions in which there is still a viable stock market, no matter how diminished, a proper financial relations strategy will serve that company in its effort in the capital markets.

There is one more overriding factor that is essential for the success of any financial relations program. This is credibility. The acoustics of Wall Street are magnificent. Misrepresentation, misdirection, inflated projections —all will ultimately come home to roost and tarnish, perhaps permanently, the reputation of even the most profitable corporate management. FRB's Ted Pincus proffers a credibility equation. Credibility, he notes, equals percentage of information completeness times consistency of communication. According to Pincus, "If corporate managements have not yet discovered that their price to earnings ratios now depend upon more than their profit performance and general market conditions, then they simply haven't learned the lesson that the 1972–74 era was supposed to teach them about the credibility factor."

In other words, no strategy is complete without all elements of the credibility equation in place.

CHAPTER 11

THE FINANCIAL RELATIONS COUNSEL

The performance of this peculiar quasi-art form and technical skill known as financial relations, it should be apparent at this point, requires at least a certain amount of attention. Many corporate executives have a natural talent and affinity for visibility. Many companies are glamorous and deserve wide attention just by virtue of their own performance. After all, when a man murders his wife he doesn't need a public relations man to get his name in the paper. When the cure for the common cold is found no news editor will have to be harangued by a public relations man to report the event in detail.

But exposure for itself, without focus and adjustment for changing circumstances, can never be more than partially effective. The truly effective public relations program is one that is well rounded, and includes at least several of the elements described in this book. Obviously it requires a measure of time and attention. The question is, who is to do it?

Setting aside for the moment those facets of a company's operations that attract attention by virtue of their own performance, there are three possibilities:

1. The company's investment banker.
2. The internal financial relations executive.
3. The external financial relations counsel.

Excluded from this discussion are those ancillary services that are sometimes called upon by virtue of their ability in one or another minor facets of communications, such as the nonfinancial public relations firm or the advertising agency. As will be seen further on in this discussion, unless there is a specifically experienced and qualified person in either of these structures, neither is in any way qualified to function effectively in financial relations. Financial relations is not, after all, merely public relations directed to the financial community. It is a separate and distinct practice, and is as different from public relations as it is from advertising. The two are not interchangeable.

THE INVESTMENT BANKER

The investment banking firm would, on the face of it, seem to be a logical candidate to assist in the area of financial relations, by virtue of its involvement with the financial community. Unfortunately, this rarely turns out to be true for several reasons:

1. The investment banker, through his own research and brokerage structure, is sometimes equipped to deal solely with one facet of the financial relations program. Rarely does an investment banking or brokerage firm have the capability to deal professionally with the financial press, nor does it have the structure to direct an effective investor relations program.

2. No investment banking or brokerage firm is financially structured to supply a full-scale service, either from a physical or an economic base. Most investment banking firms are paid a fee earned from the performance of specific investment banking services, such as underwriting. To allocate time and personnel to such a nonremunerative activity, even though it helps support their clients' stock, is uneconomical, and they are not likely to give it their greatest attention.

3. It is unfortunate but true that the perspective of most brokerage houses and investment bankers is limited to the scope or their own activity. Their view of overall market conditions tends to be pervaded by conditions at the moment, which invariably means undue optimism in an up market and undue pessimism in a down market. There is all too frequently lacking the perspective necessary to develop the kind of strategy, in its totality, described in the previous chapter.

4. The pursuit of a financial relations program requires an up-to-the-minute understanding of changes in both attitude and personnel throughout the entire financial community. Investment banking firms are not geared to do this, as *au courant* as they may be with current conditions in the industry.

5. The scope of the investment banker's contacts in the financial community is usually limited to his own circle of friends and business relationships. In some cases, this may be adequate to the needs of a program. In most cases it is not.

6. There is a great potential for conflicts of interest.

On the other hand, the good investment banker or broker does have a service to perform in behalf of his client, and can contribute in some measure to an effective total financial relations program.

He certainly has a responsibility to his client to support the after-market of a new issue, and indeed any issue he has been responsible for underwriting. This includes, when appropriate, issuing a research report qualified by the fact that he is the underwriter, sponsoring and making a market in the stock, and introducing the company to those houses and institutions he knows. Certainly, no financial relations program, whether done internally or externally, should be performed without the complete cooperation and participation of the investment banker, since he is not only a beneficiary along with the company, but he is also a valuable source of information.

INTERNAL

Internal capability, if the company is of a size to warrant it, can be tremendously useful either alone or in conjunction with external counsel. If the task is assigned to a qualified person, there is a singular advantage in that the internal counsel has an ongoing feeling for the company and its activities, operations, objectives, and plans. If he is properly qualified, he can also function as a spokesman for the company in ways that even the best qualified external counsel can not.

When there is external counsel, he serves as a liaison and as coordinator. In many cases, the internal man performs most facets of the program, usually aided by a staff, as effectively as does the external counsel. Frequently, when there is good in-house capability, an external counsel is used only to supplement the staff man in designated areas. Sometimes, the staff man is highly qualified in one or several—but not all—functions of financial relations. He may be a former financial writer whose efforts in dealing with the financial press or in writing annual reports cannot be excelled. He may be a former analyst who superbly understands the needs of analysts. Or he may be a former executive of a financial relations firm, in which case his knowledge of the total financial relations function is well rounded. In these cases, it is sometimes found that the outside counsel merely supplements efforts in those areas in which his experience is not as strong as in others, or supplies additional manpower as needed, or supplies the broader perspective and expertise that should be expected of the external counsel.

In some cases, the nature of the program itself, as well as the budget available for such a program, dictates the feasibility of using internal counsel. His skills and capabilities may be all that are required to perform a program for a company at any given time (although as demonstrated in the previous chapter, these circumstances frequently change rapidly).

In determining whether internal capability is feasible, there are only two hard and fast rules. The first is that the man be properly qualified. A public relations man with no financial background, or an advertising manager with a smattering of knowledge about public relations, is in no sense qualified to function effectively in financial relations for any company of consequence, although one or the other may certainly be effective in coordinating and assisting the efforts of external counsel.

Second, it is next to useless to retain an internal financial relations counsel who does not have the ear, the respect, and direct access to the chief executive officer. Without this, the man, no matter how well qualified he may be, is merely a clerk. If he has no respect within the company for his value and capabilities, he will quickly cause the company to lose respect in the financial community and with the financial press. The financial community and the financial press are very quick to discern the degree of authority a spokesman has. To attempt to deal with the financial community through even the most highly qualified internal financial relations executive who does not have access to the inner-councils is foolhardy and wasteful.

EXTERNAL COUNSEL

Properly qualified, the external financial relations counsel has several distinct advantages that go beyond the obvious ones of manpower and physical capability. These include:

1. He is a specialist. Not merely a public relations man practicing only those aspects of financial relations with which he is familiar, his total concentration and effort is in the area of financial relations.

2. His firm is mechanically structured to deal with all aspects of a financial relations program. He is equipped for the quick dissemination of releases, as well as for direct contact with the financial community. He is geared to maintain up-to-the-minute mailing lists and lists of appropriate personnel in both the financial community and the financial press, which changes constantly.

3. His liaison with the financial community and the financial press is constant, which should make him knowledgeable of shifts in attitude and personnel, and allows him to supply an extraordinarily valuable perspective of changing needs and changing attitudes in those areas.

4. He brings to each financial relations program the breadth of experience in serving many companies with a wide variety of problems, and a broad experience in solutions.

5. He is objective. Any financial relations counsel must serve two roles —objectivity and advocacy. One is useless without the other. Advocacy that is not based on objectivity is weak, frequently irrelevant, and often borders dangerously close to creating problems of credibility.

6. His ongoing relations with the financial community frequently allow him to serve as a source of information not directly related to financial relations, such as shifting sources of capital. In fact, for the company seeking new investment banking relationships, the experienced and qualified financial relations consultant is an excellent source of information about the capabilities of a wide variety of investment bankers.

7. He is economically feasible. Whereas there are hidden overhead factors to be added to the cost of an internal counsel, the expense of an external counsel can be budgeted and he is accountable for fees and expenses. This is particularly pertinent for those consultants whose fee is based on an hourly rate, where each month's bill itemizes the amount of time spent by each executive in each of the several categories in which he is functioning for the company.

8. He is responsible and knowledgeable in the field of SEC regulation as it pertains to financial relations and disclosure. While he is neither an attorney nor an accountant, his qualifications must include, by SEC regulation, knowledge of all SEC rules that pertain to a financial relations program.

9. His staff represents the wide variety of skills—financial press, writing, and so on—necessary for a well-rounded program.

While this would seem to weigh the argument very heavily in favor of the use of external financial relations counsel, the judgment is made, in many respects, no differently than is the decision to retain house legal counsel or internal auditing staff. The use of one does not necessarily preclude the other, and frequently they supplement one another. At the same time, it must be recognized that the nature of a particular company or of a particular financial relations problem contains factors that make the internal staff sufficiently effective to defer consideration of external counsel.

Selecting a financial relations consultant is a matter of judging qualifications. Unfortunately, unlike the law or accounting, there are no legal qualifications that define or certify the financial relations counsel. It should be noted that a move is afoot, instigated by FRB's Ted Pincus, to register financial relations counsel with the SEC. This is sound for several reasons, not the least of which is that the financial relations counsel functions in many areas that are subject to SEC regulation. Until such time as that is accomplished, however, other means are necessary to determine the qualifications of such counsel.

The problem with qualifications for financial relations is a very basic one. It may best be defined by noting that very few 15-year-olds plan to be financial relations consultants when they grow up. This means that the people in the industry are drawn from no single source that has prepared them educationally for the total financial relations counsel's role. Unlike the public relations man, the financial relations counsel cannot subsist on merely an inventive mind, an outgoing personality, and the ability to express an idea on paper.

The qualifications for a financial relations counsel, or the qualifications that should be inherent in the staff of a financial relations firm, are at least the following:

1. A sound financial background. This is primary and essential. He should understand corporate finance, accounting, the investment banking 'function, and corporate structure. While not necessarily capable of professionally performing any of these tasks, he must be able to converse easily, authoritatively, and with understanding with the chief executive officer, the vice president of finance, the attorney, and the accountant.

2. He must have an intimate knowledge of the workings of the capital markets. Not just Wall Street and the stock market, although that may be his primary area of activity, but with all the capital markets, including— and this becomes increasingly important—the Eurodollar market. He must understand both the mechanics and the elan of the market in all its subtleties. He must be experienced in dealing with the entire cast of characters to be found on Wall Street from the registered representative to the security analyst to the money manager to the trader to the investment banker.

Many financial relations counsels are themselves former analysts. While this is basically good, there is a peculiar problem here. The fact that a man is a former analyst does not of itself qualify him for financial relations. A really good security analyst can earn considerably more money practicing that craft than he can in financial relations. These are the economics of both industries. Those analysts that have made the successful transition to financial relations are the ones who have done so because they feel that financial relations offers them a broader scope for their total personal needs and desires than does security analysis. Those that are successful are the ones that bring to financial relations a range of skills and interests that supplement their financial background. An analyst who fails in his career as an analyst does not automatically become a good financial relations counsel. On the other hand, many excellent analysts have joined the ranks of financial relations successfully because they have found that the wide variety of financial relations activities offers a better outlet for their interests than does security analysis alone.

3. He should have the breadth of experience of dealing with a great many firms, and facing a great many problems under all kinds of market conditions. It takes no great skill to function successfully for a company in a raging bull market. The question is whether he can function just as effectively in a bear market.

4. He should have an understanding of the full scope of corporate activity, including management, production, research and development, marketing and distribution, and finance.

5. He should have a thorough experience and knowledge of the financial press, both in its mechanics and in its ever-changing structures.

6. He should be a capable and facile writer of releases, annual and interim reports, and speeches. And this means not merely the ability to repeat the cliches of what has been done before, but to approach each problem with a fresh viewpoint. He should, in this context, be an effective communicator.

7. His firm should have the mechanical structure and the manpower to deal effectively with all facets of the financial relations program. This includes the equipment to disseminate information at appropriate speed and with professional quality to the entire financial community and financial press. Manpower should be sufficient to allocate an appropriate amount of time to each client to effectively fulfill a program. An account executive with sole responsibility for 12 clients cannot possibly serve any one of those clients effectively.

8. He should be familiar with the financial community nationally as well as locally in every major financial center of the United States. This means being knowledgeable about the various financial centers, and physically capable of dealing effectively with each of them.

9. He should himself be a sound businessman running a sound business. While the individual practitioner is sometimes useful for his experience and wisdom, if he is to serve solely as consultant he should still function in as businesslike a way as does the largest financial relations firm.

10. The financial relations firm's people who work on any account should each be intelligent, knowledgeable, and personable. While the effective financial relations counsel can speak for the company and its executives in only a limited way, and may serve for the most part only to pave the way for communications between the financial community and the chief executive officer, each man who represents the company in any capacity is doing exactly that—representing the company. Rarely does any segment of the financial community write off an inept financial relations counsel and then accept as wise and capable the management he represents. The financial relations counsel is also exactly that, a counsel. He may have all the skills, mechanical capabilities, and experience in the

world, but he is useless to a company if his judgment cannot be respected and utilized with confidence.

11. While there are several general-purpose public relations firms with excellent financial relations staffs, the likelihood is that the greater capability will lie with the firm that specializes primarily in financial relations. The situation would be comparable to using an auditor who is on the staff of a firm of attorneys. The chances are that his role is secondary to the company's primary business, leaving him without facility and sometimes without portfolio. For the company seriously competing in the capital market, financial relations is primary—not an auxiliary. And so there is greater likelihood of finding more effectiveness in a specialized rather than a generalized firm. Moreover, as has been noted before, financial relations is not public relations to the financial community. It is a highly specialized financial function.

Selecting a financial relations firm from among the several that specialize is in a sense no different from selecting an auditor or an attorney. Qualifications must be clearly established. Reputation is important. A Dun & Bradstreet rating is essential.

In choosing a firm, a preliminary interview should demonstrate not only qualification, but also an understanding of the description of the company, its problems, and its opportunities. There is probably no better rule for judging a prospective financial relations counsel than to interview him as if he were being hired as an executive vice-president. Assuming the proper qualifications, you should be as personally impressed with his firm's representative as you would expect yourself to be with any candidate for a high managerial position. That is, after all, a function he serves.

Certainly his references should be checked very carefully. These should include a broad spectrum drawn from clients, the financial press, and the financial community itself. A great deal of trust is placed in a financial relations counsel, and his responsibility in serving the company is great. No chief executive officer should retain any financial relations counsel with whom he is not totally impressed and upon whose judgment he feels he cannot rely.

JUDGING THE PROGRAM

The results of an advertising campaign can be judged by sales. The results of a public relations campaign can be judged by favorable clippings, although ultimately the larger result is usually also sales. A financial relations program, although it may result in some rather specific things such as an increase in stock price or price/earnings ratio or volume, is judged in terms of continuous effectiveness.

The nature of the capital markets, and particularly the stock market, is such that there is no immediate result visible in terms of stock price from even the most effective financial relations program. In fact, any financial relations counsel that suggests that he can increase the price of a stock is not only misrepresenting, he is probably violating the law and should be avoided.

A financial relations program will be effective in fulfilling its objectives if it successfully communicates your story to a broad and appropriate financial community. Over a period of time, an infinitely larger segment of the financial community should know, know about, and understand your company in all its aspects. There should be a clear and discernible interest in your company as a result of the financial relations program.

The ultimate results of such an interest can be, over the long run, an improved price/earnings ratio, active sponsorship of your stock, an increased number of market-makers (for an over-the-counter company), discernibly greater liquidity, and increased trading volume. However, there is unfortunately no direct one-to-one relationship between any activity or group of activities in a financial relations program and any of these results. There are too many external factors affecting the market at any given moment to allow it to be immediately responsive to any activity in a financial relations program, other than the specific news of an event or activity of momentous nature.

This is one reason why, in order to be effective, a financial relations program must be assiduously pursued over a reasonable period of time before any judgment is made about its performance. The evidence that salutary results in the capital markets are ultimately achieved is clear, however. In fact, surveys periodically taken by one major financial relations firm, for internal use only, clearly indicate that a majority of its clients consistently outperform the market. This survey is kept internal, and for the information of the firm only, in order to avoid any unwarranted promise to any client or prospective client that its financial relations effort can in any way offset the traditional mechanics of the market.

Ultimately, the best judgment of the financial relations program is the judgment of management that the various facets of the program are being intelligently and actively performed, and that the receptiveness of the financial community is evident.

There must also be consistency. Since the market, the economy, and the company are all in a constant state of flux, and since the competition for capital is exceptionally keen, the cumulative effects of a program stopped at midpoint are very quickly lost. There is very little residual value. In order to be effective, the once discontinued program must start up again, sometimes virtually from scratch.

In the final analysis, financial relations is a function of people—their intelligence, their skills, their eagerness, and their dedication. The final judgment of the success of a financial relations program is a judgment of these elements and their application.

CHAPTER 12

COMPETING FOR CAPITAL

The thrust of this book has been toward one aspect of competing for capital—the financial relations approach. Obviously, the competition for capital is infinitely more complex than can be achieved by financial relations alone. The role of financial relations in the competition for capital is, in fact, one of marketing. No matter how good the company, if it's not well known and clearly understood by all components of the capital markets, then competition for capital becomes that much more difficult.

What, then, are the other elements, in addition to financial relations, that are necessary for successful capitalization in a competitive market?

The most significant is a well-run company. No financial relations program is capable of pure cosmetics—of making a company look better than it really is. There is no such thing as a financial relations program that will take a firm that clearly misuses its assets, is incapable of coping with its markets, whose management has not clearly demonstrated its grasp of financial, marketing, and other business principles, and is not capable of demonstrating its own clear grasp of its future—and promote it to a shrewd and skeptical financial community. In earlier chapters, those elements of a company's operation to be projected are described in great detail. But no financial relations program can project what is not true or real. Again, the accoustics of Wall Street are magnificent, and a false note reverberates mightily.

To a sophisticated financial community, profitability at any given moment is not so significant as is a company's ability to use capital properly. At first glance, the more highly visible factors of success—the earnings record each quarter, the rapid growth during a boom period in the economy, high margins, and so forth—would appear to be the elements of the company most likely to succeed in the capital markets. Not so in a period of acute capital shortage. It was one thing during the 1960s, when a gullible public bought any stock that went on the market. It is quite another thing when the capital pools have not only diminished, but shifted to more conservative and sophisticated centers.

Perhaps one of the greatest weaknesses of the peculiar period of the 1960s, when the flow of capital investment from the public was at a record high, was that so much of that invested capital was misused. It was, after all, so easy to obtain that it made no difference if much of it was misapplied. The result has been that in a tight economy, so many firms that went public in the 1960s are now undercapitalized. Moreover, they lack the ability to obtain new capital under current conditions.

Basically, the capital markets must judge a company as much by intangible and subjective factors as in tangible terms, such as the profit and loss statement and the balance sheet. The earnings record by itself does not count so much as the judgment of those factors that demonstrate the continued ability to earn. The strong balance sheet in any one period is not as significant as a clear indication that management is capable of keeping the balance sheet strong in the future.

Capitalism, after all, means a return on investment. The company that successfully competes for capital under any conditions is the one best in a position to demonstrate that the capital will be most profitably used. There is a significant difference between capitalization for expansion, growth, improvement of facilities, and so on, and capitalization for working capital when the need is for working capital to make up for the failure of earnings. In the latter case, the company is doomed to failure. This would seem obvious, except that there are too many examples of its happening. Unfortunately, many companies that did this were aided and abetted by investment bankers who should have known better.

Nor is size alone a measure of a company's success. Witness the problems of Pan American, Lockheed, and Chrysler.

The atmosphere in the capital markets has changed abruptly, as have the markets themselves. The happy times of easy and uncomplicated financing of the 1960s are gone—perhaps forever, perhaps not, but certainly for the foreseeable future. They cannot be expected to return to what they had been before, even after the 1974–1975 recession. The burgeoning economy that began shortly after World War II seems to have run its course, a fact which leaves many a businessman in a state of shock. It now faces some serious structural problems. Those companies that sprang up and became giants virtually overnight must now face the fact that the economy is, and is going to continue to be, very different. The investing public, once lulled into a euphoric feeling that the stock market would continue to rise forever, has been rudely awakened and sorely wounded. The capital markets themselves are now in rapid flux.

What is this new economic climate in which companies must function?

In the 1970s, it has become a climate characterized by uncertainty, lack of leadership on a global basis, and racked by disturbing elements bred of its own success. The growth of industry in the years following World War II, for example, led to production that outpaced its supply lines. Material shortages combined with other factors to produce raging inflation on an international scale. The inflation itself, by distorting purchasing power, combined with efforts to fight inflation, producing the deepest recession in generations and with it, the highest unemployment rate in three decades or more.

International dislocations, such as the Arab oil embargo which led to sudden sharp rises in the price of oil, not only fanned the inflation and contributed to the recession, but created a new and somewhat quixotic capital pool by drawing billions of dollars from the world's economy into the Middle East.

International food problems were exacerbated by poor crops in the United States in 1974, which created shortages that further fed the inflation and the recession.

The depth and extent of the damage to the capital pools by these and other events are difficult to assess. It is certain, though, that the new and changed climate now becomes a normal climate in which business must function for some years to come. And the attack never ceases. For example, a new pension fund law passed in 1974 places a greater fiduciary responsibility on pension fund managers. This has bred extreme caution that sharply limits the pension fund as the source of capital it once was.

With the retreat of the equities market, the needed capital has been more intensively sought from lenders, as a result of which companies are now more highly leveraged than they have ever been before.

Not the least of the problems is in the structure of the capital markets themselves.

The securities industry is in constant disarray, and has been for at least five decades. The promise of reform springs up at every downturn of the market, but has not yet been forthcoming. As a result, the industry, which has made a practice of answering major problems with minor amelioratives, is in a persistent feast or famine mode, and is never quite able to stabilize itself. In a modern world, complex and in constant flux, it is able to respond only in the perspective of a single trading day. And with the advent of negotiated rates, it seems almost certain that the securities industry will find itself in even greater trouble than it has ever been before. The failures and forced mergers of securities firms over the past five years will probably seem as nothing, compared to the future. Gustave Levy, senior partner of Goldman Sachs, has predicted that by 1980 there will be only 100 New York Stock Exchange member firms. *The Wall Street Journal* and others have run articles by prominent industry observers suggesting that under negotiated rates, the system will alter so significantly that the New York Stock Exchange will be obsolete. Even now the talk of merger between the New York and American Stock Exchanges is becoming quite serious.

It's little wonder that the securities industry is in such difficulty. In the 200-odd years of its existence, it has changed relatively little in relation to the capital needs of a burgeoning America. Its structure is predicated more on recycling stock than on its primary purpose, which is to supply capital to industry.

Banking, long self-impressed by its fiduciary responsibilities, is now straining to move into the twentieth century. As has been noted, the banking industry is pressing hard against the restrictions of the Glass-Steagall Act, which prohibits its functioning in the securities industry, and more and more is making incursions into new kinds of lending and investment banking services. The good or ill of this move will be determined by the way in which competition between banking and investment banking is fought. One thing seems likely—if both banking and investment banking attempt to compete by sabotaging one another through restrictive legislation, then industry and the economy will be the losers.

The insurance industry, with vast pools of cash, has become a major source of capital—certainly not the primary purpose of an insurance company. The investment of cash reserves was once prudent management. Now, in a great many cases, the insurance company functions with an eye more to investment of reserves and surplus than to insurance. The questions raised because of this, and because of the very real possibility that some insurance companies may be moving rather more deeply into reserve funds than they should, have made the insurance companies wary and conservative. During the 1960s, some insurance companies were among the leaders in supplying venture capital to new industries. The CATV industry, for example, received a great deal of its seed capital from farseeing and venturesome insurance companies. Now, caution and conservatism put a damper on the investment of insurance funds.

Pension funds, a product of an increasingly humane and civilized society, have in recent years become so large that they too have turned into a major source of capital. At the beginning of 1975, there was approximately $150 billion accumulated in private pension funds, with new money flowing into them at the rate of about $20 billion a year. During periods of rising stock prices, the pension funds have been a prime purchaser. Even during dips in the stock market, the pension funds have been good stock customers because they could afford to wait out the market's peaks and valleys. But it was only a matter of time before the government recognized the size that pension funds have reached and began to look to the need for regulating those funds. This, coupled with isolated abuses in the payment of pension funds to individuals, resulted in the passage of a complex new pension reform law in 1974. Aside from the myriad problems created by new regulations in any case, the new law places a tremendous responsibility on the fiduciary management of the funds. This has bred not only confusion in conformity to the regulations, but a caution in the investment of the funds that has sharply reduced pension fund participation in the stock market and moved it more heavily into the bond market.

And so, the traditional structures for flowing capital into industry are in a state of upheaval. Some segments of it are antiquated and inadequate. Other segments, filling vacuums, are growing at a rapid pace. The net effect is to make the attainment of a sound capital base that much more difficult, and the need for new and greater skill in formulating and achieving it that much more necessary.

Given a sound company, one with demonstrated ability to successfully use capital for greater appreciation, to succeed even under adverse conditions, to grow and expand its markets, what are the sources of capital available? For the growing business, there are still three major sources—retained earnings, equity, and debt.

Most growth for industry traditionally comes from retained earnings, the best use of which is intelligent reinvestment in the corporation's own business. But this calls for some keen management decisions. How much of profits must be paid out to the shareholders in dividends and how much retained so that the shareholders are kept happy and the business still remains well capitalized? Here, keeping the shareholders happy is not an arbitrary point—the shareholders represent not only current capitalization, but the potential for future capitalization. In the obvious judgment to be made as to the degree to which retained earnings shall be applied to capital investment rather than to working capital, some assessment must be made as to future capabilities of capitalization from other sources. If it seems likely that a well-planned growth program can include ultimate debt or equity capitalization, then less of the retained earnings need be used for capital growth. If, on the other hand, it appears that future debt or equity may be difficult to obtain, then a greater portion of retained earnings must be applied, and certainly a reevaluation must be made of growth plans. The point is that the decision is not only not a simple one to make, but that it requires tremendous input of intelligence, information, and expertise. Once again, the need for the skill and facilities of sound investment banking becomes significant.

Except in the rarest of circumstances, for most companies retained earnings are never sufficient for the growth spurt—for entering new markets, for building new plants, for developing new operational capability. This leaves new equity or debt as the alternative.

Competition for equity capital, so comparatively simple in the late 1960s, is no longer so. The changes in the economy and the upheaval in the securities industry dictate the need for competitive techniques that are more keenly honed than ever before in history. Not only must a company be a good one, but through the financial relations techniques described in this book, the company's strengths must be intensively and professionally projected. Even with the problems of the economy and the securities industry, there is still an equities market, and there always will be. Even if the market values of stocks have diminished to 50% of their all-time highs, a market nevertheless continues to exist. Even if there are long periods during which it is not feasible to seek capital in the equities market, the time always comes back when it can be done again. But competition in the equities market, no matter how intensive, can be successfully performed by a deserving company through the application of sound financial relations techniques. Moreover, this competition, for any company with any kind of equity base, is necessarily fought assiduously day by day, with no safe loss of momentum. When Coca Cola arbitrarily decided to stop talking to security analysts in late 1974 because they were having problems related to a sugar price increase, and did so feeling that their size precluded the necessity for communication, they deprived themselves of every advantage they might have had in keeping the plummeting price of their stock more consistent with the realities of their earnings.

Despite the shifts in the equity market, and despite the fact that equity contributes only about 15% of the total capitalization of industry, it's still a crucial source of capital and a vital part of the capitalization formula for any consequential company. As such, it colors and affects capitalization from any source. Merely because equity capital is scarce and difficult at any given moment, there is no sound basis for reducing the effort. There is no sound basis for downgrading either its importance to total capitalization or the necessity for consistent projection of a company's potential to the equities market through the use of sound financial relations techniques.

As the capital markets shrink in other aspects, so does debt capital. Short-term debt from banks and through other debt instruments such as commercial paper becomes not only harder to get, but harder to use intelligently in the corporate capital structure. As every company president knows, rarely does one form of capitalization serve as a substitute for another. Short-term debt may solve a company's problem at any given moment, but it is no substitute, in the long run, for equity or long-term debt when either of the alternatives is dictated. The corporate bond, which flourishes out of proportion to its value to a sound capital program when the stock market is down, is still sought in a competitive milieu. When money is scarce and bond yields are high, then the public buys bonds. When there is a greater potential for return from the stock market, then the public buys stock. It is significant to note, however, that bond yields have been higher then stock yields for at least 17 years—the longest period in the last 100 years in which bonds have yielded more than stocks. During a recession, when corporate profits tend to be lower, many investors fear dividend cuts, and, therefore, distrust historical stock yields. This further enhances the attractiveness of bonds. When debt must be sought under adverse conditions, the terms of that debt can sometimes be traumatic on the long-range plans of a growing company. It becomes extremely important, then, that the company that must seek debt in a tight market do so under the most favorable conditions. This, too, is a function of financial relations, in that the company must be clearly understood for its ability to use the debt properly and to thrive under adverse conditions. A company's ability to do so and to repay the debt without sapping earnings must be as assiduously projected as in the case of equity. There is virtually no technique in this book that does not equally apply for a company seeking capitalization through debt as well as one using equity.

There is also the private placement, venture capital, and the small business investment company (SBIC).

The private placement most often accomplished by the investment banker is a debt issue, most frequently used for its flexibility of terms and for the fact that it can often be done without dilution of equity. It is the channel of large pools of capital, ranging from insurance companies to Eurodollars, into the corporation. It is in the private placement that the investment banker shows his mettle, not merely in finding it, but in the terms that he is able to develop. For the growing company, the private placement is frequently the best tool for capitalization for the least disturbance of the balance sheet and the lowest mortgage on the future. But if the skill of the investment banker in arranging for the private placement can make for a good one, it should be remembered also that it can make for a bad one. Would that this were an unnecessary caution to note.

Venture capital is most frequently thought of in terms of an individual or an institution that advances money in expectation of a greater return than it might normally get through other investments. Venture capital has been responsible for the beginning and sustenance of many now successful businesses in the United States. The sources of venture capital may be the individual investor, the venture capital arm of an investment banking firm or a bank, a venture capital affiliate of an insurance company, or a SBIC. Some major corporations, such as Textron, Exxon, Johnson & Johnson, and Dow Chemical, have made venture capital funds available either directly or through affiliates. SBICs are government sponsored and are, of course, regulated under that sponsorship.

The venture capital market is as affected by the economy as is any other pool of capital. While the term itself implies greater risk, all sources of venture capital are reflecting the conservatism and caution of all other sources of capital. Here, too, the ability to project a company's potential is an essential element in competing for venture capital.

The big question, at this writing, is the billions of dollars now in Arab hands. There seems to be no question that this money will be invested, and a large part of it in the United States, but the Arabs are being cautious and are giving little indication as to how that money will be deployed. Some of it has already found its way into the United States in the form of purchases of securities in American companies and real estate investment. It's still an enigma.

Prior to December 31, 1974, the date at which it became legal for Americans to own gold, there was considerable concern by the investment community that a lot of the money that might have otherwise been available for corporate investment would be diverted to gold and would, therefore, not be available for productive use in the economic system. Indications as of this writing are that this concern was not warranted. On January 6, 1975, the U.S. Treasury, in order to contain the price of gold by speculators, put two million ounces of it up for public auction. Such was the public apathy that only 750,000 ounces were sold, at prices considerably lower than gold's recent all-time high price.

Entering 1975, stock prices were still severely depressed and offered a hostile climate for new equity issues. At the same time, the calendar for new bond issues for the year was loaded. Thus there stands a severe danger that American industry will be more highly leveraged than ever.

And so the competition for capital, never simple, becomes infinitely more difficult and complex. Many companies have long-standing banking and financial community relationships which make their jobs easier. For the majority of American corporations, however, capitalization becomes that much more difficult. The role of the investment banker and the need for his services become infinitely more acute. His knowledge and experience are now important not just for finding capital, but to analyze and determine the company's real needs for short- and long-term capital, to assist even the most intelligent management in developing techniques for the proper use of that capital, and to supply overall economic data that allow management to make intelligent decisions objectively in a difficult economic climate. The investment banker must be keenly aware of all sources of capital, including cost, so that as the capital markets shrink and shift, he still retains choice. Now more than ever he must be imaginative and skillful in putting together deals that make sense for the corporation not only for the present but for the future. It's doubtful that very many companies can either succeed in competing for capital nor use that capital to the greatest advantage without some very sophisticated help.

And one thing is also certain. No company can successfully compete for capital if it is not known and understood for its superior ability to appreciate that capital—and this is the proper role of financial relations.

APPENDICES

COSTS AND BUDGETS

In a well-run financial relations program, there is no question that the greater and more extensive the effort, the greater the effectiveness. Nevertheless, the cost of a financial relations program is not a measure of its potential success. Programs that cost a great deal may be no more effective than programs that are moderately priced. The measure is the program— not the cost. Virtually every cost factor may be foreseen. And at least, a program should be budgetable.

Essentially, the expense elements of a financial relations program are the following:

1. Consulting fees.
2. Design and printing.
3. Mailing.
4. Analyst meetings.
5. Travel costs to meetings, major press interviews, and so forth.
6. Out-of-pocket and miscellaneous expenses, including phones, teletype, Dow Jones and Reuters, entertainment, and so on.
7. Contingencies.

FEES

For companies using outside consultants, the fee structure is determined at the outset.

Fee structures vary from one consulting firm to another, although basically there are only two types used by most consultants—straight fee and hourly rate. Fees for an effective program are usually in the range of $9000 to $50,000 a year. Although some programs can exceed that amount, it's unlikely that an effective and well-rounded program can be performed professionally for less than $9000.

The straight fee basis is usually a simple fixed amount, paid monthly. This has the advantage of simpler budgeting. .

The hourly rate functions much the same as with accountants and attorneys. Usually a basic minimum fee is agreed upon, with hours charged against that fee, and the client is billed for hours in excess of the minimum. Sometimes a maximum is also agreed upon. The maximum also allows for overall budgeting. The hourly basis functions best if there is a clear understanding beforehand of the hourly rate of each person who is to work on the account. The Financial Relations Board uses the hourly rate, with several distinct advantages to the plan. Each month, the client is billed on a printout which indicates each person who worked on the account, his hourly rate, and the time he put in. Each person's time is broken down in each of 14 categories, to the quarter hour. This allows the client the added advantage of seeing how the time was spent on his account, which enables him to measure the effectiveness of the effort in each of the categories. FRB also uses the hourly rate to advantage by budgeting time for each account at the beginning of every month. Specific hours may be budgeted to each executive and each of the several FRB offices. The interoffice allocation makes it possible for the firm to function more effectively on a national basis by virtue of clear-cut, time-budgeted assignments from office to office.

Most firms bill a month in advance, with firms that use the hourly rate billing the agreed-upon minimum. Because it generally takes at least a year to measure the effects of a program, most contracts are for that period.

Considering the complexities of evaluating the effectiveness of a program, any fee structure, whether it be a monthly flat fee or the hourly rate, depends for its success on some kind of detailed reporting system. Since much of the financial relations effort is done in the consultant's rather than the company's offices, only a sound reporting system allows the client to know that his fee is actually going to effective effort.

DESIGN AND PRINTING COSTS

Printing, in a financial relations program, is primarily for annual and interim reports, reprints of speeches, and post-meeting reports. Other printing may be brochures, reprints, or background reports.

The design of an annual report, which is probably the most expensive printing item in a financial relations budget, ranges from $75 a page to a total of $5000 or more for the extensive report of a major company. It includes design, layout, typography, galley proofs, and camera-ready mechanicals. Photography and other expenses attendant to the report, such as travel and research, are extra. Photographers generally charge $200 to $500 a day for their services, plus expenses. The cost of printing the report depends, of course, on the size of the report, the number of copies, the quality of paper, and so on. It's a good idea to get several bids from printers, selecting only those whose quality of work has been judged on the basis of samples. Printing costs vary from one locale to another, and price is not necessarily a key to quality. Printing costs in New York, for example, can be considerably higher than in Cincinnati, despite the fact that Cincinnati is one of several major cities with excellent printers.

An element of cost enters into the selection of the designer for a company located in a different city than its consultant. If there is sound reason for a New York consultant to use a New York designer, even if the report is to be printed elsewhere, then expenses for the consultant to deal with the designer are lower. Sometimes, however, a company will find it more convenient to use a local designer, in which case the consultant will have to visit with him once or twice to supervise the production of the report.

Design costs for interim reports and other material are usually considerably lower, not only because of the size, but because of the simplicity of the format. Interim reports normally follow the same format from one to the other, at least during the course of any one year. Speeches and similar printed matter, while usually just straight text, still require a measure of design and production expense, since they must be attractive in their appearance no matter how simple the makeup. Background reports generally follow a predetermined format, with very little design factor involved. While they are usually offset from typed copy, there's frequently a measure of professional pasteup to be done, usually at negligible cost. Reprints are usually photo-offset from pasteups of the original copy. Here, too, while the pasteup cost is negligible, it's still a factor. Offset printing costs vary, but are easily determined. Brochures that may occasionally be part of a financial relations program are designed and produced in essentially the same way, and at essentially the same cost, as annual reports.

MAILING

The elements to be calculated in mailings to shareholders and the financial community include:

1. Mailing lists.
2. Envelopes.
3. Postage.
4. Labor.

Mailing lists, it has been noted, are very difficult to maintain, and therefore, consume a measure of time—whether it be internal or external. In mailings to the ever–mobile financial community, what often may seem to be an undue amount of time and attention go into a constant updating, checking, and changing mailing lists, including the return postcard technique.

When an outside mailing house is used, these costs are incorporated into the basic price of mailing, since it is assumed that the mailing house keeps its lists updated for all its clients. Mailing lists are usually maintained on plates or computer, and each plate or computer listing changed is an expense. It's less of an expense, however, than the very high cost of mailing material to the wrong address.

The cost of envelopes must be considered as an additional expense of any mailing. Most consulting firms use their own envelopes for releases and may charge clients for exact cost. Annual reports, quarterly reports, and so on are usually mailed in company envelopes, sometimes especially printed for the purpose. In the design of any printed material unusual sizes mean special and expensive envelopes. It's infinitely cheaper to design for a standard size envelope.

There's really nothing to be said about postage, except that it keeps going up.

As in any corporate effort, labor is an element that must be calculated in any budget, from stuffing envelopes to maintaining mailing lists. Except if it's broken out separately for mailing list maintainance, it's usually incorporated in the total cost of mailing.

Most financial consultants, whether they use an outside mailing house or their own internal structure, are able to supply a rate schedule for reproduction of material and mailing. It's usually billed as a separate expense item. While advertising agencies and some financial relations consultants add a fixed percentage charge to all costs, most consultants rebill such expenses at exact cost.

ANALYST MEETINGS

Luncheon meetings are the largest expense in dealing with analysts in a financial relations program. It's simply the cost of lunch for any group of people. Most financial relations consultants hold meetings in restaurants and clubs normally familiar with serving group meetings, and their costs are readily predetermined.

Expenses beyond the cost of meals are negligible, although they may include sound system and audiovisual equipment rental. Displays especially designed for meetings are usually arranged for with display firms, and are a separate expense.

The program may include visits by analysts, press, and others to the company's office or plant. Normally, the expenses involved are travel costs, housing, meals, and local transportation.

MAJOR TRAVEL COSTS TO MEETINGS

The cost of travel by executives to meetings held in other than their own cities must be calculated. A normal financial relations practice, designed to save expenses, is to arrange meetings to coincide with executive travel for other reasons. Thus it's sound practice to keep the financial relations consultant advised of out-of-town travel by management.

OUT-OF-POCKET AND MISCELLANEOUS EXPENSES

Normally, out-of-pocket and routine expenses include:

1. Clipping services.
2. Photography and art work.
3. Telephone, telegrams, and teletype.
4. Wire services, such as PR Newswire.
5. News bulletins and other lettershop charges for printing, collating, and mailing.
6. Transportation.
7. Promotional expenses for meetings with press, analysts, and so on.
8. Postage.
9. Messenger services.
10. Photocopier and telecopier.
11. Subscriptions to trade publications.
12. Dow Jones and Reuters newswires.
13. Travel expenses.
14. Secretarial overtime on special projects.
15. Miscellaneous minor expenses.

Clipping services charge a fixed monthly fee plus a cost for each clipping. Clipping services are necessary to determine the extent to which any publicity issued by the company is printed. Unfortunately, no method has yet been devised to mechanize what is essentially a human job—scanning thousands of publications. As a result, the percentage of clipping is usually a small representation of any material that appears.

Telephones, teletype, and other means of communication are usually billed at exact cost, as determined from both records and bills.

PR Newswire and local, state, and city news services normally charge a fixed rate for each day of operation. In other words, two separate releases for one company on the same day are charged the same basic rate as for one release. There are variations of cost if the release exceeds 500 words.

Transportation expenses usually include transportation within a city, such as cabs, buses, subway, and so on.

During the course of a financial relations program, it's frequently necessary to conduct business with members of the press and the financial community over lunch, dinner, or cocktails. These expenses are usually documented by receipts.

In addition to postage for regular mailings, there is postage normally used in mailing letters, fulfilling analyst's information requests, packaging and shipping quantities of background material, and so forth.

Costs for messenger service are usually incurred within one city, although occasionally messengers must be used to transmit important material between cities. These expenses are supported by copies of bills from the messenger service.

Photocopying and telecopying are tremendous conveniences that are now part of every office operation. They are usually calculated on a predetermined rate based on costs.

In order for a financial relations firm to function, it must keep abreast of the industry of which its client is a part, as well as the trade press for that industry. Subscriptions to publications necessary for that purpose are normally billed to the client.

Larger financial relations consultants usually maintain Dow Jones and Reuters tickers to monitor news releases and other material of importance to the client. The cost of this service is usually apportioned to each of the consultant's clients.

The costs of travel—indeed all expenses in behalf of a client—are usually allocated on the same basis as determined by the Internal Revenue Service. This includes transportation, meals, hotel expenses, transportation within a city, auto mileage, tips, and miscellaneous out-of-pocket expenses, and so forth.

While normal secretarial and office services are considered part of a consultant's or company's own internal operating expenses, special projects frequently require additional expense, such as secretarial overtime or the use of temporary office help. Consulting firms normally include these costs in expense billings.

In the normal course of a program, miscellaneous minor expenses are sometimes incurred. These include additional copies of publications, tips, phone calls made away from the office, and so on.

CONTINGENCIES

Even in the best planned program, circumstances frequently arise, often in the form of opportunities, for special projects or activities. This may include an opportunity to participate as a panelist in a seminar, the need for a special brochure or pamphlet, and so forth.

While these occasions are normally unexpected, their value can sometimes be measured in terms of cost, and may be perfectly valid as additional expenses.

Granted the flexibility of expenses that tend to be variable, it's still possible to review a program well in advance and generally estimate what the expenses relative to that program are likely to be. This should make it possible for any company or experienced financial relations consultant to budget appropriately for the cost of the program.

SUMMARY OF NEW SEC REGULATIONS FOR ANNUAL REPORTS

With the issuance of Release 11079 of the SEC Act, the SEC virtually opened a new era of control over the annual report to shareholders. While still a document that need not be filed with the SEC, the annual report is felt to be of such significance in the protection of investors that the SEC now moves heavily into control of its content.

Essentially, much of the information now required is drawn from the Form 10K, although the SEC has tried to make it clear that they are not interested in turning the annual report from an artful and literate document to be read and understood by nonfinancial people into a legal document with the formal language and presentation of the 10K. They are primarily concerned that certain information found in the 10K also be made available to investors in the annual report.

The new regulations require that, within the traditional structures of the annual report, the following information be included:

1. Financial statements and notes must be printed in type at least 10 points in size, or a comparable size type that is at least as legible. Eight-point type may be used for tables within footnotes.

2. Any differences in accounting principles or practices between the financial statements in the report must be clearly indicated.

3. The report must include audited financial statements for the past two years instead of just the year of the report. While this is now common practice, if a company has changed auditors in the interim period, the report must now include the auditors' certificate from the prior year.

4. The report must now include an historical table of operating data for at least five years. This must contain information identical to that shown in the 10K. Where applicable, the table must show the following items:

Sales or revenues
Costs of goods sold or gross profit
Interest expense
Income tax expense
Income from continuing operations
Discontinued operations less applicable tax
Income or loss before extraordinary items
Extraordinary items, less applicable tax
Cumulative effects of changes in accounting principles
Net income or loss
Earnings applicable to common stock
Per share earnings
Per share dividends
The ratio of earnings to fixed charges (optional)

5. The text must go into substantial detail regarding "material changes." The SEC staff has defined a material change as one that affects any item of revenue or expense by more than 10% and/or affects net income by more than 2% in the past year, or during the past three years. The main point is that the SEC is no longer satisfied to see companies cover these items in the *Notes to Financial Statements,* but instead insists that they be directly covered in the letter to shareholders, or accompanying text.

6. A separate description of business must appear in the text portion of the report, clearly indicating the nature and scope of the company's operations and that of its subsidiaries.

7. The list of directors and officers must include a one-line description of their outside business affiliation.

8. A summary of quarterly dividends paid and quarterly high and low prices for each of the company's public securities must be presented on at least a two-year basis.

9. The report must include a prominent notice that the company's latest 10K is available free upon request by shareholders (companies may charge for exhibits, however).

10. Although it has now become standard practice for most corporations, it is now mandatory that annual reports include the same breakdown of sales and earnings by lines of business in which the company reports in its 10K.

MAJOR BUSINESS AND FINANCIAL PERIODICALS

Barron's National Business and Financial Weekly
22 Cortlandt Street, New York, N.Y. 10007

Black Enterprise
295 Madison Avenue, New York, N.Y. 10017

Business Week
1221 Avenue of the Americas, New York, N.Y. 10020

Commercial and Financial Chronicle
110 Wall Street, New York, N.Y. 10005

Credit Executive
71 West 23rd Street, New York, N.Y. 10010

Credit and Financial Management
475 Park Avenue South, New York, N.Y. 10016

Dow Digest
10 Main Center, Kansas City, Mo. 64105

Dun's
666 Fifth Avenue, New York, N.Y. 10019

The Exchange
11 Wall Street, New York, N.Y. 10005

Finance
P.O. Box G, Lenox Hill Station, New York, N.Y. 10021

Financial World
919 Third Avenue, New York, N.Y. 10022

Forbes
60 Fifth Avenue, New York, N.Y. 10011

Fortune
1271 Avenue of the Americas, New York, N.Y. 10020

Harvard Business Review
Soldiers Field, Boston, Mass. 02163

Industry Week
Penton Plaza, 1111 Chester Avenue, Cleveland, Ohio 44114

Institutional Investor
488 Madison Avenue, New York, N.Y. 10006

Journal of Accountancy
666 Fifth Avenue, New York, N.Y. 10019

Journal of Commerce
99 Wall Street, New York, N.Y. 10005

The M/G Financial Weekly
P.O. Box 26991, Richmond, Va. 23261

The Money Manager
1 State Street Plaza, New York, N.Y. 10004

Nation's Business
1615 H Street, N.W., Washington, D.C. 20006

The O-T-C Market Chronicle
25 Park Place, New York, N.Y. 10007

Over-The-Counter Securities Review
P.O. Box 110, Jenkintown, Pa. 19046

Pensions and Investments
708 Third Avenue, New York, N.Y. 10017

The Stock Market Magazine
16 School Street, Yonkers, N.Y. 10701

United States Investor/Eastern Banker
286 Congress Street, Boston, Mass. 02210

Wall Street Journal
22 Cortlandt Street, New York, N.Y. 10007

Wall Street Reports
120 Wall Street, New York, N.Y. 10005

The Wall Street Transcript
120 Wall Street, New York, N.Y. 10005

DIRECTORIES

These are major directories useful in the execution of a financial relations program.

Ayer Directory of Publications—a list of virtually every periodical publication in the United States and Canada, including key publication information about each (Ayer Press, Philadelphia, annual)

Bacon's Publicity Checker—a directory of virtually every magazine and daily newspaper published in the United States and Canada, including editors' names and general editorial requirements (Bacon's Publishing Company, Chicago, annual)

Editor & Publisher International Year Book—a directory of every daily newspaper in the United States, arranged by state, major foreign newspapers, wire and news services, columnists, correspondents, press associations, and so on, including key editorial and executive personnel (Editor & Publisher, New York, annual)

The E-Z Telephone Directory of Brokers and Banks—an alphabetical listing of the New York financial community, with addresses and telephone numbers (E-Z Telephone Directory Corp., New York, quarterly)

Hudson's Washington News Media Contacts Directory—a directory of Washington, D.C. area news media, including editors (Hudson Associates, Rhinebeck, N.Y., annual)

Institutions—a directory of portfolio managers, analysts, and traders at major financial institutions in the United States and Canada (Technometrics, Inc., New York, three times a year)

Middle West Publicity Media Directory—a directory of Chicago area publications and news media, including key editorial personnel (St. Clair Press, Chicago, annual)

New York Publicity Outlets—a directory of New York City area-based newspapers, major magazines, news services, radio and television stations, and trade publications, including departmental editorial breakdown (Public Relations Plus, Inc., Washington Depot, Conn., annual)

News Bureaus in the U.S.—a directory of the locations and personnel of all news bureaus in the United States and their branch offices (Richard Weiner, Inc., New York)

Nominee List—a directory of nominee names and their identification (American Society of Corporate Secretaries, New York)

Security Dealers of North America—a complete directory of all brokers, dealers, underwriters, investment bankers, exchanges, and so on, arranged by states in the United States and Canada, including key personnel (Standard and Poor's Corporation, New York, annual)

Simon's Editorial Offices in the West—a directory of Western media and editorial personnel (David H. Simon, Los Angeles)

While not directories, there are several newsletters that may be of interest:

PR Aids Party Line—a weekly newsletter of current placement opportunities in all media (PR Aids Periodicals, Inc., New York, weekly)

The Corporate Shareholder—an inside report on investor relations (Corporate Shareholders, Inc., New York, semi-monthly)

Investor Relations Newsletter—reports current thinking on problems in investor relations, as well as new regulations (Enterprise Publications, Chicago, Ill., monthly)

The Corporate Communications Report—reports and discusses latest problems in corporate communication with the financial community (Corporate Communications Services, Inc., New York, bi-monthly)

Myron Kandel's Review of the Financial Press—a topnotch summary of major stories gleaned from business and financial publications (Kandel Publications, Inc., New York, weekly)

Jack O'Dwyer's Newsletter—a comprehensive report of activities in the public relations and financial relations fields (Jack O'Dwyer, New York, weekly)

PR Reporter—a newsletter of activities of public relations and financial relations practitioners, including frequent discussions of current public relations problems (PR Reporter, Meridan, Conn., weekly)

Public Relations News—a newsletter of activities of public relations and financial relations practitioners, including frequent case histories of successful programs (Public Relations News, New York, weekly)

APPENDIX V

NEWS BULLETIN

RE: DEVCON INTERNATIONAL CORP.
1125 S.W. Third Street
Pompano Beach, Florida 33061
(RICHARD HORNSBY - V.P. Fin.)

From: *The Financial Relations Board, Inc.*   Traded: OTC/Symbol DEVC

Financial Relations Board, Inc. serves as financial relations counsel to this company, is acting on the company's behalf in issuing this bulletin and receiving compensation therefor. The information contained herein is furnished for information purposes only and is not to be construed as an offer to buy or sell securities.

For Further Information:

ST. PETERSBURG:	NEW YORK:	CHICAGO:	LOS ANGELES:
Earle B. Brown	Bruce W. Marcus	Bill Miller	Virginia M. Lowe
Mrg. - Southeast	Sr. Vice President	Sr. Vice President	Vice President
3151 Third Avenue No.	44 Beaver Street	150 East Huron St.	626 Wilshire Blvd.
813/822-8585	212/422-7250	312/266-7800	213/680-9750

FOR IMMEDIATE RELEASE
Monday, March 25, 1974

DEVCON INTERNATIONAL CORP. REPORTS RECORD HIGH 1973 REVENUES, EARNINGS

POMPANO BEACH, FLA., MAR. 25 -- Record revenues and earnings for 1973 were reported today by Devcon International Corp. (OTC), with further earnings increases projected for 1974, according to Donald L. Smith, Jr., President.

Net earnings for the year ended December 31, 1973, increased 20 per cent to $2,568,000, equal to $2.21 per share, from $2,143,000 or $1.91 per share a year earlier. Total revenues gained 26 per cent to $24,819,000 from $19,705,000 in 1972.

Smith said, "Record high earnings reflect substantially increased activity in both public and private construction plus a greater contribution to corporate earnings from our real estate development division.

"At the same time," Smith added, "we effectively absorbed sharp increases in interest expenses and fuel costs combined with a higher overall tax rate." The company's effective tax rate, after tax subsidies and consolidation with the results of offshore, lower-taxed operations, equalled 18 per cent of income before taxes in 1973, versus 13 per cent in 1972.

Results for 1974 are expected fo fall within Devcon's stated five-year objective of 20 to 25 per cent average annual earnings growth, Smith said. "Our optimism is supported by a $31 million construction services backlog of work in process or yet to get under way, a major acquisition which should

More...

double the concrete products volume, and recently obtained favorable zoning
on 40 percent of our 2,500 acre inventory of prime development property.

"This five-year growth target remains a reasonable objective," Smith
continued. "At the same time, we anticipate a continuation of comparatively
high interest costs and substantially higher fuel costs, and we recognize
the uncertainties in the economy generally."

DEVCON INTERNATIONAL CORP. AND SUBSIDIARIES
CONSOLIDATED STATEMENT OF INCOME FOR THE YEARS ENDED DECEMBER 31

	1973	1972	Per Cent Increase
Revenues...................	$24,819,000	$19,705,000	+26%
Income from Operations....	3,151,000	2,455,000	+28%
Provision for Income Taxes	583,000	312,000	+87%
Net Earnings..............	2,568,000	2,143,000	+20%
Per Share...........	$2.21	$1.91	+16%
Weighted Average			
Shares Outstanding...	1,164,000	1,121,000	

A BACKGROUND REPORT FROM

 SAUNDERS LEASING SYSTEM, INC.

August 1973

Prepared on behalf of the company by

The Financial Relations Board, Inc.

CHICAGO   NEW YORK   LOS ANGELES
TAMPA   MINNEAPOLIS
TORONTO

```
LISTED:  American Stock Exchange (SAU)     1972 REVENUES:  $45,211,383

RECENT PRICE:  9-3/8                        1972 NET INCOME:  1,867,162

1973 PRICE RANGE:  7-3/4 - 17-1/8           1972 PER SHARE:    $1.33

DIVIDEND:  $.20                             NET PER SHARE:
                                            $1.33 vs. $0.72 in 1971
                                            Trailing 12 months
                                            $1.63 vs. $1.08 in 1972

CURRENT YIELD:  0.9%                        PRICE/EARNINGS MULTIPLE
                                            (Based on 1972 Net
                                             Income) 7X

SHARES OUTSTANDING:  1,507,945              FISCAL YEAR ENDS:  December 31

APPROXIMATE FLOAT:  658,000
```

	Quarter Ended June 30 (Unaudited)		Six Months Ended June 30 (Unaudited)	
	1973	1972	1973	1972
Total Revenue	$13,601,949	$11,207,151	$26,338,335	$21,442,962
Net Income	$ 710,615	$ 500,214	$ 1,359,062	$ 786,613
Average common and common equivalent shares	1,514,723	1,351,161	1,519,956	1,350,211
Net income per share	$.47	$.37	$.89	$.58

Summary

Based on current performance trends, the management of this full-
service truck leasing company believes that 1973 will be the third
successive year that Saunders will increase net margins as well as
attain record earnings. The company earned 4.1 percent on gross
revenues in 1972. For the first six months of 1973, that percentage
increased to 5.2 percent.

Saunders' compounded growth rate in revenues has averaged 26 percent
annually in the ten years since 1962, and 27 percent in earnings.

Saunders' revenues in 1972 increased more than 25 percent. Improved margins brought a 61 percent jump in pre-tax earnings from the 1971 level.

Results reflect an active cost control program to reduce overhead, focus on efficiencies, concerted emphasis on service in leasing operations, and the growth of maintenance services for fleets of trucks not on lease.

Saunders has concentrated its business in the heavy truck transport sector of the vehicle leasing industry, which also includes Ryder, Leaseway, and Feld among the independents, as well as Hertz and Avis. Saunders differs not only in its emphasis on long-term heavy truck transportation, but in its full-service capabilities, which are tailored specifically to the customer's needs. This service concept is a function of Saunders' long-term arrangement.

The industry, founded by Saunders in 1916, accelerated its growth after World War II. This growth rate is largely a result of the clear economic advantages that specialized truck fleet leasing affords American industry.

Since fewer than 10 percent of trucks are under lease today, sizable opportunities for expansion continue. To hold down distribution costs in the face of rising common carrier rates, a firm must either tie up capital in its own trucks and in servicing facilities, or choose the leasing alternative. Leasing gives all the advantages of ownership without such problems as vehicle inspections, repairs and servicing.

Recent Developments

FIRST SIX MONTHS NET UP 73 PERCENT ON 23 PERCENT IN REVENUES

Record net income (unaudited) for the first six months amounted to $1,359,052, or $.89 per share, compared with $786,613, or $.58 per share in the year earlier period. Revenues also increased to a record high of $26,338,335 in the first six months of 1973, compared with $21,442,962 in the first six months of 1972.

Earnings were based on the 1,519,956 average common and common equivalent shares outstanding, up 13 percent over the 1,350,211 shares in the first six months of 1972. The larger number of shares currently outstanding was due principally to the company's public offering (at $16) of 172,500 shares on August 18, 1972.

COMPANY'S AUTHORIZED COMMON STOCK DOUBLED TO 4,000,000 SHARES

Shareholders, at their annual meeting on April 17, 1973, voted to increase the number of authorized common stock, supporting management's opinion that "it (is) in the best interests ... to have a larger number of authorized shares available ... although the company has no present plans to issue any of these shares."

COMPANY PURCHASES ITS OWN STOCK

During the first half of 1972, the company repurchased 29,200 shares of its own common stock at prices ranging from 9-5/8 to 11-1/2 per share. These shares will be held in the treasury for possible use in connection with stock options or acquisitions.

NEW ACQUISITIONS

The company acquired Acme Truck Leasing System, Inc. of Mansfield, Ohio on June 21, 1973, and PhilRich, Inc., a Tuscaloosa, Alabama-based leasing concern in July, 1973.

NET INCOME FOR 1972 ALMOST DOUBLED ON 25 PERCENT INCREASE IN REVENUES

Saunders earned a record $1,867,162 for 1972, up 97 percent over 1971's net income of $949,051. Revenues for 1972 were $45,211,383, compared with $36,037,016 a year ago.

Current Outlook

MINIMUM OF $55-MILLION REVENUES SEEN FOR 1973

At the close of the second quarter, President Harris Saunders, Jr., announced that the company's existing long-term lease contracts and new contracts going into effect indicate at least a $10,000,000 rise in revenues for all of 1973.

LABOR SITUATION MORE PREDICTABLE WITH NATIONAL TEAMSTERS' CONTRACT SIGNED WITH FREIGHT LINES

Union contracts are in effect in approximately 15 percent of Saunders' maintenance and service facilities. Management believes that renewal contracts can be negotiated without strikes or other labor difficulties experienced in 1970.

GASOLINE SHORTAGE

So far, the fuel shortage has not adversely affected the company, nor does it anticipate a serious problem in the near future. The company believes it has sufficient sources of fuel. Most increases in fuel costs are contractually passed on to the company's customers at no detriment to the company.

COMPANY'S EARNINGS NOT GROSSLY AFFECTED BY CHANGES IN PRIME RATE

Less than 30 percent of Saunders revenue is derived from the financial aspects of leases. Despite the fact that Saunders is a leasing company, it is not, as might be assumed, mostly a finance company whose earnings will be seriously affected by fluctuations in interest rates. Interest cost is only approximately 6.7 percent of total costs. Since only a portion of its loans are tied to prime, the net effect on per share earnings of a one percent change in prime is $.07. Current interest rates are built into new lease contracts.

Basic Position

Saunders' concept of vehicle leasing is designed so that the customer can pay his transportation costs out of current income generated by the fleet without dipping into capital. It serves the customer by first helping in the selection of the vehicle or fleet ideal for the job and then applying expertise in preventive maintenance, repairs, servicing. The company also furnishes consultation services in connection with driver selection procedures, driver training, safety.

While all vehicle leasing companies overlap in some of their services, each has its own approach to the industry and serves its customers differently. Saunders, for example, does not lease non-commercial vehicles. Its business is primarily to service long-term industrial and commercial transportation needs, with heavy emphasis on over-the-road truck-tractors and trailers. Virtually all leases are long-term, and an increasing number of Saunders' fleet customers are multi-location users. It does, however, maintain a substantial short-term rental fleet which also contributes standby units to cover unusual customer needs for either additional vehicles or to minimize customer downtime while vehicles are being serviced. The short-term and standby vehicles contribute about 13 percent of the company's revenue.

If the prospect or customer has an existing fleet which must be upgraded for maximum efficiency, Saunders will purchase and dispose of the old vehicles, and purchase and lease back any comparatively new vehicles that meet the high standards of Saunders.

Saunders' full-service lease contracts require the customer to purchase the vehicles -- should he choose to cancel a contract -- at a price exceeding the vehicle's depreciated value, including specific cancellation expenses. Increasingly, Saunders' leases specify purchase by the customer in the event Saunders cancels.

Lease contracts include escalator clauses to cover operating variables such as increased maintenance charges, fuel prices, etc. Typically, they are based on a fixed amount per week or month, plus a mileage charge, or they may specify a flat mileage rate with a guaranteed minimum miles per year.

Related services provided 7 percent of Saunders' 1972 revenues. These are specialized transportation services, originally developed for and provided to Saunders' full-service leasing customers, which are now

available to non-Saunders fleets. These services are not only a
secondary source of income and a guarantee to Saunders' customers
of improved service, but also have promotional value for the company.

Saunders' fuel stop program offers the services of more than 900 fuel
stops. Saunders constantly negotiates for good fuel prices.

The Saunders fuel tax reporting system attacks a problem of specific
consequence to the industry in that it helps the system's clients comply
efficiently with the full and complex spectrum of all fuel taxing bodies.

This includes initial registration, fuel permits and renewal, required
periodic tax reports, refund applications, reciprocity and proration
distribution -- every aspect of taxation faced by the truck or fleet
operator. Saunders will even file and store tax records in a central
warehouse.

Saunders' management feels that the company has been highly successful
not only in tailoring its services to meet the specific transportation
peculiarities of a given client, but to do so without overextending
itself. For example, as a matter of policy, Saunders does not construct
a branch facility unless there are contracts in hand to cover the
largest portion of the overhead. Once a branch facility becomes
feasible, the company moves quickly to establish a convenient garage
and parking facility consisting of fuel and service islands, spare
parts inventory and complete repair shops. The company currently
has 105 fully equipped and staffed maintenance and service facilities
and plans to add a minimum of seven more this year.

Management believes its leases have proven to be well protected and
the level of credit worthiness among its customers has remained high.
Historically, Saunders' bad-debt write-off has been less than 1/5 of
1 percent.

Customers

Presently, Saunders' ten largest customers provide 39 percent of total
revenues and no single lessee generates more than 6 percent.

Among the company's largest customers -- each leasing a fleet valued at
more than $1-million -- are Western Auto Supply (div. Beneficial
Finance Corp.), Champion International, State Stove Company, The Mead
Corporation, Arkansas Cement Corp. (sub. of Arkansas-Louisiana Gas Co.),
Iowa Beef Processors, Northwestern Steel and Wire Company, J. I. Case
Company (sub. of Tenneco, Inc.), Rose's Stores, Inc., Massey-Ferguson
Industries, Ltd., Union Carbide Corp., and Futorian Mfg. Corp. (sub.
of Mohasco Industries, Inc.).

Marketing

Most long-term leases historically have been sold through the home office's national account sales staff with the assistance of branch managers. In 1971, however, a new program was begun to partially decentralize the sales effort. At no large increase in overhead, a new emphasis was placed on utilizing the branch management staff -- proven extremely capable at displaying full-service leasing benefits to a potential customer at the local level -- as additional salesmen.

In management's opinion, price competition in the leasing of trucks, truck-tractors, and trailers is secondary to the quality of service and maintenance. The number of customers lost over the past five years as a result of competitors' price cutting has been very small.

Saunders' management looks for increased revenues directly from the following sources:

* Growth of existing customers resulting in their need to enlarge their fleets.

* Tendency of customers to reduce their usage of common carriers and increase their use of full-service leasing.

* The addition of new leases through their home office based sales force.

* Additional related services such as management and maintenance of vehicles for customers who prefer to own their equipment, and fuel and state tax services.

Saunders is instituting an improved national industrial advertising campaign utilizing major business media, which it believes will generate considerable business. The advertising campaign will stress those major sales points which Saunders believes give it competitive advantage over those in the field. The points to be stressed are:

* Periodic Branch Inspection. This program involves a team of auditors and inspectors and is an extraordinarily complex and detailed system of maintaining the highest level of efficiency and performance in the industry.

* Rate Making Procedures. Saunders believes that its procedures for developing rates for its customers is the most sophisticated in the industry, resulting in rates that are the most

favorable for the customer and the most efficient
and profitable for Saunders.

* Instant Power. Saunders' Instant Pcwer plan
  means a reserve of truck-tractors that preclude
  downtime loss to customers. These truck-tractors
  are made available as needed on virtually a
  moment's notice. They are also used to supplement
  the company's short-term rental inventory.

* Manpower Planning. This is a continuous training
  program to increase the size of the manpower
  reserve and the quality of its performance.
  While this training program has a primary use
  to Saunders, it also guarantees customer service
  from a growing stock of specially qualified
  personnel.

Competition

Saunders, as opposed to some of the major segments of its competition,
has concentrated or specialized on long-term heavy duty, over-the-road
trucks, truck-tractors and trailers. Ryder System, for example, derives
a larger amount of its volume from short-term, transit rentals. Avis
and Hertz, at the same time, are much more heavily involved in auto
rentals. Saunders' management believes there is an inherent advantage
in its concentrating on offering outstanding service in one specialized
area rather than diversifying into several. This, the company believes,
coupled with its branch network, has provided a distinct competitive
edge in selling its services to large national corporations operating
in various parts of the U.S.

Headquartered in the Southeastern section of the United States, the
company has an equal number of branch facilities both above and below
the Mason-Dixon line, and operates on a national basis. In addition
to the larger national firms, Saunders is also directly competitive
with smaller regional firms that are often associated with auto or
truck dealerships.

Like all leasing firms, Saunders also competes with all forms of common
carriers for shares of the total transportation dollar. Another important
competitive area, of course, is the owner-operated fleet, where the
shipper purchases, operates and maintains his own vehicles.

Industry Demand

Federal government statistics on leasing, on a monthly or even a year-
to-year basis, are not available. The main source for year-to-year

information concerning leasing growth -- particularly in the area of truck-tractor and trailer leasing -- is found through automotive industry sources. Conclusions are developed primarily through the use of nationwide questionnaires and special studies that are sponsored by associations and published in periodicals.

According to a study published in <u>Automotive Fleet</u> magazine in 1971, there were then a total of 584,000 trucks under some form of lease in the United States compared with 353,000 five years earlier, a 65 percent increase. In that span, trucks under lease have increased at a 13 percent average annual rate, establishing a trend which is expected to continue well into the future.

The study indicates that the rate at which trucks are being put under full-service lease also is growing substantially. For example, in 1971, a total of 330,000 trucks in the United States were known to be under full-service contracts compared with 221,000 five years before. This represents an annualized increase of 11 percent.

Early in 1970, Bobit Publishing Co. executed the first in-depth study on the impact of vehicle leasing on the trucking industry. The following were considered the major findings:

* 65 percent of the companies responding were already leasing their truck fleets.

* Of the companies leasing, 65 percent indicated they leased on a full-service basis, while 23 percent used only a finance lease. The remainder leased on a short-term or daily rental basis only.

* Of these 17 percent considering leasing, 54 percent were considering using full-service leasing, while 25 percent were thinking of a finance lease arrangement.

* The survey's respondents indicated they leased for two reasons: 33 percent to release capital, and 67 percent to obtain maintenance and repair service.

Industry experts point to today's heavy costs of physical distribution as a major reason behind the growing stress placed on full-service leasing. These costs are estimated to exceed $100-billion annually and can account for as much as 40 percent to 50 percent of retail price. The amount paid for physical distribution is often twice the cost of manufacturing. While distribution adds nothing to physical value, it is a costly necessity and a target for continual appraisal. Full-service leasing offers industry an opportunity to transfer a significant share of the problem to an independent specialist and gain proven savings.

Ten Year Financial Review

	1972	%*	1971	%*	1970	%*	1969	%*
Rental and lease revenues:								
Passenger cars	$ 407.245	21.3	$ 335.759	10.3	$ 374.358	20.5	$ 470.959	(6.2)
Trucks, tractors and trailers	41.579.908	24.8	33.323.651	19.6	27.872.086	8.0	25.796.635	18.8
Other revenue	3.224.230	36.8	2.357.606	31.6	1.790.966	18.6	1.510.742	77.6
Total revenue	45.211.383	25.5	36.037.016	20.0	30.037.410	8.1	27.778.336	20.5
Costs and expenses:								
Operating expenses, exclusive of depreciation	25.741.005	25.5	20.516.198	17.9	17.404.670	14.6	15.193.668	20.9
Depreciation	8.846.510	21.4	7.289.105	12.6	6.474.946	7.7	6.013.745	16.9
Net (gain) on sale of rental vehicles	(802.920)	45.5	(551.688)	95.2	(282.683)	26.2	(223.986)	49.5
Selling, administrative and general expenses	5.865.258	33.8	4.383.875	15 5	3.794.563	(1.8)	3.863.101	16.7
Provision for doubtful notes and accounts receivable	106.440	309.4	25.999	(31.2)	37.777	(57.9)	89.699	68.8
Total costs	39.756.293	25.6	31.663.489	15.4	27.429.273	10.0	24.936.227	19.2
Interest expense	2.817.928	3.0	2.736.476	25.6	2.179.368	17.0	1.862.414	29.3
Income before provision for income taxes	2.637.162	61.1	1.637.051	281.8	428.769	(56.2)	979.695	40.4
Provision for income taxes:								
Current	215.000	141.6	89.000	535.7	14.000	(94.2)	240.000	2.081.8
Deferred	555.000	(7.4)	599.000	205.6	196.000	133.9	83.800	(48.3)
Net income	1.867.162	96.7	949.051	333.8	218.769	(66.7)	655.895	25.0
Net income per Common and Common Equivalent Share **	$1.33	84.7	$0.72	323.5	$0.17	(66.7)	$0.51	27.5
Stockholders' Equity	$11.775.082	65.8	$ 7.103.085	13.8	$ 6.241.346	2.2	$ 6.109.889	10.3
Return on Revenues	4.1%	57.7	2.6%	271.4	0.7%	(70.8)	2.4%	4.3
Return on Stockholders' Equity	15.9%	17.2	13.4%	280.0	3.5%	(67.3)	10.7%	12.6

* Percentages shown represent increases or (decreases) over the previous year.
** After giving effect to the 3-for-2 stock split in March, 1972.

1968	%*	1967	%*	1966	%*	1965	%*	1964	%*	1963	%*
$ 501.817	425.4	$ 95.507	190.0	$ 32.935	9.4	$ 36.347	5.7	$ 34.396	124.9	$ 15.292	19.6
21.706.067	43.8	15.090.534	18.3	12.751.852	25.4	10.168.071	30.2	7.810.351	44.3	5.413.023	28.5
850.780	286.9	219.892	23.7	177.779	46.3	121.532	45.7	83.434	16.4	71.671	14.6
23.058.664	49.7	15.405.933	18.8	12.962.566	25.5	10.325.950	30.2	7.928.181	44.1	5.499.986	28.3
12.562.977	56.9	8.006.622	17.3	6.823.179	29.6	5.263.359	30.3	4.039.868	45.7	2.772.611	28.8
5.144.617	49.0	3.453.051	19.4	2.892.861	24.2	2.328.926	28.4	1.813.760	37.2	1.321.857	23.6
(149.794)	(29.2)	(211.626)	898.4	(21.197)	(33.1)	(31.700)	3.4	(30.654)	17.3	(26.127)	20.7
3.309.317	45.8	2.270.045	35.0	1.681.940	24.5	1.350.571	28.3	1.052.688	35.5	776.856	26.0
53.150	90.4	27.917	37.8	20.258	(42.0)	34.954	117.2	16.093	(19.5)	19.987	6.3
20.920.267	54.4	13.546.009	18.9	11.397.041	27.4	8.946.110	29.8	6.891.755	41.7	4.865.184	27.2
1.440.581	56.0	923.181	23.5	747.645	20.0	622.889	26.3	493.137	42.7	345.636	31.0
697.816	(25.5)	936.743	14.5	817.880	8.0	756.951	39.3	543.289	87.9	289.166	43.8
11.000	(91.3)	126.000	75.8	71.670	156.0	28.000	419.7	(6.672)	(119.8)	33.722	615.2
162.000	47.3	110.000	(44.4)	198.000	(1.0)	200.000	(.3)	200.672	217.0	63.306	128.1
524.816	(25.1)	700.743	27.8	548.210	3.6	528.951	51.4	349.289	81.8	192.138	14.0
$0.40	(36.5)	$0.63	12.5	$0.56	3.7	$0.54	50.0	$0.36	80.0	$0.20	17.6
$ 5.541.345	8.1	$ 5.127.277	103.2	$ 2.522.740	27.8	$ 1.974.530	36.6	$ 1.445.579	31.9	$ 1.096.290	21.3
2.3%	(48.9)	4.5%	7.1	4.2%	(17.6)	5.1%	15.9	4.4%	25.7	3.5%	(10.3)
9.5%	(30.7)	13.7%	(36.9)	21.7%	(19.0)	26.8%	10.7	24.2%	38.3	17.5%	(5.9)

235

Financial Review

From 1962 to 1972, revenue increased at an annual compounded growth
rate of 26 percent, from $4.29-million in 1962 to $45.2-million in
1972. The company currently estimates that revenues during fiscal 1973
should range between $55-and-$58-million.

There are certain characteristics related to Saunders' financial position
as a leasing company that management feels are significant.

* At the close of 1972, total debt was $29,599,214.
  The current ratio was 2.55-to-1. (Industry accounting
  standards exclude rental equipment obligations due
  within one year from current liabilities and also
  exclude depreciated value of equipment covered by
  these obligations from current assets.) Although
  leasing companies must necessarily carry a high
  debt-to-equity ratio, the debt is backed by
  equipment with immediate resale value.

  Further protection is provided by contract
  provisions under which lessees will purchase
  the leased equipment in the event of cancellation. Saunders' management, therefore,
  believes the company's capital structure is
  sufficiently strong to permit favorable
  negotiation of long-term debt when required.
  The capital base also has been further
  strengthened by the recent sale of common
  shares and the retention of profits.

* Saunders currently has borrowing arrangements
  with a number of banks, with additional lines
  of credit available from finance subsidiaries
  of vehicle manufacturers. Loan agreements are
  collateralized by the vehicles purchased with
  the proceeds and by pledging the lease agreements.
  As a result, Saunders' balance sheet shows heavy
  amounts related to equipment obligations and
  correspondingly less funded debt.

* The company depreciates its revenue-generating
  equipment on a straight-line basis over their
  estimated useful lives. Estimates and depreciation
  schedules are conservative, management points out,
  so the sale of used equipment consistently produces
  more than the depreciated value. Accelerated
  depreciation is used for tax purposes only.

* Saunders has historically handled the investment
  tax credit on a flow-through basis. Under this
  method, the company takes the full amount of the
  credit in the same year in which the applicable
  piece of equipment is purchased. While the truck
  leasing industry is divided over this accounting
  treatment, several other major companies also are
  using it. Saunders believes that this method is
  consistent with accurate reporting since the credit
  is taken at the time of purchase of vehicle.

* Saunders uses the operating method of accounting
  which recognizes income as rental becomes receivable.
  Vehicles purchased for lease to customers are
  recorded as fixed assets on the date of purchase.

Management

*HARRIS SAUNDERS
    Chairman of the Board

*HARRIS SAUNDERS, JR.
    President, Chief Executive Officer
    and Treasurer

*JOHN R. SAUNDERS
    Executive Vice President

*CHARLES C. McLANE
    Senior V. P. and Secretary

*CARL CARSON
    Vice President
    Union Plaza Building
    Memphis, Tennessee 38104

*ALLEN W. MATHIS, JR.
    Montgomery, Alabama

*FRANK P. SAMFORD, JR.
    Chairman of the Board
    Liberty National Life Ins. Co.
    Birmingham, Alabama

*LEE STYSLINGER
    President, Altec, Inc.
    Birmingham, Alabama

MILTON G. HAUSER
    Vice President-Industrial
    Relations

MELVIN A. KOCH
    Vice President-Branch Operations

CHARLES D. PIERCE
    Vice President-Group Manager

JAMES L. RYAN
    Vice President-Group Manager

RON HICKMAN
    Asst. Vice President-Group
    Manager

JAMES F. SHIKLE
    Asst. Vice President-Group
    Manager

GEORGE H. CAUGHEY
    Asst. V.P.-National Accounts
    Sales Manager

ROBERT S. HUCKESTEIN
    Asst. V.P.-Branch Accounts
    Sales Manager

J. H. FLEMMING
    Asst. V.P. - Comptroller

*Member, Board of Directors

FOR FURTHER INFORMATION CONTACT: Harris Saunders
                                   Chairman of the Board
                                   Saunders Leasing System, Inc.
                                   201 Office Park Drive
                                   Birmingham, Alabama 35223
                                   PHONE: (205) 879-2131

OR...   The Financial Relations Board, Inc.

New York: Chicago: Los Angeles:

B. W. Marcus   W. Burkhart   V. Lowe
Sr. Vice President   Senior Associate   Vice President
25 Broad Street (10004) 75 E. Wacker Dr. (60601)   626 Wilshire Blvd.(90017)
PHONE: (212)422-7250   PHONE: (312)641-2100   PHONE: (213)680-9750

                        St. Petersburg, Florida:

                        E. B. Brown
                        Director of Southeastern Operations
                        Exec. Bldg. - Suite 340
                        1135 Pasadena Ave. South (33707)
                        PHONE: (813)344-2644

239

A sample return postcard for updating mailing lists.

FIRST CLASS
Permit No. 44475
New York, N.Y.

BUSINESS REPLY MAIL

NO POSTAGE STAMP NECESSARY IF MAILED IN THE UNITED STATES

—POSTAGE WILL BE PAID BY—

THE FINANCIAL RELATIONS BOARD, INC.
44 BEAVER STREET
NEW YORK, NEW YORK   10004

I do not wish to continue
receiving financial reports
from DEVCON INTERNATIONAL CORP.

I wish to continue receiving
financial reports from DEVCON
INTERNATIONAL CORP.

Note name and/or address change

name_____

firm_____

street_____

city_____ **state**_____ **ZIP**_____

YOUR POSITION
____ partner, officer or
      resident manager
____ research director
____ analyst
____ sales manager
____ trading manager
____ registered rep
____ editor
____ reporter
____ librarian
____ proxy clerk
____ other, pls. specify

TYPE OF FIRM
____ brokerage firm
____ invest. counsellors
____ mutual fund research
____ staff or mgmt. co.
____ bank
____ insurance company
____ advisory service
____ financial publication
____ trade publication
____ newspaper or wire
____ radio or TV
____ other, pls. specify

If this postcard is not returned to us by
        June 30   , we will presume you
wish to have your name deleted from the list.

OUTLINE OF PRESENTATION BEFORE THE NEW YORK SOCIETY OF SECURITY ANALYSTS

The following is an outline of a presentation by a chief executive officer before The New York Society of Security Analysts.

A. INTRODUCTION

   1. It's an honor to come here from the land of International Harvester, John Deere, and other famous farm implement people, and to address the same audience that they've addressed many times in the past. Unfortunately, that's where the similarity ends!

   2. Although Allied has not quite become the household word that these others have become, Allied is indeed carving out a special and profitable niche for itself within North America's farm implement market. Today's remarks are designed to acquaint you with the most significant points about Allied:
       a. Our specialized role within the industry.
       b. Our operations and how they generate profits.
       c. Our recent restructuring of those operations toward higher profitability.
       d. How we see the outlook for our market place.
       e. Our competitive position within that market place.

B. ALLIED AND THE SPECIALTY IMPLEMENT FIELD

   1. Allied's role as North America's largest wholesale distributor of specialty farm equipment and a manufacturer of several implement lines.

2. How the specialty implement field differs from the eight major manufacturers of tractors and combines.

3. Description of specialty implement manufacturing, worldwide— small and medium-sized manufacturers with limited resources for marketing.

4. The normal channels of distribution—either company owned warehouses or franchised distribution organizations . . . selling to several thousand retail dealers who are affiliated with one of the eight major tractor makers.

5. Stress the reasons why the specialty implement producers and distributors do not really compete with the "Big Eight."

6. A description of typical specialty implements and how they have helped to mechanize the modern North American farm.

7. The defensive characteristics of the specialty implement field— broad diversification; the tendency of farmers to upgrade existing implements during a soft economic period.

8. Allied's present scope in providing warehouses, distribution, and marketing services for about 50 major lines of specialty implements. Discuss franchise territory arrangements and stress Allied's coverage of all Canadian provinces, coast to coast, and 33 key farming states of the United States.

9. Discuss Allied's competition—name the companies and estimate the kind of coverage they offer implement suppliers. Stress Allied's competitive advantages.

C. ALLIED'S RECENT RESTRUCTURING

1. Discuss Allied's expansion period of 1965 to 1969. Present rationale for the expansion and the need to retrench.

2. Point out Allied's unusually high return on sales in the mid-1960s and the reasons for declining margins in the later 1960s.

3. Review the figures leading to Allied's deficit years and discuss reasons for the deficits.

4. Allied's consolidation program—its goals and techniques.

5. The results of the consolidation program—loss reduction in 1971, profitability in 1972, and a sharp increase in profits for 1973.

6. Review 1973 operating statement in detail (use round figure estimates in case final year-end figures are not yet ready for release).
   a. Why sales rose in 1973.
   b. Decreasing ratio of operating expenses to sales.

   c. Decrease in direct selling cost.
   d. Increasing dollar sales per salesman.
   e. Decreasing percent of interest costs to sales.
   f. Vastly improved net margins.
7. Review of Allied's year-end position.
   a. Working capital.
   b. Net equity ratio—stress a leverage that this affords the common shareholder.
   c. Short-term credit available and amount currently in use.
   d. Long-term debt arrangements, including significant restrictions.
   e. Preferred stock—be sure to call attention to convertibility and potential dilution. (This is important to impart total candor.)

D. THE OUTLOOK FOR THE SPECIALTY IMPLEMENT MARKET IN THE NEXT FIVE YEARS.

1. Everybody in our business woke up one morning about a year ago and found that we were being looked on as a growth industry!
2. The more we looked at the global statistics that were unfolding, the more we tended to believe that this was true.
3. None of you have to be introduced to the repeated headlines proclaiming a worldwide food shortage. What is notable is that North America is increasingly becoming the breadbasket of the world and sees a rather unbroken uptrend in demand for many years to come.
4. This is a strange position for an industry traditionally looked on as highly cyclical.
5. Consider that in the past year, according to the United Nation's Food and Agriculture Organization, farm output in 42 developing nations around the world actually dropped by 1%. Meanwhile, many economists estimate that—just to keep up with its own demand for food—the U.S. farm community will have to increase production by 32% to meet projected 1985 demand.
6. This production increase is quite possible. The trend of the past 15 years is continuing. Innovations developed by Allied and other specialty implement producers, plus the major farm equipment makers and those companies developing more potent seeds, pesticides, and fertilizers, the yield per acre in the United States

and Canada has been soaring. For example, in 15 years the average corn yield has almost doubled to 92 bushels per acre. On some experimental farms, yields have already reached 300 bushels per acre. Meanwhile, soybean yields have risen to 30 bushels per acre and U.S. government projections show that the yield will increase by another 30% by 1985.

7. This productivity has helped boost the U.S. and Canadian harvest of 1973 to record levels. In the United States, the wheat crop reached an all-time high of 1.7 billion bushels and soybeans reached 1.5 billion bushels, another all-time high.

8. This kind of output is enough to far surpass domestic needs and has enabled the United States to boost its farm exports by 60% in the past year, to an estimated $13 billion.

9. These trends have combined to give the U.S. and Canadian farmer a degree of unprecedented prosperity and an outlook for a steady uptrend in demand. This in turn has given him the cash and the confidence to invest in new capital equipment and upgrade existing equipment as well.

10. On the other hand, we do recognize certain problems still facing the North American farm community:
    a. Fertilizer shortages—which experts say could last for two years or more with supplies running about 15% below demand in many categories.
    b. Fuel shortages—which will affect farmers that rely on higher horsepower engines for their machinery. The National Allocation Program on fuel is giving the farm community high priority, but the energy crisis will have some effect in dampening the farmers' ability to take maximum advantage of crop expansion opportunities.
    c. Railroad car shortages—which will tend to slow down the movement of supplies to the farmer and the movement of their products to the market place. Hopefully, the crash program to produce a sizable number of additional covered hopper cars by the railroad car building industry should catch up with the car shortage some time in late 1974 or early 1975.

11. Despite these problems, the U.S. Department of Agriculture is convinced that 1974 will bring another record year in farm production, and a similar new record is expected in Canada. Accordingly, most companies involved in farm implement pro-

duction and distribution are looking for record high demand once again next year.

E. ALLIED'S COMPETITIVE POSITION

1. Allied's unique ability to put a manufacturer in business, virtually overnight, across Canada and the major U.S. farming states.
2. Description of Allied's distribution centers and sales forces.
3. Describe Allied's capacity to funnel higher sales through its existing structure, enabling further increases in sales per salesman.
4. A detailed description of Allied's franchisors—who they are, their size range, their location, and the average territorial franchise awarded to Allied.
5. Description of the major Allied product lines—distributed:
   a. Material-handling equipment.
   b. Tillage equipment.
   c. Harvesting equipment.
   d. Hay, forage, and feed preparation.
   e. Agricultural hydraulics.
   f. Tractors (small and medium size).
   g. Earth-moving equipment.
   h. Orchard equipment.
   i. Small motors and other miscellaneous equipment.
6. Description of Allied's manufactured products:
   a. Harrow.
   b. Grain augers.
   c. Bale elevators and conveyors.
   d. Farm loaders.
   e. Hydraulic equipment.
7. New franchises recently won by Allied.

F. ALLIED'S PERFORMANCE OUTLOOK FOR 1974

1. Allied's ability to pass on higher product costs to its customers with minimal time-lag.
2. Estimated Allied money costs in 1974.
3. Remaining opportunities for Allied to reduce even further its ratios of operating costs to sales.
4. Record sales expected for 1974.
5. Record profits expected for 1974.

QUESTION AND ANSWER PERIOD

OUTLINE OF PRESENTATION BEFORE AN ANNUAL MEETING

The following is a sample outline of a presentation by a chief executive officer before his company's annual meeting.

Verbal Presentation	Visual	Time Span
1. Review of past fiscal year performance	• 10-year graph of total sales with breakdown by foreign and domestic • 10-year graph of sales with breakdown by branches and licensees • 10-year graph of net revenues • 10-year graph of net income with breakdown by foreign and domestic • 10-year chart of earnings per share	5 minutes
2. Announcement of fiscal 1974 foreign expansion plans—worldwide totals only	None	5 minutes

3. Report from London
  a. Announcement of U.K. expansion plans
  b. Outlook for general business conditions and temporary ser-
	Slide of Secretan photo	3 minutes

vices market in the
United Kingdom

4. Report from Paris 　a. Announcement of France expansion plans 　b. Announcement of expansion plans elsewhere on the Continent	Grunelius photo slide	2 minutes
c. Comments on outlook for general business conditions and temporary services market in France and the Continent	Carton photo slide	3 minutes
5. Announcement of international expansion in other specific nations	World map showing nations where new offices are planned	1 minute
6. Announcement of interoffice expansion plans	U.S. map showing cities where expansion is planned	
7. Manpower posture for 1974—discussion of defensive factors —broader multinational base —prevailing early warning system among corporations now better streamlined for softer 1974	• Graph showing foreign GNP growth during 1953 U.S. recession • Graph showing foreign GNP growth during 1957 U.S. recession • Graph showing foreign GNP growth during 1970 U.S. recession	2 minutes
8. First quarter results	• Graph showing first quarter sales versus last year, with breakdown of foreign and domestic • Graph showing first quarter revenues versus last year • Graph showing first quarter earnings versus last year,	1 minute

with breakdown of foreign
and domestic

9. The fiscal 1974 outlook
    a. Expansion of services   • 10-year graph showing num-   4 minutes
                                    ber of offices per year pro-
                                    viding each major category
                                    of service
    b. Client longevity   • Graph showing client lon-
                                    gevity trend
                                  • Sample listing of prominent
                                    clients of five years or more
                                    tenure
    c. Expanded   revenues   • Chart showing rising reve-
        per client   nues per client per year
    d. New office start-up   • Chart showing decreasing
        costs   time span for new office to
                                    attain profitability
    e. Further geographical   • World map showing key lo-
        expansion potential   cations where company is
                                    not yet based

10. New building   • Slide of new building ex-   1 minute
                                    terior

11. Question and answer pe-
     riod with foreign office
     managers via telephone

End of telephone connection

12. Question and answer pe-
     riod, Milwaukee only

A SAMPLE SCRIPT FOR
A SLIDE FILM PRESENTATION FOR
USE BEFORE ANALYSTS AND OTHERS

Video	Audio
1	DEVCON INTERNATIONAL CORP. HAS ENJOYED 23 YEARS OF CONTINUOUS GROWTH IN BOTH PROFITS AND VOLUME, COMPETING IN THE CONSTRUCTION, CONCRETE PRODUCTS, AND REAL ESTATE DEVELOPMENT FIELDS. MANAGEMENT IS ESPECIALLY PLEASED TO HAVE THIS OPPORTUNITY TO TELL YOU ABOUT THE COMPANY'S RECENT DEVELOPMENTS AND CURRENT POSITION, ALONG WITH OUR GROWTH STRATEGY AND POTENTIAL.
2	IN RECENT YEARS, DEVCON HAS CHANGED FROM PRIMARILY A HIGHWAY AND LAND DEVELOPMENT CONTRACTOR.
3	... TO A MULTIDIVISIONAL ORGANIZATION WITH MAJOR OPERATIONS IN CONCRETE PRODUCTS.
4	... AND REAL ESTATE DEVELOPMENT. WHILE EACH DIVISION STANDS ON ITS OWN AS A PROFIT CENTER ...
5	... THE DIVISIONS ARE SO CLOSELY INTERRELATED THAT EACH LENDS IMMEASURABLE SUPPORT TO THE OTHERS, THEREBY CREATING A SINGLE DYNAMIC ORGANIZATION.
6	THE SUCCESS OF THE COMPANY CAN BE ILLUSTRATED THROUGH NET EARNINGS GROWTH. OVER THE PAST FIVE YEARS NET EARNINGS HAVE BEEN COMPOUNDING AT AN AVERAGE OF MORE THAN 25% PER YEAR.
7	TODAY, DEVCON'S CONSTRUCTION SERVICES DIVISION, UTILIZING SOME 175 PIECES OF HEAVY EQUIPMENT—A MORE THAN $14 MILLION INVESTMENT, PERFORMS CONSTRUCTION SERVICES ...
8	... THROUGHOUT AN AREA SPANNING SOUTH FLORIDA ...

Video	Audio
9	... THE CARRIBEAN, AND CENTRAL AMERICA. WHAT CONTINUES TO SET DEVCON APART FROM OTHER HEAVY EQUIPMENT CONTRACTORS IS THE CRITICAL BALANCE BETWEEN PRIVATE AND PUBLIC CONSTRUCTION WHICH WAS MAINTAINED IN THE PAST YEAR ...
10	... AS SUCCESSFUL BIDDING OF INTERSTATE HIGHWAY CONTRACTS TOTALING MORE THAN $30 MILLION WAS COMPLEMENTED BY NEGOTIATING MORE THAN $5 MILLION IN PRIVATE CONSTRUCTION CONTRACTS.
11	WE HAVE CONSISTENTLY PENETRATED THE CARRIBEAN MARKET AND DEVELOPED BOTH STRENGTH AND CONFIDENCE IN OFFSHORE LOWER TAX AREAS. THE COMPANY FURTHER LIMITS ITS RISK BY SPECIALIZING IN MEDIUM-SIZE CONTRACTS AS INDIVIDUAL CONSTRUCTION CONTRACTS RARELY EXCEED 10 MILLION.
12	THE WIDE RANGE OF DEVCON CONSTRUCTION SERVICES IS EVIDENT IN OUR DIVERSE PROJECTS. IN ONE YEAR THE COMPANY BUILT A PORTION OF THE FLORIDA TURNPIKE IN MIAMI AND TWO SECTIONS OF I-95 ...
13	... COMPLETED A 70-KILOMETER SECTION OF THE PAN AMERICAN HIGHWAY IN COSTA RICA, AND STARTED CONSTRUCTION ON A HIGHWAY IN THE REPUBLIC OF PANAMA CONNECTING THE ATLANTIC AND PACIFIC COASTS.
14	LAST YEAR LAND WAS PREPARED FOR SEVERAL LARGE DEVELOPERS. AT WELLEBY WEST OF FT. LAUDERDALE, DEVCON EQUIPMENT PREPARED LAND FOR A PLANNED UNIT DEVELOPMENT THAT IS BECOMING A CITY UNTO ITSELF. SIMILAR WORK IS CURRENTLY IN PROGRESS IN BONAVENTURE IN BROWARD COUNTY AND BENT TREE IN DADE COUNTY.
15	DEVCON'S SPECIALIZED SKILLS IN WATERFRONT DEVELOPMENT AND OUR WATERWAY CONSTRUCTION CAPABILITIES HAVE FOR YEARS BEEN UTILIZED ...
16	... AT EXCLUSIVE DEVELOPMENTS BOTH IN FLORIDA AND THROUGHOUT THE CARRIBEAN.
17	DURING ALL OF ITS 23 YEARS, DEVCON HAS ENGAGED IN HEAVY CONSTRUCTION SERVICES, MOVING AND RESHAPING THE EARTH, BUILDING EXPRESSWAYS ...
18	... AIRPORT RUNWAYS, AND PLANE PARKING FACILITIES ...
19	... CONSTRUCTING GOLF COURSES, WATER AND SEWAGE FACILITIES, PREPARING RAW LAND FOR COMPLETE MODERN COMMUNITIES.
20	SINCE 1955 DEVCON HAS BEEN BUILDING GOLF COURSES AND IN RECENT YEARS CONSTRUCTED WELL-KNOWN

Video	Audio

	GOLF COURSES FOR SUCH LEADING ARCHITECTS AS ROBERT TRENT JONES, ROBERT VON HAGGE, AND JOE LEE.
21	IN CONJUNCTION WITH THE INVERARY GOLF COURSES, DEVCON ALSO CONSTRUCTED ROADS, CANALS, BULKHEADS, BRIDGES, AND OTHER IMPROVEMENTS.
22	IN THE BAHAMAS, DEVCON SIMULTANEOUSLY DREDGED A MARINA AND BUILT A GOLF COURSE ON ELEUTHERA ISLAND . . .
23	. . . FOR A RESORT AND CONDOMINIUM DEVELOPER. FEDERAL, STATE, AND FOREIGN GOVERNMENTS HAVE MADE USE OF THE DIVISIONS CAPABILITIES IN CONSTRUCTING PUBLIC PROJECTS.
24	WE ARE ESPECIALLY PROUD OF OUR WORK ON BREWER'S BEACH ON ST. THOMAS WHERE WE RECONSTRUCTED A WIDE SAND BEACH FOR PUBLIC USE. HERE, DREDGING DID NOT HARM THE AREA'S ENVIRONMENT BUT RATHER ENHANCED IT.
25	DOCKS, DEEP WATER PIERS, AND PORT FACILITIES HAVE BEEN COMPLETED IN OTHER CARRIBEAN LOCALES INCLUDING MONTEGO FREEPORT, JAMAICA; BRITISH VIRGIN ISLANDS, ANTIGUA, WEST INDIES . . .
26	. . . AND MOST RECENTLY BY THE WATER AND POWER AUTHORITY ON ST. THOMAS.
27	DEVCON CONSTRUCTION SERVICES CONTINUES TO GENERATE A SUBSTANTIAL PORTION OF THE COMPANY'S NET EARNINGS. CONSTRUCTION SERVICES REVENUE IN 1973 WAS IN EXCESS OF $18 MILLION. ON MARCH 31, 1974, MORE THAN $30 MILLION REMAINED ON CURRENT PROJECTS OR CONTRACTS STILL TO GET UNDER WAY. ABOUT 80% OF THIS BACKLOG IS EXPECTED TO BE COMPLETED WITHIN 18 MONTHS AND ADDITIONAL CONTRACTS ARE ANTICIPATED.
28	DEVCON'S SECOND MAJOR FIELD OF ENDEAVOR IS THE CONCRETE PRODUCTS DIVISION. AS A NATURAL OUTGROWTH OF OUR CONSTRUCTION SERVICES, READY-MIX CONCRETE AND CONCRETE BLOCK ARE PRODUCED IN THE CARRIBEAN.
29	THE COMPANY MAINTAINS READY-MIX CONCRETE BATCH PLANTS, A ROCK QUARRY, AND . . .
30	. . . A FLEET OF READY-MIX TRUCKS IN ST. THOMAS IN THE U.S. VIRGIN ISLANDS.
31	ON ST. MAARTEN IN THE NETHERLAND ANTILLES, THE COMPANY ALSO OPERATES A READY-MIX BATCH PLANT, A FLEET OF TRUCKS, QUARRIES, PLUS A CONCRETE BLOCK PLANT.

Video	Audio
32	WE RECENTLY ACQUIRED THE MASONRY PRODUCTS DIVISION OF WHITTAKER CORPORATION WHICH WILL DOUBLE OUR CONCRETE PRODUCTS VOLUME IN 1974. THIS MAJOR ADDITION FURTHER EXTENDS OUR CONCRETE PRODUCTS SERVICE AREA TO ST. CROIX, U.S. VIRGIN ISLANDS, WHERE WE HAVE MAJOR INDUSTRIAL CUSTOMERS . . .
33	. . . AND TO ANTIGUA AND MONTSERRAT IN THE BRITISH WEST INDIES. THE COMPANY NOW SERVES MUCH OF THE CARRIBEAN WITH READY-MIX CONCRETE, CONCRETE BLOCK, AND QUARRY MATERIALS FROM EXTENSIVE FACILITIES ON FIVE ISLANDS.
34	WE ARE ESPECIALLY OPTIMISTIC ABOUT MASONRY PRODUCTS, WHERE TURNAROUND STEPS INITIATED DURING THE FIRST TWO MONTHS OF OPERATION UNDER OUR CONCRETE PRODUCTS MANAGEMENT RESULTED IN OUR CURRENT CONFIDENCE THAT MASONRY PRODUCTS WILL CONTRIBUTE SIGNIFICANTLY TO COMPANY EARNINGS FOR THE YEAR.
35	DEVCON ORIGINALLY WENT TO THE VIRGIN ISLANDS TO EXTEND ST. THOMAS AND ST. CROIX AIRPORTS. CONTROLLED CONCRETE PRODUCTS WAS PURCHASED AT THAT TIME TO FACILITATE THE ST. THOMAS AIRPORT CONTRACT.
36	CURRENTLY WE ARE THE SOLE SUPPLIER OF READY-MIX CONCRETE FOR HOUSING, ROADS, AND COMMERCIAL CONSTRUCTION ON THE ISLAND.
37	DEVCON NOT ONLY PREPARED THE SITE FOR A LUXURY HOLIDAY INN, RECENTLY OPENED NEAR CHARLOTTE AMALIE ON ST. THOMAS, BUT ALSO SUPPLIED ALL THE CONCRETE FOR THIS PROJECT.
38	DEVCON EXTENDED ITS CONCRETE MANUFACTURING TECHNOLOGY 125 MILES EAST OF ST. MAARTEN IN THE WINDWARD ISLANDS. ST. MAARTEN, HALF DUTCH ANTILLEAN, HALF FRENCH. . .
39	. . . IS ONE OF THE FASTEST GROWING ISLANDS IN THE CARRIBEAN. DEVCON'S NETHERLAND ANTILLES AND FRENCH SUBSIDIARIES ARE THE MAJOR SUPPLIERS OF READY-MIX CONCRETE . . .
40	. . . AND OF CONCRETE BLOCK ON THAT ISLAND. AS WE DID IN SOUTH FLORIDA . . .
41	. . . DEVCON POSITIONED ITSELF IN THE MIDST OF ONE OF THE WORLD'S MOST RAPIDLY DEVELOPING AREAS— THE CARRIBEAN.
42	THE POPULATION OF THE U.S. VIRGIN ISLANDS HAS INCREASED FROM APPROXIMATELY 55,000 FIVE YEARS AGO TO MORE THAN 90,000 NOW.

Video	Audio
43	AIRLINES AND SHIPS BRING MORE THAN 1.2 MILLION PASSENGERS TO THESE ISLANDS ANNUALLY. IN THE PAST FIVE YEARS . . .
44	. . . BUILDING PERMITS HAVE MULTIPLIED TWO AND A HALF TIMES. ALL OF THIS REQUIRES SAND, ROCK AND GRAVEL . . .
45	. . . CONCRETE, AND CONCRETE BLOCK. WE DREDGE OUR OWN SAND . . .
46	. . . CRUSH OUR OWN ROCK, ACCURATELY MIX OUR OWN CONCRETE . . .
47	. . . TO RIGID STRUCTURAL SPECIFICATIONS—AND WE EVEN CONSTRUCTED OUR OWN CATCHMENT AREA AS A SOURCE OF FRESH WATER—AN ESSENTIAL INGREDIENT IN CONCRETE.
48	THE CONCRETE PRODUCTS DIVISION HAS BEEN A MAJOR CONTRIBUTOR TO THE COMPANY'S NET EARNINGS IN RECENT YEARS, AND NOW WE HAVE DOUBLED OUR BASE AND GAINED A STRONG POSITION FOR FUTURE GROWTH.
49	THE THIRD AND MOST RAPIDLY GROWING DIVISION OF DEVCON INTERNATIONAL IS THE REAL ESTATE DEVELOPMENT COMPANY. IN 1972, DEVCON REALTY CORPORATION WAS FORMED AS A WHOLLY OWNED SUBSIDIARY TO CONDUCT OUR REAL ESTATE DEVELOPMENT BUSINESS.
50	SINCE ITS FORMATION, DEVCON REALTY HAS ACQUIRED OR CONTRACTED TO ACQUIRE VALUABLE ACREAGE IN BROWARD, BREVARD, ORANGE, AND DADE COUNTIES IN FLORIDA. PRIME DEVELOPMENT PROPERTY, INCLUDING JOINT VENTURE HOLDINGS, NOW EXCEEDS 2500 ACRES WITH MORE THAN 1200 ACRES OF THIS PROPERTY IN THE MIAMI AREA ALONE.
51	ADDITIONAL ACREAGE HAS BEEN ACQUIRED IN THE CARRIBEAN INCLUDING AN 80% INTEREST IN THE CORPORATION WHICH OWNS HANS LOLLIK ISLAND. IN FACT, DEVCON CONSTRUCTED THE MANDAHL BAY MARINA ON ST. THOMAS WHICH WHEN COMPLETED WILL PROVIDE ACCESS TO HANS LOLLIK ISLAND.
52	RECENTLY THE COMPANY ENTERED INTO A JOINT VENTURE ON THE FRENCH SIDE OF ST. MAARTEN FOR THE DEVELOPMENT OF 60 ACRES WITH IT'S OWN PROTECTED CUL-DE-SAC ON THE CARRIBEAN SEA. WE ARE PARTICULARLY OPTIMISTIC ABOUT ST. MAARTEN . . .
53	. . . WE ARE PARTICIPATING IN A 500-HOME MIDDLE-INCOME HOUSING DEVELOPMENT ON THE DUTCH SIDE OF THIS TWO-COUNTRY ISLAND. WE ALSO HOLD FOR FUTURE DEVELOPMENT A SMALLER 12-ACRE PARCEL COMPRISED OF TWO ACRES OF BEACHFRONT AND AN ISLAND IN

SIMPSON'S BAY CONNECTED TO THE MAINLAND BY A CAUSEWAY.

54 FROM OUR REAL ESTATE DEVELOPMENT DIVISION'S AC-CUMULATED LAND INVENTORY, THE MARGATE PROPERTY IN BROWARD COUNTY WAS THE FIRST TO GENERATE SUBSTANTIAL SALES AND CONTRIBUTION TO CORPORATE EARNINGS. EXISTING SALES CONTRACTS ON PROPERTY WHICH DEVCON PURCHASED, ENGINEERED, ZONED, AND IS SELLING TO BUILDERS WILL CONTRIBUTE SIGNIFI-CANTLY TO EARNINGS DURING THE SECOND AND SUB-SEQUENT QUARTERS OF 1974.

55 WHILE DEVCON REALTY APPEARS TO BE THE COMPANY'S YOUNGEST DIVISION, ITS MANAGEMENT CAN POINT TO-WARD 15 YEARS OF INCREASING PROFITABLE REAL ES-TATE DEVELOPMENT. DEMONSTRATING DEVCON RE-ALTY'S DEPTH OF EXPERIENCE AND ABILITY TO ACQUIRE VALUABLE REAL ESTATE WAS THE ACCUMULATION OF MORE THAN 2500 ACRES OF PRIME DEVELOPMENT PROP-ERTY, THE OBTAINING OF REQUESTED ZONING ON 40% OF THIS LAND INVENTORY, AND THE ENTERING INTO SEVERAL IMPORTANT JOINT VENTURES.

56 THE JOINT VENTURES OF DEVCON REALTY AND LENNAR CORPORATION, ONE OF THE NATION'S LARGEST HOME BUILDERS, RECENTLY OBTAINED REQUESTED ZONING FOR A PLANNED UNIT DEVELOPMENT OF OUR LARGEST DADE COUNTY TRACT. WHILE DEVCON WILL PREPARE THE LAND FOR SINGLE FAMILY HOMES, TOWN HOUSES, CON-DOMINIUMS, AND COMMERCIAL PROPERTIES, LENNAR WILL DESIGN, CONSTRUCT, AND MARKET THE INDIVID-UAL UNITS. NOT FAR FROM THIS PROPERTY, DEVCON REALTY HAS ENTERED INTO ANOTHER JOINT VENTURE OF 480 ACRES AND HAS ALSO OBTAINED THE DESIRED ZONING ON 85 ACRES OF NEARBY LAND.

57 DEVCON MANAGEMENT HAS STATED THAT THE THRUST OF THE COMPANY IS SHIFTING, AS PLANNED, TOWARD THE REAL ESTATE DIVISION WHICH HAS ALREADY BEGUN TO PRODUCE AN ACCELERATING PROPORTION OF THE COMPANY'S NET INCOME. AT THE SAME TIME, MANAGE-MENT ANTICIPATES CONTINUED GROWTH OF CONSTRUC-TION SERVICES AND CONCRETE PRODUCTS WHILE FOCUS-ING ON THE INCREASING RETURN IN THE DEVELOPMENT OF REAL ESTATE.

58 WE HAVE SAID THAT DEVCON'S THREE DIVISIONS OPER-ATE AS DISTINCT PROFIT CENTERS. HOWEVER, MANAGE-MENT INSURES TOP-LEVEL COORDINATION IN SEEKING, EVALUATING, AND CAPITALIZING UPON NEW VENTURE OPPORTUNITIES. THIS DIVISIONAL SYNERGISM IS BEST ILLUSTRATED BY THE COMPANY'S U.S. INTERSTATE HIGH-WAY PROJECT NEAR THE CORPORATE HEADQUARTERS IN POMPANO BEACH, FLORIDA.

59   PRIOR TO BIDDING FOR THE CONSTRUCTION OF ITS I-95 PROJECT, THE COMPANY OBTAINED AN OPTION TO PURCHASE A NEARBY 90 ACRES WHICH WOULD SOON SERVE A DUAL PURPOSE. ALREADY DETERMINED TO BE THE MOST ECONOMICAL SOURCE OF REQUIRED FILL MATERIALS, THIS TRACT FIRST SUPPLIED SAND WHICH WAS PUMPED FROM A LOW AREA DIRECTLY TO THE HIGHWAY SITE.

60   LATER, THE LAKE CREATED BY THIS DREDGING ENHANCED THE VALUE OF BOTH THE REMAINING ACREAGE PLUS THE ADDITIONAL ADJACENT LAND PURCHASED BY DEVCON REALTY TO EXPAND THIS DEVELOPMENT TO 130 ACRES.

61   BY PLANNING AND EXECUTING THE I-95 PROJECT TOGETHER, TWO DEVCON DIVISIONS PROFITABLY ACCOMPLISHED TWO SIZABLE CONSTRUCTION PROJECTS AND AN ATTRACTIVE REAL ESTATE DEVELOPMENT. A SIMILAR ENDEAVOR IS NOW UNDER WAY IN PALM BEACH COUNTY.

62   WE BELIEVE THAT WE CAN CONTINUE TO MAXIMIZE PROFITS BY CONTINUING TO COORDINATE ACTIVITIES OF OUR CONSTRUCTION SERVICES, CONCRETE PRODUCTS, AND REAL ESTATE DEVELOPMENT DIVISIONS. JUST AS OUR NET EARNINGS HAVE GROWN SO HAVE OUR EARNING PER SHARE BEEN CLIMBING STEADILY INCLUDING 1972—THE YEAR DEVCON BECAME PUBLICLY OWNED—AND 1973—THE YEAR OF THE ENERGY CRISIS CONFRONTATION AND SERIOUS ECONOMIC DISLOCATIONS.

63   AT THE SAME TIME, STOCKHOLDERS' EQUITY PER SHARE HAS ALSO BEEN MOVING AHEAD AND JUMPED FROM $4.39 IN 1971 TO $7.98 IN 1972 AND FURTHER TO $10.14 IN 1973. MANAGEMENT BELIEVES THAT EARNINGS GROWTH WILL CONTINUE AND THAT THE COMPANY SHOULD BE ABLE TO MAINTAIN AN AVERAGE EARNINGS GROWTH RATE OVER THE NEXT FIVE YEARS OF AT LEAST 20% PER YEAR.

64   DEVCON'S MANAGEMENT DEPTH HAS BEEN BUILDING FOR 20 YEARS UNDER THE GUIDANCE OF DONALD SMITH, JR., PRESIDENT, AND INCLUDES . . .

65   . . . THE COMPANY'S SECOND LARGEST SHAREHOLDER, ALEC P. COURTELIS, PRESIDENT OF DEVCON REALTY CORPORATION.

66   AN EIGHT-MAN OFFICER GROUP GIVES DEVCON AN AVERAGE EXECUTIVE AGE OF 46 . . .

67   . . . SEVEN ENGINEERING DEGREES, PLUS AN AVERAGE OF 18 YEARS CONSTRUCTION CONTRACTING . . .

68   . . . OR REAL ESTATE DEVELOPMENT EXPERIENCE. SEASONED BUT YOUTHFUL EXPERIENCE . . .

69   . . . BLENDED WITH AN ENTREPRENEURIAL APPROACH TO

DIVISION MANAGEMENT IS A KEY STRENGTH OF THE COMPANY.

70   TODAY, DEVCON INTERNATIONAL CORPORATION CONSISTS OF A GROUP OF INTERRELATED COMPANIES FUNCTIONING THROUGHOUT THE WORLD TO CAPITALIZE UPON HIGH RETURN OPPORTUNITIES FOR CONSTRUCTION—BOTH SERVICES AND MATERIALS—AND REAL ESTATE DEVELOPMENT WHICH REQUIRE IMAGINATION, CAPACITY, AND UNCOMMON SKILL.

71   MIX MORE THAN 20 YEARS OF HEAVY CONSTRUCTION SERVICES WITH SIX YEARS OF CONSTRUCTION MATERIALS MANUFACTURING, THEN ADD AN ENVIABLE RECORD OF REAL ESTATE DEVELOPMENT—THE RESULT IS DEVCON INTERNATIONAL CORPORATION TODAY.

SUGGESTED READINGS

The Anatomy of Wall Street—edited by Charles J. Rolo and George J. Nelson (Lippincott, 1968)

Annual Report of Stockholder Activities and Corporation Meetings—Lewis D. Gilbert and John J. Gilbert (Corporate Democracy, Inc., annually)

The Bankers—Martin Mayer (Weybright and Talley, 1974)

The Big Board—Robert Sobel (Free Press, 1965)

Business Man's Guide to Washington—William Ruder and Ray Nathan (MacMillen, Second Edition, 1975)

A Complete Guide to Making a Public Stock Offering—Elmer L. Winter (Prentice-Hall, Second Edition, 1972)

Economics—Paul A. Samuelson (McGraw-Hill, Ninth Edition, 1973)

Financial Analysts Journal—(The Financial Analysts Federation, bimonthly)

Management—Peter F. Drucker (Harper & Row, 1974)

The Money Game—Adam Smith (Random House, 1968)

News and The Market—Frederick C. Klein and John A. Prestbo (Henry Regnery Company, 1974)

The Over-The-Counter Securities Market—Leo M. Loll and Julien G. Buckley (Prentice-Hall, Third Edition, 1973)

Professional Guide to Public Relations Services—Richard Weiner (Richard Weiner, Inc., Third Edition, 1975)

Public Relations Law—Morton J. Simon (Appleton-Century-Crofts, 1969)

Security Analysis—Benjamin Graham, David L. Dodd, et al. (McGraw-Hill, Fourth Edition, 1962)

The Sophisticated Investor: A Guide to Stock Market Profits—Burton Crane (Simon & Schuster, 1964)

The Stock Market—George C. Leffler and Loring C. Farwell (Roland, Third Edition, 1963)

The Stock Market Handbook—edited by Frank G. Zarb and Gabriel T. Kerekes (Dow Jones-Irwin, 1970)

INDEX